NF

D1582748

SPALDING LIBRARY OF RELIGION

THE KORAN INTERPRETED

by A. J. Arberry

SCHEHEREZADE
SUFISM
THE HOLY KORAN
REVELATION AND REASON IN ISLAM
THE SEVEN ODES
CLASSICAL PERSIAN LITERATURE
ROMANCE OF THE RUBAIYAT
ORIENTAL ESSAYS

THE KORAN INTERPRETED

By

ARTHUR J. ARBERRY
Litt.D., F.B.A.

*

VOLUME TWO

SURAS XXI-CXIV

LONDON: GEORGE ALLEN & UNWIN LTD
NEW YORK: THE MACMILLAN COMPANY

First Published 1955
Second Impression 1963
Third Impression 1971

© *George Allen & Unwin Ltd* 1955

ISBN 0 04 297005 9

PRINTED IN GREAT BRITAIN
BY PHOTOLITHO
in 11-*point Bell type*
BY UNWIN BROTHERS LTD
WOKING AND LONDON

CONTENTS

CONTENTS

PREFACE

This volume contains the second half of a new version of the Koran; it thus marks the completion of one phase of a labour which is in the nature of things unending. Over a period of many months the Koran has been my constant companion, the object of my most attentive study. Though many can certainly claim to have read the Koran, indeed over and over again, and to know it well, I think it may be reasonably asserted that their understanding and appreciation of the book will always fall short of what may be attained by one who undertakes to translate it in full and with all possible fidelity. I had myself studied the Koran and perused it from end to end over many years, before I embarked upon making a version of it; assuredly the careful discipline of trying to find the best English equivalent for every meaning and every rhythm of the original Arabic has profoundly deepened my own penetration into the heart of the Koran, and has at the same time sharpened my awareness of its mysterious and compelling beauty. For this reason, if for no other, I think it is justifiable to adopt the unusual procedure of adding a separate preface to the second instalment of a two-volume work. I suppose I shall never again recapture the freshness and excitement of the experience just now completed; the passing months and years will inevitably blur the image; this is the moment, or never, to attempt to record the impact which a sustained and concentrated exploration of the Koran has left on my mind and my heart.

First let us look again at the rhythm; for it is to the rhythm that I constantly return as I grope for a clue to the arresting, the hypnotic power of the Muslim scriptures. I was talking about this power to an Arab friend; before I could say what I would have said he spoke in terms that expressed exactly what was in my mind. 'Whenever I hear the Koran chanted, it is as though I am listening to music; underneath the flowing melody there is sounding all the time the insistent beat of a drum.' Then he added, 'It is like the beating of my heart.' A keen sense of rhythm is of course one of the most outstanding

8

characteristics of the Arab genius; it has displayed itself in a great variety of ways. No other people has evolved a prosody of comparable richness and complexity; the metres in which Arab poets have composed from earliest times exhibit a wide range of rhythmic patterns, all used with seemingly effortless ease, and each eliciting a distinctive response from the listener. Arab music reveals the same quality. I well recall a wonderful evening, many years ago, when somewhere in the Egyptian desert I sat in the gathering darkness and heard far off—it may have been a mile, it may have been two miles distant—an encampment of Bedouins singing to the accompaniment of their primitive drums and strings; the theme was being repeated endlessly, each repetition showing a subtle variation of melodic line and rhythm. So it is with architectural ornament; so it is with arabesque design. The wellnigh impenetrable maze of delicate tracery dances to the beat of a strong and urgent rhythm.

Rhythm runs insistently through the entire Koran; but it is a changeful, fluctuating rhythm, ranging from the gentle, lulling music of the narrative and legislative passages, through the lively counterpoint of the hymns of praise, to the shattering drum-rolls of the apocalyptic movements. Almost all Western scholars who have ever written about the Koran have made the comment, with a slavish repetitiveness, that the early revelations—those received at Mecca before the Hegira, mostly descriptive of the imminent end of the world and the coming Day of Doom—are more poetical than the later parts. Thus R. A. Nicholson remarked, in his *Literary History of the Arabs:* 'The preposterous arrangement of the Koran is mainly responsible for the opinion almost unanimously held by European readers that it is obscure, tiresome, uninteresting; a farrago of long-winded narratives and prosaic exhortations, quite unworthy to be named in the same breath with the Prophetical Books of the Old Testament. One may, indeed, peruse the greater part of the volume, beginning with the first chapter, and find but a few passages of genuine enthusiasm to relieve the prevailing dullness. It is in the short Suras placed at the end of the Koran that we must look for evidence of Muhammad's prophetic gift. These are the earliest of all; in these the flame of inspiration burns

9

purely and its natural force is not abated.' This was the verdict of a great scholar justly renowned for his fairmindedness; it betrays a deafness, shared by him with all too many, to that very rhythmical quality which marks the Koran apart from all other books. It is therefore all the more refreshing to read, in a very recent work by Professor A. Guillaume (*Islam:* Penguin Books), an appreciation so notably nonconformist. 'The Koran is one of the world's classics which cannot be translated without grave loss. It has a rhythm of peculiar beauty and a cadence that charms the ear. Many Christian Arabs speak of its style with warm admiration, and most Arabists acknowledge its excellence. When it is read aloud or recited it has an almost hypnotic effect that makes the listener indifferent to its sometimes strange syntax and its sometimes, to us, repellent content. It is this quality it possesses of silencing criticism by the sweet music of its language that has given birth to the dogma of its inimitability; indeed it may be affirmed that within the literature of the Arabs, wide and fecund as it is both in poetry and in elevated prose, there is nothing to compare with it.' These two contrasting statements epitomise the gulf which divides a musically sensitive from a musically insensitive reading of one and the same book. Aesthetically judged, there should be no question of the superiority or the inferiority of certain parts of the Koran. The rhythm changes, admittedly; yet it never ceases. The cataract transforms itself into a softly running stream; but the broad later sweep of the waters of inspiration is no less beautiful or majestic than the tumultuous thunder of their earlier flow.

Disciples of the Higher Criticism, having watched with fascinated admiration how their masters played havoc with the traditional sacrosanctity of the Bible, threw themselves with brisk enthusiasm into the congenial task of demolishing the Koran. Taking as their point of departure that rough classification of the Suras, a crude analysis preserved from far antiquity, which marked some as having been revealed at Mecca before A.D. 622 and some thereafter at Medina, and pursuing eagerly the faint clues emerging out of the mists of time that certain verses received during Muhammad's later years were inserted into contexts of a much earlier date, these brilliant detectives sought to assign every Sura, and every section, almost every verse or half-verse of each individual Sura, to a particular incident in the Prophet's career. Much of their work was done on sound lines, and the boundaries of knowledge have been notably enlarged by their labours; not even the most sensitive Muslim believer needs to take offence at the well-intentioned and well-conducted investigations of pure scholarship. But having cut to pieces the body of Allah's revelation, our erudite sleuths have found themselves with a corpse on their hands, the spirit meanwhile eluding their preoccupied attention. So they have been apt to resort to the old device of explaining away what they could not explain; crushed between their fumbling fingers, the gossamer wings of soaring inspiration have dissolved into powder.

The most extreme representative of this school of thought, which once tyrannised over Koranic studies in the West, was no doubt the late Dr Richard Bell. A man of great kindliness and the utmost integrity, he devoted his last years of ripe scholarship to a remarkable essay to place every verse of the Koran in its historical context (*The Qur'an*, 2 vols.). He was too scrupulous a scholar to claim anything like finality; indeed he often felt obliged to make such vague judgments as that which he prefixed to his translation of Sura CVI: 'This little surah, though rhythmic in style, is uncertain in rhyme. It must either be very early or very late—more probably early.' He was generally cautious in expressing his favourite hypothesis; that what he, with most critics, regarded as the incoherency of the Koran was due in no small measure to the fact (or rather the presumption, for there is no shred of proof) that parts of the Suras were originally written down, more or less at random, on the backs of other parts, and then tacked on to follow them by the later editors. Occasionally however his satisfaction with this ingenious theory tempted him almost to dogmatize, as on page 450: 'The end of the surah, vv. 67–88, which may not be in itself a unity, is in a different rhyme and does not properly belong to it. Its presence may be due to vv. 49–66 having been written on the back of it.' On page 476 he is even more positive: 'Vv. 23, 24, and vv. 30, 31, 32, 35 contrast the fates of unbelievers and believers, and are probably the latest parts of the

11

surah. They have been written on the back of scraps, of which
vv. 25–28 form a connected piece.' Dr Bell's preliminary com-
ments on Sura LXVI well illustrate the boldness, and incident-
ally the irreverence, of his approach: 'This surah is very dis-
jointed, and seems to consist of a collection of discarded passages of various dates. Vv. 1 and 2 go together, but as they are
addressed to the prophet personally, they possibly were not
publicly recited. It is very unlikely that vv. 3 and 4 were published. If recited at all, they were probably addressed to the two
wives. They refer in all probability—as vv. 1 and 2 also—to the
episode of Muhammad having been discovered with Mary the
Copt, by Hafsa, who then in spite of having been pledged to
secrecy, told the story to Ayesha. But the matter is anything but
clear, and v. 3 is so vague and silly that we might almost suspect
someone—Ayesha?—of having parodied Muhammad. Verse 5
joins well enough in sense with the preceding verses, but the
rhyme and the different pronoun of address show that originally
at least it belonged to some other context (cf. XXXIII, 28ff.).
The rest of the pieces of which the surah is made up belong to
early Medinan times. Verse 9 must be later than Uhud. The fact
that the examples quoted in vv. 10–12 are women might argue
a connection between them and the beginning of the surah, but
in language they seem much earlier.'

Such is the position which champions of the Higher Criticism
of the Koran eventually reach. It is against this excess of
anatomical mincing that I argue the unity of the Sura and the
Koran; instead of offering the perplexed reader *disjecta membra*
scattered indifferently over the dissecting table, I ask him to
look again at the *cadaver* before it was carved up, and to imagine
how it might appear when the lifeblood of accepted inspiration
flowed through its veins. I urge the view that an eternal compo-
sition, such as the Koran is, cannot be well understood if it is
submitted to the test of only temporal criticism. It is simply
irrelevant to expect that the themes treated in the individual
Sura will be marshalled after some mathematical precision to
form a rationally ordered pattern; the logic of revelation is not
the logic of the schoolmen. There is no 'before' or 'after' in the
prophetic message, when that message is true; everlasting
truth is not held within the confines of time and space, but every

moment reveals itself wholly and completely. Such was the experience that Henry Vaughan described in those famous lines:

> I saw Eternity the other night
> Like a great Ring of pure and endless light,
>   All calm, as it was bright,
> And round beneath it, Time in hours, days, years
>   Driv'n by the spheres
> Like a vast shadow moved, in which the world
>   And all her train were hurl'd.

Sublime expression was given to the same mystical reality by Thomas Traherne:

> I felt no dross nor matter in my soul,
> No brims nor borders, such as in a bowl
> We see. My essence was capacity,
>   That felt all things;
>   The thought that springs
> Therefrom's itself. It hath no other wings
>   To spread abroad, nor eyes to see,
>   Nor hands distinct to feel,
>   Nor knees to kneel;
> But being simple like the Deity
>   In its own centre is a sphere
>   Not shut up here, but everywhere.
>   It acts not from a centre to
>   Its object as remote,
>   But present is when it doth view,
>   Being with the Being it doth note
>   Whatever it doth do . . .
>   But yet of this I was most sure,
>   That at the utmost length,
>   (So worthy was it to endure)
>   My soul could best express its strength.
>   It was so quick and pure,
> That all my mind was wholly everywhere,
> Whate'er it saw, 'twas ever wholly there;

The sun ten thousand legions off, was nigh:
    The utmost star,
    Though seen from far,
Was present in the apple of my eye.

It was this experience of multiplicity-in-unity, this momentary flight of the eternal spirit out of the prison of life-in-time into the boundless plain of life everlasting, that moved the Egyptian mystic Ibn al-Farid to write in his great epic of the soul's ascent to God:

The whole of me performing what the Path
Provideth, in the manner that the Truth
Of me required, when I had joined the rift
So that the cracks that split the unity
(Through difference of attribute) (no more
Dispersed) were closed, and naught remained (to cause
Estrangement) as between myself and my
Firm trust in love's familiarity,
I realized that we in truth were one
And the sobriety of unison
Confirmed the blotting-out of scatteredness.
My all: a tongue, an eye, an ear, a hand:
To speak, to see, to hear, to seize withal.
Mine eyes conversed, the while my tongue beheld,
My hearing uttered, and my hand gave ear;
My hearing was an eye considering
Whate'er appeared, mine eyes an ear to heed
Silently if the folk broke forth in song;
Upon my benefits my tongue became
A hand, as too my hand became a tongue
For converse and for preaching; so my hand
Became an eye, to see whate'er appeared,
Mine eye a hand outspread wherewith to strike;
Mine ear became a tongue in my address,
My tongue an ear for silent listening;
The smell too had its rules agreeable
To general analogy as in
The fusion of my attributes, or by

Reversal of the case. No limb in me
Was specialized as being singled out
To the exclusion of the rest for one
Description, as to wit a seeing eye:
My every atom, notwithstanding its
Own singularity, itself comprised
The sum of all the organs' faculties,
Whispering and attending, consequent
On contemplation of one taking charge
(By virtue of a hand omnipotent)
Disposing of his whole totality
In one brief moment. So it is I read
The various knowledge of all learned men
Summed in one word, and with a single glance
Reveal to me all beings in the world:
I hear the voices of all men at prayer,
And every language, in a space of time
Less than an instant's flash: I summon up
Before me, what could scarcely be conveyed
From its far distance, ere mine eye can wink:
So in one inhalation I breathe in
The perfumes of all gardens, and the scent
Of every herb clutching the breezes' skirts:
And I review all regions of the earth
Before me in one thought, and with one bound
Traverse the seven layers of the skies.

The mystic's experience, attested as it is by a cloud of witnesses, surely provides the key to the mysterious inconsequence of the Koranic rhetoric. All truth was present simultaneously within the Prophet's enraptured soul; all truth, however fragmented, revealed itself in his inspired utterance. The reader of the Muslim scriptures must strive to attain the same all-embracing apprehension. The sudden fluctuations of theme and mood will then no longer present such difficulties as have bewildered critics ambitious to measure the ocean of prophetic eloquence with the thimble of pedestrian analysis. Each Sura will now be seen to be a unity within itself, and the whole Koran will be recognised as a single revelation, self-consistent in the highest degree. Though half a mortal lifetime was needed for the message to be received and communicated, the message itself, being of the eternal, is one message in eternity, however heterogeneous its temporal expression may appear to be. This, the mystic's approach, is surely the right approach to the study of the Koran; it is an approach that leads, not to bewilderment and disgust—that is the prerogative of the Higher Critic—but to an ever deepening understanding, to a wonder and a joy that have no end.

XXI

THE PROPHETS

In the Name of God, the Merciful, the Compassionate

Nigh unto men has drawn their reckoning,
while they in heedlessness are yet turning away;
no Remembrance from their Lord comes to them
lately renewed, but they listen to it yet playing,
diverted their hearts. The evildoers whisper
one to another, 'Is this aught but a mortal
like to yourselves? What, will you take to sorcery
   with your eyes open?'
He says: 'My Lord knows what is said in the heavens
and the earth, and He is the All-hearing,
   the All-knowing.'
5 Nay, but they say: 'A hotchpotch of nightmares!
Nay, he has forged it; nay, he is a poet!
Now therefore let him bring us a sign, even
as the ancient ones were sent as Messengers.'

Not one city that We destroyed before them
believed; what then, will they not believe?
And We sent none before thee, but men to whom
We made revelation—question the People
of the Remembrance, if you do not know—
nor did We fashion them as bodies
that ate not food, neither were they immortal;
then We made true the promise We gave them
and We delivered them, and whomsoever We would;
   and We destroyed the prodigal.

10 Now We have sent down to you a Book wherein
is your Remembrance; will you not understand?
How many a city that was evildoing
We have shattered, and set up after it

17

another people! Then, when they perceived
Our might, behold, they ran headlong out of it.
'Run not! Return you unto the luxury
that you exulted in, and your dwelling-places;
       haply you shall be questioned.'
They said, 'Alas for us! We have been evildoers.'
15   So they ceased not to cry, until We made them
       stubble, silent and still.

We created not the heaven and the earth,
and whatsoever between them is, as playing;
had We desired to take to Us a diversion
We would have taken it to Us from Ourselves,
       had We done aught.
Nay, but We hurl the truth against falsehood
and it prevails over it, and behold,
falsehood vanishes away. Then woe to you
       for that you describe!

To Him belongs whosoever is in the heavens
and the earth; and those who are with Him
wax not too proud to do Him service
       neither grow weary,
20   glorifying Him by night and in the daytime
       and never failing.
Or have they taken gods out of the earth
       who raise the dead?
Why, were there gods in earth and heaven
other than God, they would surely go to ruin;
so glory be to God, the Lord of the Throne,
       above that they describe!
He shall not be questioned as to what He does,
       but they shall be questioned.
Or have they taken gods apart from Him?
Say: 'Bring your proof! This is the Remembrance
of him who is with me, and the Remembrance
of those before me. Nay, but the most part
of them know not the truth, so therefore they
       are turning away.'

25   And We sent never a Messenger before thee
except that We revealed to him, saying,
'There is no god but I; so serve Me.'

They say: 'The All-merciful has taken to Him
a son.' Glory be to Him! Nay, but they
        are honoured servants
that outstrip Him not in speech, and perform
        as He commands.
He knows what is before them and behind them,
        and they intercede not
save for him with whom He is well-pleased, and they
        tremble in awe of Him.

30   If any of them says, 'I am a god
apart from Him', such a one We recompense
with Gehenna; even so We recompense
        the evildoers.

Have not the unbelievers then beheld
that the heavens and the earth were a mass
all sewn up, and then We unstitched them
and of water fashioned every living thing?
        Will they not believe?
And We set in the earth firm mountains
lest it should shake with them, and We set in it
ravines to serve as ways, that haply so
        they may be guided;
and We set up the heaven as a roof
well-protected; yet still from Our signs
        they are turning away.
It is He who created the night and the day,
        the sun and the moon,
        each swimming in a sky.

35   We have not assigned to any mortal before thee
to live forever; therefore, if thou diest,
        will they live forever?
Every soul shall taste of death; and We try you
with evil and good for a testing, then unto Us

you shall be returned.

When the unbelievers behold thee, they take thee
only for mockery: 'Ha, is this the one
who makes mention of your gods?' Yet they
in the Remembrance of the All-merciful
      are unbelievers.
Man was created of haste. Assuredly
I shall show you My signs; so demand not
      that I make haste.
They say, 'And when shall the promise come to pass,
      if you speak truly?'
40   If the unbelievers but knew when that they
shall not ward off the Fire from their faces
nor from their backs, neither shall they be helped!
Nay, but it shall come upon them suddenly,
dumbfounding them, and they shall not be able
to repel it, nor shall they be respited.

Messengers indeed were mocked at before thee,
but those that scoffed at them were encompassed
      by that they mocked at.
Say: 'Who shall guard you by night and in the daytime
from the All-merciful?' Nay, but from the Remembrance
of their Lord they are turning away.
Or have they gods that shall defend them
apart from Us? Why, they are not able
to help themselves, nor shall they be guarded
      in safety from Us.
45   Nay, but Ourselves gave these and their fathers
enjoyment of days, until their life had lasted
long while upon them. What, do they not see
how We come to the land, diminishing it
in its extremities? Or are they the victors?
Say: 'I warn you only by the Revelation';
but they that are deaf do not hear the call
      when they are warned.
If but a breath of thy Lord's chastisement
touched them, they would surely say, 'Alas for us!

    We were evildoers.'
And We shall set up the just balances
for the Resurrection Day, so that not one soul
shall be wronged anything; even if it be
the weight of one grain of mustard-seed
We shall produce it, and sufficient are
        We for reckoners.

We gave Moses and Aaron the Salvation
and a Radiance, and a Remembrance
      for the godfearing
50   such as fear God in the Unseen, trembling
      because of the Hour.

    And this is a blessed Remembrance
that We have sent down; so are you
      now denying it?

    We gave Abraham aforetime
his rectitude—for We knew him—
when he said to his father and his people,
 'What are these statues unto which
      you are cleaving?'
They said, 'We found our fathers
      serving them.'
55   He said, 'Then assuredly you
and your fathers have been in
      manifest error.'
They said, 'What, hast thou come to us
with the truth, or art thou one of
      those that play?'
He said, 'Nay, but your Lord
is the Lord of the heavens and the earth
who originated them, and I
am one of those that bear witness
      thereunto.
And, by God, I shall assuredly
outwit your idols, after you have gone away
      turning your backs.'

So he broke them into fragments,
all but a great one they had, for haply they
would return to it.

60 They said, 'Who has done this
with our gods? Surely he is one of
the evildoers.'
They said, 'We heard a young man
making mention of them, and he was called
Abraham.'
They said, 'Bring him before the people's eyes;
haply they shall bear witness.'
They said, 'So, art thou the man
who did this unto our gods,
Abraham?'
He said, 'No; it was this great one
of them that did it. Question them, if they
are able to speak!'

65 So they returned one to another,
and they said, 'Surely it is you who are
the evildoers.'
Then they were utterly put to confusion
saying, 'Very well indeed thou knowest
these do not speak.'
He said, 'What, and do you serve,
apart from God, that which profits you
nothing, neither hurts you? Fie upon you
and that you serve apart from God!
Do you not understand?'
They said, 'Burn him, and help your gods, if
you would do aught.'
We said, 'O fire, be coolness and safety
for Abraham!'

70 They desired to outwit him; so We made
them the worse losers,
and We delivered him, and Lot,
unto the land that We had blessed
for all beings.
And We gave him Isaac and Jacob
in superfluity, and every one

made We righteous
and appointed them to be leaders
guiding by Our command, and We revealed
to them the doing cf good deeds, and
to perform the prayer, and to pay the alms,
and Us they served.

And Lot—to him We gave judgment
and knowledge; and we delivered him
from the city that had been doing
deeds of corruption; they were an evil people,
truly ungodly;
75   and We admitted him into Our mercy; he
was of the righteous.

And Noah—when he called before, and We answered
him, and delivered him and his people
from the great distress,
and We helped him against the people
who cried lies to Our signs; surely
they were an evil people, so We drowned them
all together.

And David and Solomon—when they gave
judgment concerning the tillage, when the sheep
of the people strayed there, and We bore witness
to their judgment;
and We made Solomon to understand it,
and unto each gave We judgment
and knowledge. And with David We subjected
the mountains to give glory, and the birds,
and We were doers.
80   And We taught him the fashioning of garments
for you, to fortify you against your violence;
then are you thankful?
And to Solomon the wind, strongly blowing,
that ran at his command unto the land
that We had blessed; and We had knowledge
of everything;

and of the Satans some dived for him
and did other work besides; and We were
          watching over them.

And Job—when he called unto his Lord,
'Behold, affliction has visited me,
and Thou art the most merciful
          of the merciful.'
So We answered him, and removed
the affliction that was upon him,
and We gave his people, and the like of them
with them, mercy from Us, and a Reminder
          to those who serve.

85   And Ishmael, Idris, Dhul Kifl—each
                    was of the patient,
          and We admitted them into Our mercy; they
                    were of the righteous.

And Dhul Nun—when he went forth enraged
and thought that We would have no power
over him; then he called out in the darkness,
'There is no god but Thou. Glory be to Thee!
          I have done evil.'
So We answered him, and delivered him
out of grief; even so do We deliver
          the believers.

And Zachariah—when he called
unto his Lord, 'O my Lord, leave me not
solitary; though Thou art the best
          of inheritors.'
So We answered him, and bestowed on him
John, and We set his wife right for him;
truly they vied with one another, hastening
to good works, and called upon Us
out of yearning and awe; and they were
          humble to Us.

And she who guarded her virginity,

so We breathed into her of Our spirit
and appointed her and her son to be a sign
      unto all beings.
'Surely this community of yours
is one community, and I am your Lord;
      so serve Me.'
But they split up their affair between them;
      all shall return to Us.

95   And whosoever does deeds of righteousness,
being a believer, no unthankfulness
shall befall his endeavour; We Ourselves
      write it down for him.

There is a ban upon any city that We have destroyed;
      they shall not return
till, when Gog and Magog are unloosed, and they slide down
      out of every slope,
and nigh has drawn the true promise, and behold, the eyes
of the unbelievers staring: 'Alas for us! We were heedless
      of this; nay, we were evildoers.'
'Surely you, and that you were serving apart from God,
      are fuel for Gehenna; you shall go down to it.'
If those had been gods, they would never have gone down
yet every one of them shall therein abide forever;   [to it;
100 there shall be sighing for them therein, and naught they
                               [shall hear.
But as for those unto whom already
the reward most fair has gone forth from Us,
      they shall be kept far from it
neither shall they hear any whisper of it,
and they shall dwell forever in that
      their souls desired;
the greatest terror shall not grieve them,
and the angels shall receive them: 'This is
      your day that you were promised.'
On the day when We shall roll up heaven as a scroll is rolled
for the writings; as We originated the first creation,
so We shall bring it back again—a promise binding on Us;
      so We shall do.

105 For We have written in the Psalms, after the
Remembrance, 'The earth shall be the inheritance
   of My righteous servants.'
Surely in this is a Message delivered
   unto a people who serve.

We have not sent thee, save as a mercy
   unto all beings.
Say: 'It is revealed unto me only that
your God is One God; do you then surrender?'
Then, if they should turn their backs, say:
'I have proclaimed to you all equally,
even though I know not whether near or far
   is that you are promised.'

110 Surely He knows what is spoken aloud
   and He knows what you hide.
I know not; haply it is a trial for you
   and an enjoyment for a time.

He said: 'My Lord, judge Thou with truth!
   And our Lord is the All-merciful;
His succour is ever to be sought against
   that you describe.'

XXII

THE PILGRIMAGE

In the Name of God, the Merciful, the Compassionate

O men, fear your Lord!
Surely the earthquake of the Hour is a mighty thing;
on the day when you behold it, every suckling woman shall
neglect the child she has suckled, and every pregnant woman
shall deposit her burden, and thou shalt see mankind drunk,
yet they are not drunk, but God's chastisement is terrible.

And among men there is such a one
that disputes concerning God without knowledge
        and follows every rebel Satan,
against whom it is written down that
whosoever takes him for a friend, him he
leads astray, and he guides him to the
        chastisement of the burning.
5   O men,
if you are in doubt as to the Uprising,
        surely We created you of dust
                then of a sperm-drop,
                then of a blood clot,
then of a lump of flesh, formed and unformed
        that We may make clear to you.
        And We establish in the wombs
        what We will, till a stated term,
        then We deliver you as infants,
        then that you may come of age;
                and some of you die,
        and some of you are kept back
unto the vilest state of life, that after
knowing somewhat, they may know nothing.
And thou beholdest the earth blackened,
then, when We send down water upon it,

27

it quivers, and swells, and puts forth
    herbs of every joyous kind.
That is because God—He is the Truth,
and brings the dead to life, and is powerful
    over everything,
and because the Hour is coming, no doubt of it, and
God shall raise up whosoever is within the tombs.

And among men there is such a one
that disputes concerning God without knowledge
or guidance, or an illuminating Book,
turning his side to lead astray
from God's way; for him is degradation
in this world, and on the Resurrection Day
We shall let him taste the chastisement
    of the burning:
10   'That is for what thy hands have forwarded
and for that God is never unjust
    unto His servants.'

And among men there is such a one
as serves God upon the very edge—
if good befalls him he is at rest in it,
but if a trial befalls him he turns
completely over; he loses this world
and the world to come; that is indeed
    the manifest loss.
He calls, apart from God, upon that
which hurts him not, and which neither
profits him anything; that is indeed
    the far error.
He calls upon him who is likelier
to hurt him, rather than to profit him—
an evil protector indeed, he,
    an evil friend!

God shall surely admit those who believe
and do righteous deeds into gardens
underneath which rivers flow; surely God does

that He desires.

15 Whosoever thinks God will not help him
in the present world and the world to come,
let him stretch up a rope to heaven,
then let him sever it, and behold
whether his guile does away with what
enrages him.

Even so We have sent it down as signs,
clear signs, and for that God guides
whom He desires.
Surely they that believe, and those of Jewry,
the Sabaeans, the Christians, the Magians
and the idolaters—God shall distinguish
between them on the Day of Resurrection;
assuredly God is witness
over everything.
Hast thou not seen how to God bow all who are in the
and all who are in the earth,   [heavens
the sun and the moon, the stars and the mountains,
the trees and the beasts,
and many of mankind? And many merit the chastisement;
and whom God abases,
there is none to honour him. God does whatsoever He will.

20 These are two disputants who have disputed
concerning their Lord. As for the unbelievers,
for them garments of fire shall be cut,
and there shall be poured over their heads
boiling water
whereby whatsoever is in their bellies
and their skins shall be melted; for them await
hooked iron rods;
as often as they desire in their anguish
to come forth from it, they shall be restored
into it, and: 'Taste the chastisement
of the burning!'
God shall surely admit those who believe

and do righteous deeds into gardens
underneath which rivers flow; therein
they shall be adorned with bracelets of gold
and with pearls, and their apparel there
        shall be of silk;
and they shall be guided unto goodly speech,
and they shall be guided unto the path
        of the All-laudable.

25   Those who disbelieve, and bar from God's way
and the Holy Mosque that We have appointed
equal unto men, alike him who cleaves to it
        and the tent-dweller,
and whosoever purposes to violate it
wrongfully, We shall let him taste
        a painful chastisement.

And when We settled for Abraham the place
of the House: 'Thou shall not associate
with Me anything. And do thou purify
My House for those that shall go about it
and those that stand, for those that bow
        and prostrate themselves;
and proclaim among men the Pilgrimage,
and they shall come unto thee on foot
and upon every lean beast, they shall come from
        every deep ravine
that they may witness things profitable to them
and mention God's Name on days well-known
over such beasts of the flocks as He has
provided them: "So eat thereof, and feed
        the wretched poor."

30   Let them then finish with their self-neglect
and let them fulfil their vows, and go about
        the Ancient House.'
All that; and whosoever venerates
the sacred things of God, it shall be better
for him with his Lord. And permitted
to you are the flocks, except that which is
recited to you. And eschew the abomination

come upon them the chastisement of
a barren day.
The Kingdom upon that day shall belong
to God, and He shall judge between them.
As for those who believe, and do deeds
of righteousness, they shall be in
Gardens of Bliss.
But as for the unbelievers, who cried
lies to Our signs, for them awaits
a humbling chastisement.
And those who emigrated in God's way
and were slain, or died, God shall provide them
with a fair provision; and surely God is the
best of providers.
He shall admit them by a gate that is
well-pleasing to them; and surely God is
All-knowing, All-clement.
All that; and whosoever chastises
after the manner that he was chastised
and then again is oppressed, assuredly
God will help him; surely God is
All-pardoning, All-forgiving.

That is because God makes the night to enter into the day
and makes the day to enter into the night; and that God is
All-hearing, All-seeing.
That is because God—He is the Truth, and that they call
apart from Him—that is the false; and for that God is [upon
the All-high, the All-great.
Hast thou not seen how that God has sent down out of heaven
water, and in the morning the earth becomes green? God is
All-subtle, All-aware.
To Him belongs all that is in the heavens and in the earth
surely God—He is the All-sufficient, the All-laudable.
Hast thou not seen how that God has subjected to you
all that is in the earth
and the ships to run upon the sea at His commandment,
and He holds back heaven
lest it should fall upon the earth, save by His leave?

of idols, and eschew the speaking
of falsehood,
being men pure of faith unto God,
not associating with Him anything;
for whosoever associates with God anything,
it is as though he has fallen from heaven
and the birds snatch him away, or the wind
sweeps him headlong into a place
far away.
All that; and whosoever venerates
God's waymarks, that is of the godliness
of the hearts.
There are things therein profitable
to you unto a stated term; thereafter
their lawful place of sacrifice is by
the Ancient House.

35

We have appointed for every nation
a holy rite, that they may mention
God's Name over such beasts of the flocks
as He has provided them. Your God is One God,
so to Him surrender. And give thou good tidings
unto the humble
who, when God is mentioned, their hearts
quake, and such as endure patiently
whatever visits them, and who perform
the prayer, and expend of what We have
provided them.
And the beasts of sacrifice—We have appointed
them for you as among God's waymarks;
therein is good for you. So mention
God's Name over them, standing in ranks;
then, when their flanks collapse, eat of them
and feed the beggar and the suppliant.
So We have subjected them to you; haply
you will be thankful.
The flesh of them shall not reach God,
neither their blood, but godliness from you
shall reach Him. So He has subjected them

to you, that you may magnify God for that
He has guided you. And give thou good tidings
   unto the good-doers.

Assuredly God will defend those
who believe; surely God loves not any
   ungrateful traitor.
40 Leave is given to those who fight because
they were wronged—surely God is able
   to help them—
who were expelled from their habitations
without right, except that they say
'Our Lord is God.' Had God not driven back
the people, some by the means of others,
there had been destroyed cloisters and churches,
oratories and mosques, wherein God's Name
is much mentioned. Assuredly God will
help him who helps Him—surely God is
   All-strong, All-mighty—
who, if We establish them in the land,
perform the prayer, and pay the alms,
and bid to honour, and forbid dishonour;
and unto God belongs the issue
   of all affairs.
If they cry lies to thee, so too before them
the people of Noah cried lies, and Ad
and Thamood, and the people of Abraham,
the people of Lot, and the men of Midian;
to Moses also they cried lies. And I respited
the unbelievers, then I seized them; and
   how was My horror!
How many a city We have destroyed
in its evildoing, and now it is fallen down
upon its turrets! How many a ruined well,
   a tall palace!
45 What, have they not journeyed in the land
so that they have hearts to understand with
or ears to hear with? It is not the eyes
that are blind, but blind are the hearts

   within the breasts.
And they demand of thee to hasten
the chastisement! God will not fail
His promise; and surely a day
with thy Lord is as a thousand year
   of your counting.
How many a city I have respited
in its evildoing; then I seized it, an
   Me was the homecoming.
Say: 'O men, I am only for you
   a plain warner.'
Those who believe, and do deeds o
righteousness—theirs shall be forgi
   and generous provision.
And those who strive against Our s
to void them—they shall be the inh
   of Hell.

We sent not ever any Messenger
or Prophet before thee, but that Sa
cast into his fancy, when he was far
but God annuls what Satan casts, tl
God confirms His signs—surely G
   All-knowing, All-wise—
that He may make what Satan casts
a trial for those in whose hearts
is sickness, and those whose hearts
are hard; and surely the evildoers a
   in wide schism;
and that they who have been given
may know that it is the truth from
and believe in it, and so their heart
be humble unto Him; and assuredly
God ever guides those who believe
   to a straight path.

And the unbelievers will not cease
to be in doubt of it, until the Hour
comes on them suddenly, or there s

Surely God is All-gentle to men, All-compassionate.
It is He who gave you
65   life, then He shall make you dead, then He shall give you life.
Surely man is ungrateful.

We have appointed for every nation
a holy rite that they shall perform.
Let them not therefore wrangle with thee
upon the matter, and do thou summon
unto thy Lord; surely thou art upon
    a straight guidance.
And if they should dispute with thee,
do thou say, 'God knows very well
    what you are doing.
God shall judge between you on the Day
of Resurrection touching that whereon
    you were at variance.'
Didst thou not know that God knows all
that is in heaven and earth? Surely that
is in a Book; surely that for God is
    an easy matter.
70   They serve, apart from God, that whereon
He has sent down never authority
and that whereof they have no knowledge;
and for the evildoers there shall be
    no helper.
And when Our signs are recited to them,
clear signs, thou recognisest in the faces of
the unbelievers denial; wellnigh they
rush upon those who recite to them
Our signs. Say: 'Shall I tell you of
something worse than that? The Fire—God
has promised it to the unbelievers—
    an evil homecoming!'

O men, a similitude is struck; so
give you ear to it. Surely those upon
whom you call, apart from God, shall never
create a fly, though they banded together

to do it; and if a fly should rob them
of aught, they would never rescue it from him.
Feeble indeed alike are the seeker
                  and the sought!
They measure not God with His true measure; surely God is
                  All-strong, All-mighty.

God chooses of the angels Messengers
and of mankind; surely God is
                  All-hearing, All-seeing.
75   He knows whatsoever is before them
and behind them, and unto God all
                  matters are returned.

O men, bow you down and prostrate yourselves,
and serve your Lord, and do good; haply so
                  you shall prosper;
and struggle for God as is His due, for
He has chosen you, and has laid on you
no impediment in your religion,
being the creed of your father Abraham; He
                  named you Muslims
aforetime and in this, that the Messenger
might be a witness against you, and that
you might be witnesses against mankind.
So perform the prayer, and pay the alms,
and hold you fast to God; He is your
Protector—an excellent Protector,
                  an excellent Helper.

XXIII

THE BELIEVERS

In the Name of God, the Merciful, the Compassionate

Prosperous are the believers
who in their prayers are humble
and from idle talk turn away
and at almsgiving are active
5   and guard their private parts
save from their wives and what their right hands own
then being not blameworthy
(but whosoever seeks after more than that,
those are the transgressors)
and who preserve their trusts
and their covenant
and who observe their prayers.
10   Those are the inheritors
who shall inherit Paradise
therein dwelling forever.

We created man of an extraction
of clay,
then We set him, a drop, in a receptacle
secure,
then We created of the drop a clot
then We created of the clot a tissue
then We created of the tissue bones
then We garmented the bones in flesh;
thereafter We produced him as another creature.
So blessed be God, the fairest of creators!
15   Then after that you shall surely die,
then on the Day of Resurrection you
shall surely be raised up.
And We created above you seven ways,
and We were not heedless of creation.

And We sent down out of heaven water
in measure and lodged it in the earth;
and We are able to take it away.
Then We produced for you therewith
    gardens of palms and vines
    wherein are many fruits for
    you, and of them you eat,

20   and a tree issuing from the Mount of Sinai that
    bears oil and seasoning
      for all to eat.
And surely in the cattle there is a lesson for you;
    We give you to drink of
    what is in their bellies,
and many uses there are in them for you,
    and of them you eat;
and upon them, and on the ships, you are borne.

And We sent Noah to his people;
and he said, 'O my people, serve God!
You have no god other than He.
    Will you not be godfearing?''
Said the Council of the unbelievers
of his people, 'This is naught but
a mortal like yourselves, who desires
to gain superiority over you. And
if God willed, He would have sent down
angels. We never heard of this among
    our fathers, the ancients.

25   He is naught but a man bedevilled; so
    wait on him for a time.'
He said, 'O my Lord, help me,
    for that they cry me lies.'
Then We said to him, 'Make thou the Ark
under Our eyes and as We reveal,
and then, when Our command comes
    and the Oven boils,
insert in it two of every kind
and thy family—except for him
against whom the word already

has been spoken; and address Me not
concerning those who have done evil;
    they shall be drowned.
Then, when thou art seated in the Ark
and those with thee, say, "Praise belongs to
God, who has delivered us from the people
    of the evildoers."

30   And say, "O my Lord, do Thou harbour
me in a blessed harbour, for Thou art
    the best of harbourers." '
Surely in that are signs, and surely
    We put to the test.

Thereafter, after them, We produced
    another generation,
and We sent amongst them a Messenger
of themselves, saying, 'Serve God!
You have no god other than He.
    Will you not be godfearing?'
Said the Council of the unbelievers
of his people, who cried lies to the
encounter of the world to come,
and to whom We had given ease in the
present life, 'This is naught but
a mortal like yourselves, who eats
    of what you eat

35   and drinks of what you drink.
If you obey a mortal like yourselves,
    then you will be losers.
What, does he promise you that when you are
dead, and become dust and bones, you
    shall be brought forth?
    Away, away
    with that you are promised!
There is nothing but our present life;
we die, and we live, and we shall
    not be raised up.

40   He is naught but a man who has forged
against God a lie, and we will

not believe him.'
He said, 'O my Lord, help me,
    for that they cry me lies.'
He said, 'In a little they will
    be remorseful.'
And the Cry seized them justly, and We
made them as scum; so away with the people
    of the evildoers!

Thereafter, after them, We produced
    other generations;
45   no nation outstrips its term, nor
    do they put it back.
Then sent We Our Messengers successively;
whenever its Messenger came to a nation
they cried him lies, so We caused some
of them to follow others, and We made them
as but tales; so away with a people
    who do not believe!

Then We sent Moses and his brother
Aaron with Our signs and a manifest
    authority
unto Pharaoh and his Council;
but they waxed proud, and they were
    a lofty people,
and they said, 'What, shall we believe
two mortals like ourselves, whose people
    are our servants?'
50   So they cried them lies, and they were
    among the destroyed.

And We gave Moses the Book, that haply
    they would be guided;
and We made Mary's son, and his mother,
to be a sign, and gave them refuge
upon a height, where was a hollow
    and a spring:
'O Messengers, eat of the good things

and do righteousness; surely I know
the things you do.
Surely this community of yours
is one community, and I am your Lord;
so fear Me.'
55   But they split in their affair between them
into sects, each party rejoicing in
what is with them.
So leave thou them in their perplexity
for a time.
What, do they think that We succour them with
of wealth and children
We vie in good works for them? Nay, but
they are not aware.

Surely those who tremble in fear of their Lord
60   and those who believe in the signs of their Lord
and those who associate naught with their Lord
and those who give what they give, their hearts
quaking that they are returning to their Lord—
those vie in good works, outracing to them.

We charge not any soul save to its capacity,
and with Us is a Book speaking truth, and
they shall not be wronged.
65   Nay, but their hearts are in perplexity
as to this, and they have deeds besides that
that they are doing.
Till, when We seize with the chastisement
the ones of them that live at ease,
behold, they groan.
'Groan not today; surely you shall not be
helped from Us.
My signs were recited to you, but upon your
heels you withdrew,
waxing proud against it, talking foolish
talk by night.'
70   Have they not pondered the saying, or came there
upon them that which came not upon their

x

fathers, the ancients?
Or did they not recognise their Messenger
and so denied him?
Or do they say, 'He is bedevilled'? Nay,
he has brought them the truth, but most of them are
averse from the truth.
Had the truth followed their caprices,
the heavens and the earth and whosoever
in them is had surely corrupted. Nay, We
brought them their Remembrance, but from their
Remembrance they turned.
Or dost thou ask them for tribute? Yet the
tribute of thy Lord is better, and He is the
best of providers.

75   Assuredly thou art calling them
to a straight path;
and surely they that believe not
in the world to come are deviating
from the path.
Did We have mercy on them, and remove
the affliction that is upon them,
they would persist in their insolence
wandering blindly.
We already seized them with the chastisement,
yet they abased not themselves to their Lord
nor were they humble;
until, when We open against them a door
of terrible chastisement, lo, they are sore
confounded at it.

80   It is He who produced for you hearing, and eyes, and
little thanks you show.   [hearts;
It is He who scattered you in the earth, and to Him
you shall be mustered.
It is He who gives life, and makes to die, and to Him
belongs the alternation of night and day; what,
will you not understand?

Nay, but they said the like of what

the ancients said.
They said, 'What, when we are dead
and become dust and bones, shall we be
    indeed raised up?

85   We and our fathers have been promised this
before; this is naught but the fairy-tales
    of the ancients.'
Say: 'Whose is the earth, and whoso is in it,
    if you have knowledge?'
They will say, 'God's.' Say: 'Will you not
    then remember?'
Say: 'Who is the Lord of the seven heavens
    and the Lord of the mighty Throne?'
They will say, 'God's.' Say: 'Will you not
    then be godfearing?'

90   Say: 'In whose hand is the dominion of
everything, protecting and Himself unprotected,
    if you have knowledge?'
They will say, 'God's.' Say: 'How then
    are you bewitched?'
Nay, but We brought them the truth, and they
    are truly liars.
God has not taken to Himself any son,
nor is there any god with Him; for then
each god would have taken off that he created
and some of them would have risen up
over others; glory to be God, beyond
    that they describe,
who has knowledge of the Unseen and the
Visible; high exalted be He, above
    that they associate!

95   Say: 'O my Lord, if Thou shouldst show me
    that they are promised,
O my Lord, put me not among the people
    of the evildoers.'
Assuredly, We are able to show thee
    that We promise them.
Repel thou the evil with that which is

fairer. We Ourselves know very well
    that they describe.
And say: 'O my Lord, I take refuge
in Thee from the evil suggestions
    of the Satans,
100   and I take refuge in Thee, O my Lord,
    lest they attend me.'

Till, when death comes to one of them, he says,
    'My Lord, return me;
haply I shall do righteousness in that
I forsook.' Nay, it is but a word
he speaks; and there, behind them,
is a barrier until the day that they
    shall be raised up.

For when the Trumpet is blown, that day there shall be no
    ⌈kinship
any more between them, neither will they question one
    ⌈another.
Then he whose scales are heavy—they are the prosperers,
105   and he whose scales are light—they have lost their souls
in Gehenna dwelling forever, the Fire smiting their faces
the while they glower there. 'What, were My signs not
    ⌈recited
to you, and you cried them lies?' They shall say, 'Our Lord,
our adversity prevailed over us; we were an erring people.
Our Lord, bring us forth out of it! Then, if we revert,
110   we shall be evildoers indeed.' 'Slink you into it,'
He shall say, 'and do not speak to Me. There is a party
of My servants who said, "Our Lord, we believe; therefore
forgive us, and have mercy on us, for Thou art the best
of the merciful." But you took them for a laughing-stock,
till they made you forget My remembrance, mocking at them.
Now today I have recompensed them for their patient
    ⌈endurance;
115   they are the triumphant.' He shall say, 'How long have you
tarried in the earth, by number of years?' They shall say,
'We have tarried a day, or part of a day; ask the numberers!'

He shall say, 'You have tarried but a little, did you know.
What, did you think that We created you only for sport,
and that you would not be returned to Us?'

> Then high exalted be God,
> the King, the True!
> There is no god but He, the
> Lord of the noble Throne.

> And whosoever calls upon another god
> with God, whereof he has no proof,
> his reckoning is with his Lord;
> surely the unbelievers shall not prosper.

> And say: 'My Lord, forgive
> and have mercy, for Thou art the best
> of the merciful.'

XXIV

LIGHT

A sura that We have sent down
and appointed; and We have sent down
in it signs, clear signs, that haply
                you will remember.

The fornicatress and the fornicator—
scourge each one of them a hundred stripes,
and in the matter of God's religion
let no tenderness for them seize you
if you believe in God and the Last Day;
and let a party of the believers
                witness their chastisement.
The fornicator shall marry none but
a fornicatress or an idolatress,
and the fornicatress—none shall marry her
but a fornicator or an idolator;
that is forbidden to the believers.

And those who cast it up on women in
wedlock, and then bring not four witnesses,
scourge them with eighty stripes, and do not
accept any testimony of theirs ever; those—
                they are the ungodly,
5   save such as repent thereafter and
make amends; surely God is All-forgiving,
                All-compassionate.
And those who cast it up on their wives
having no witnesses except themselves,
the testimony of one of them shall be
to testify by God four times that he
                is of the truthful,

and a fifth time, that the curse of
God shall be upon him, if he should
     be of the liars.
It shall avert from her the chastisement
if she testify by God four times that he
     is of the liars,
and a fifth time, that the wrath of
God shall be upon her, if he should
     be of the truthful.

10   But for God's bounty to you and His mercy
and that God turns, and is All-wise—

Those who came with the slander are a
band of you; do not reckon it evil
for you; rather it is good for you.
Every man of them shall have the sin
that he has earned charged to him; and
whosoever of them took upon himself
the greater part of it, him there awaits
     a mighty chastisement.
Why, when you heard it, did the believing
men and women not of their own account
think good thoughts, and say, 'This is
     a manifest calumny'?
Why did they not bring four witnesses
against it? But since they did not
bring the witnesses, in God's sight
     they are the liars.
But for God's bounty to you and His mercy
in the present world and the world to come
there would have visited you for your mutterings
a mighty chastisement. When you received it
on your tongues, and were speaking with your mouths
that whereof you had no knowledge, and
reckoned it a light thing, and with God it
     was a mighty thing—
15   And why, when you heard it, did you not
say, 'It is not for us to speak about

this; glory be to Thee! This is
　　a mighty calumny'?
God admonishes you, that you shall
never repeat the like of it again, if
　　you are believers.
God makes clear to you the signs; and God is
　　All-knowing, All-wise.
Those who love that indecency
should be spread abroad concerning
them that believe—there awaits them
　　a painful chastisement
in the present world and the world to come;
and God knows, and you know not.

20　　But for God's bounty to you and His mercy
and that God is All-gentle, All-compassionate—

O believers, follow not the steps of
Satan; for whosoever follows
the steps of Satan, assuredly he
bids to indecency and dishonour.
But for God's bounty to you and His mercy
not one of you would have been pure ever;
but God purifies whom He will; and God is
　　All-hearing, All-knowing.

Let not those of you who possess bounty
and plenty swear off giving kinsmen
and the poor and those who emigrate
in the way of God; but let them pardon
and forgive. Do you not wish that God
should forgive you? God is All-forgiving,
　　All-compassionate.

Surely those who cast it up on women
in wedlock that are heedless but believing
shall be accursed in the present world
and the world to come; and there awaits them
　　a mighty chastisement

on the day when their tongues, their hands and
their feet shall testify against them touching
  that they were doing.
25 Upon that day God will pay them in full
their just due, and they shall know that God
  is the manifest Truth.

Corrupt women for corrupt men,
and corrupt men for corrupt women;
good women for good men,
and good men for good women—
these are declared quit of what they
say; theirs shall be forgiveness
  and generous provision.

O believers, do not enter houses
other than your houses until you first
ask leave and salute the people
thereof; that is better for you; haply
  you will remember.
And if you find not anyone therein,
enter it not until leave is given
to you. And if you are told, 'Return,'
return; that is purer for you; and God knows
  the things you do.
There is no fault in you that you enter
houses uninhabited wherein enjoyment is
for you. God knows what you reveal
  and what you hide.

30 Say to the believers, that they cast down
their eyes and guard their private parts;
that is purer for them. God is aware of
  the things they work.
And say to the believing women, that they
cast down their eyes and guard their private
parts, and reveal not their adornment
save such as is outward; and let them cast
their veils over their bosoms, and not reveal

their adornment save to their husbands,
or their fathers, or their husbands' fathers,
or their sons, or their husbands' sons,
or their brothers, or their brothers' sons,
or their sisters' sons, or their women,
or what their right hands own, or such men
as attend them, not having sexual desire,
or children who have not yet attained knowledge
of women's private parts; nor let them stamp
their feet, so that their hidden ornament
may be known. And turn all together
to God, O you believers; haply so
         you will prosper.

Marry the spouseless among you, and your
slaves and handmaidens that are righteous;
if they are poor, God will enrich them
of His bounty; God is All-embracing,
         All-knowing.
And let those who find not the means to
marry be abstinent till God enriches them
of His bounty. Those your right hands own
who seek emancipation, contract with
them accordingly, if you know some good
in them; and give them of the wealth of God
that He has given you. And constrain not
your slavegirls to prostitution, if they
desire to live in chastity, that you may
seek the chance goods of the present life.
Whosoever constrains them, surely God,
after their being constrained, is All-forgiving,
         All-compassionate.

Now We have sent down to you signs
making all clear, and an example
of those who passed away before you,
and an admonition for the godfearing.

35   God is the Light of the heavens and the earth;

the likeness of His Light is as a niche
wherein is a lamp
(the lamp in a glass,
the glass as it were a glittering star)
kindled from a Blessed Tree,
an olive that is neither of the East nor of the West
whose oil wellnigh would shine, even if no fire touched it;
Light upon Light;
(God guides to His Light whom He will.)
(And God strikes similitudes for men,
and God has knowledge of everything.)
in temples God has allowed to be raised up,
and His Name to be commemorated therein;
therein glorifying Him, in the mornings and the evenings,
are men whom neither commerce nor trafficking
diverts from the remembrance of God
and to perform the prayer, and to pay the alms,
fearing a day when hearts and eyes shall be turned about,
that God may recompense them for their fairest works
and give them increase of His bounty;
and God provides whomsoever He will, without reckoning.

And as for the unbelievers,
their works are as a mirage in a spacious plain
which the man athirst supposes to be water,
till, when he comes to it, he finds it is nothing;
there indeed he finds God,
and He pays him his account in full; (and God is swift
at the reckoning.)
40   or they are as shadows upon a sea obscure
covered by a billow
above which is a billow
above which are clouds,
shadows piled one upon another;
when he puts forth his hand, wellnigh he cannot see it.
And to whomsoever God assigns no light,
no light has he.

Hast thou not seen how that whatsoever is in the heavens

and in the earth extols God,
and the birds spreading their wings?
Each—He knows its prayer and its extolling; and God knows
the things they do.
To God belongs the Kingdom of the heavens and the earth,
and to Him is the homecoming.
Hast thou not seen how God drives the clouds, then composes
       then converts them into a mass,   [them,
then thou seest the rain issuing out of the midst of them?
And He sends down out of heaven mountains, wherein is hail,
so that He smites whom He will with it, and turns it aside
       from whom He will;
wellnigh the gleam of His lightning snatches away the sight.
       God turns about the day and the night;
     surely in that is a lesson for those who have eyes.
       God has created every beast of water,
       and some of them go upon their bellies,
       and some of them go upon two feet,
       and some of them go upon four; God
       creates whatever He will; God is powerful
         over everything.

45   Now We have sent down signs making all
       clear; God guides whomsoever He will
         to a straight path.
       They say, 'We believe in God and the
       Messenger, and we obey.' Then after that
       a party of them turn away; those—
         they are not believers.
       When they are called to God and His Messenger
       that he may judge between them, lo, a party of them
         are swerving aside;
       but if they are in the right, they will come to
         him submissively.
       What, is there sickness in their hearts,
       or are they in doubt, or do they fear
       that God may be unjust towards them
       and His Messenger? Nay, but those—
         they are the evildoers.

50   All that the believers say, when they
are called to God and His Messenger, that he
may judge between them, is that they say,
'We hear, and we obey'; those—
     they are the prosperers.
Whoso obeys God and His Messenger,
and fears God and has awe of Him, those—
     they are the triumphant.
They have sworn by God the most earnest oaths,
if thou commandest them they will go forth.
Say: 'Do not swear; honourable obedience
is sufficient. Surely God is aware of
     the things you do.'
Say: 'Obey God, and obey the Messenger;
then, if you turn away, only upon
him rests what is laid on him, and
upon you rests what is laid on you.
If you obey him, you will be guided.
It is only for the Messenger to deliver
     the manifest Message.'

God has promised those of you who believe
and do righteous deeds that He will surely
make you successors in the land, even as He
made those who were before them successors,
and that He will surely establish their
religion for them that He has approved for them,
and will give them in exchange, after
their fear, security: 'They shall serve Me,
not associating with Me anything.'
Whoso disbelieves after that, those—
     they are the ungodly.
55   Perform the prayer, and pay the alms,
and obey the Messenger—haply so
     you will find mercy.
Think not the unbelievers able to frustrate
God in the earth; their refuge is the Fire—
     an evil homecoming.

O believers, let those your right hands own
and those of you who have not reached puberty
ask leave of you three times—before
the prayer of dawn, and when you put off
your garments at the noon, and after
the evening prayer—three times of nakedness
for you. There is no fault in you or them, apart
from these, that you go about one to the other.
So God makes clear to you the signs; and God is
        All-knowing, All-wise.
When your children reach puberty, let them
ask leave, as those before them asked leave.
So God makes clear to you His signs; and God is
        All-knowing, All-wise.
Such women as are past child-bearing
and have no hope of marriage—there is no
fault in them that they put off their clothes,
so be it that they flaunt no ornament;
but to abstain is better for them; and God is
        All-hearing, All-knowing.

60   There is no fault in the blind, and there is
no fault in the lame, and there is no fault
in the sick, neither in yourselves, that you
eat of your houses, or your fathers' houses,
or your mothers' houses, or your brothers' houses,
or your sisters' houses, or the houses of
your uncles or your aunts paternal, or
the houses of your uncles or your aunts
maternal, or that whereof you own the keys,
or of your friend; there is no fault in you
that you eat all together, or in groups
        separately.
But when you enter houses, greet one another
with a greeting from God, blessed and good.
So God makes clear to you the signs; haply
        you will understand.

Those only are believers, who believe

in God and His Messenger and who, when they
are with him upon a common matter,
go not away until they ask his leave.
Surely those who ask thy leave—those are
they that believe in God and His Messenger;
so, when they ask thy leave for some affair
of their own, give leave to whom thou wilt
of them, and ask God's forgiveness
for them; surely God is All-forgiving,
        All-compassionate.
Make not the calling of the Messenger
among yourselves like your calling
one of another. God knows those of you
who slip away surreptitiously; so let those
who go against His command beware, lest
a trial befall them, or there befall them
        a painful chastisement.

Why, surely to God belongs whatsoever is in the heavens
and the earth; He ever knows what state you are upon;
and the day when they shall be returned to Him, then He
will tell them of what they did; and God knows everything.

XXV

SALVATION

In the Name of God, the Merciful, the Compassionate

Blessed be He
who has sent down the Salvation upon
His servant, that he may be a warner
to all beings;
to whom belongs the Kingdom of the heavens
and the earth; and He has not taken
to Him a son, and He has no associate
in the Kingdom; and He created
every thing, then He ordained it
very exactly.
Yet they have taken to them gods, apart
from Him, that create nothing and themselves
are created,
and have no power to hurt or profit
themselves, no power of death or life or
raising up.

5   The unbelievers say, 'This is naught but a
calumny he has forged, and other folk have
helped him to it.' So they have committed
wrong and falsehood.
They say, 'Fairy-tales of the ancients
that he has had written down, so that
they are recited to him at the dawn
and in the evening.'
Say: 'He sent it down, who knows the secret
in the heavens and earth; He is All-forgiving,
All-compassionate.'

They also say, 'What ails this Messenger
that he eats food, and goes in the markets?

Why has an angel not been sent down to him, to be
    a warner with him?
Or why is not a treasure thrown to him,
or why has he not a Garden to eat of?'
The evildoers say, 'You are only following
    a man bewitched!'
10   Behold, how they strike similitudes
for thee, and go astray, and are unable
    to find a way!

Blessed be He
who, if He will, shall assign to thee
better than that—gardens underneath
which rivers flow, and he shall assign
    to thee palaces.

Nay, but they cry lies to the Hour; and We have prepared
for him who cries lies to the Hour a Blaze. When it sees them
from a far place, they shall hear its bubbling and sighing.
And when they are cast, coupled in fetters, into a narrow place
of that Fire, they will call out there for destruction.
15   'Call not out today for one destruction, but call for many!'

Say: 'Is that better, or the Garden
of Eternity, that is promised to
the godfearing, and is their recompense
    and homecoming?'
Therein they shall have what they will
dwelling forever; it is a promise
binding upon thy Lord, and of Him
    to be required.

Upon the day when He shall muster them and that they
                ⌈serve, apart
from God, and He shall say, 'Was it you that led these My
                ⌈servants
astray, or did they themselves err from the way?' They shall
'Glory be to Thee! It did not behove us to take unto ⌈say,
ourselves protectors apart from Thee; but Thou gavest them

57

and their fathers enjoyment of days, until they forgot
20   the Remembrance, and were a people corrupt.' So they cried
lies touching the things you say, and you can neither [you
turn it aside, nor find any help. Whosoever of you
does evil, We shall let him taste a great chastisement.

> And We sent not before thee any
> Envoys, but that they ate food, and went
> in the markets; and We appointed
> some of you to be a trial for others:
> 'Will you endure?' Thy Lord is ever
> All-seeing.
> Say those who look not to encounter Us,
> 'Why have the angels not been sent down
> on us, or why see we not our Lord?'
> Waxed proud they have within them, and become
> greatly disdainful.

Upon the day that they see the angels, no good tidings
that day for the sinners; they shall say, 'A ban forbidden!'
25   We shall advance upon what work they have done, and make it
a scattered dust. The inhabitants of Paradise that day,
better shall be their lodging, fairer their resting-place.
Upon the day that heaven is split asunder with the clouds
and the angels are sent down in majesty, the Kingdom
that day, the true Kingdom, shall belong to the All-merciful,
and it shall be a day harsh for the unbelievers.
Upon the day the evildoer shall bite his hands, saying,
'Would that I had taken a way along with the Messenger!
30   Alas, would that I had not taken So-and-so for a friend!
He indeed led me astray from the Remembrance, after
it had come to me; Satan is ever a forsaker of men.'

> The Messenger says, 'O my Lord, behold,
> my people have taken this Koran as a
> thing to be shunned.'
> Even so We have appointed to every
> Prophet an enemy among the sinners;
> but thy Lord suffices as a guide

and as a helper.
The unbelievers say, 'Why has the Koran
not been sent down upon him all at once?'
Even so, that We may strengthen thy
heart thereby, and We have chanted it
very distinctly.
35   They bring not to thee any similitude
but that We bring thee the truth, and better
in exposition.
Those who shall be mustered to Gehenna
upon their faces—they shall be worse
in place, and gone further astray
from the way.

We gave Moses the Book, and appointed
with him his brother Aaron as minister
and We said, 'Go to the people
who have cried lies to Our signs';
then We destroyed them utterly.
And the people of Noah, when they
cried lies to the Messengers, We
drowned them, and made them to be
a sign to mankind; and We
have prepared for the evildoers
a painful chastisement.
40   And Ad, and Thamood, and the men
of Er-Rass, and between that
generations a many—for each
We struck similitudes, and each
We ruined utterly.
Surely they have come by the city
that was rained on by an evil rain;
what, have they not seen it? Nay,
but they look for no uprising.
And when they see thee, they take thee
in mockery only: 'What, is this he
whom God sent forth as a Messenger?
Wellnigh he had led us astray
from our gods, but that we kept

steadfast to them.' Assuredly
they shall know, when they see
the chastisement, who is further
astray from the way.

45   Hast thou seen him who has taken
his caprice to be his god?
Wilt thou be a guardian over them?
Or deemest thou that most of them
hear or understand? They are but
as the cattle; nay, they are further
astray from the way.

Hast thou not regarded thy Lord, how He has stretched out
the shadow? Had He willed,
He would have made it still.
Then We appointed the sun, to be a guide to it;
thereafter We seize it to
Ourselves, drawing it gently.
It is He who appointed the night for you to be a garment
and sleep for a rest, and day
He appointed for a rising.

50   And it is He who has loosed the winds, bearing good tidings
before His mercy; and We
sent down from heaven pure water
so that We might revive a dead land, and give to drink
of it, of that We created,
cattle and men a many.

We have indeed turned it about
amongst them, so that they may
remember; yet most men refuse all
but unbelief.

If We had willed, We would have raised up
in every city a warner.
So obey not the unbelievers, but struggle with
them thereby mightily.

55   And it is He who let forth the two seas, this one sweet,

grateful to taste, and this
salt, bitter to the tongue,
and He set between them a barrier, and a ban forbidden.
And it is He who created of
water a mortal, and made him
kindred of blood and marriage; thy Lord is All-powerful.

And they serve, apart from God, what neither
profits them nor hurts them; and the
unbeliever is ever a partisan
against his Lord.
We have sent thee not, except good tidings
to bear, and warning.
Say: 'I do not ask of you a wage for this,
except for him who wishes to take to
his Lord a way.'

60   Put thy trust in the Living God,
the Undying,
and proclaim His praise.
Sufficiently is He aware of His servants' sins
who created the heavens and the earth,
and what between them is, in six days,
then sat Himself upon the Throne,
the All-compassionate: ask any informed of Him!

But when they are told, 'Bow yourselves
to the All-merciful,' they say, 'And what
is the All-merciful? Shall we bow ourselves
to what thou biddest us?' And it increases
them in aversion.

Blessed be He
who has set in heaven constellations, and has set
among them a lamp, and
an illuminating moon.
And it is He who made the night and day a succession
for whom He desires to remember
or He desires to be thankful.

The servants of the All-merciful are
those who walk in the earth modestly
and who, when the ignorant address them,
    say, 'Peace';
65   who pass the night prostrate to their Lord
    and standing;
who say, 'Our Lord, turn Thou from us
the chastisement of Gehenna; surely
its chastisement is torment most terrible;
evil it is as a lodging-place
    and an abode';
who, when they expend, are neither prodigal
nor parsimonious, but between that is
    a just stand;
who call not upon another god with God,
nor slay the soul God has forbidden
except by right, neither fornicate,
for whosoever does that shall meet
    the price of sin—
doubled shall be the chastisement for him
on the Resurrection Day, and he shall dwell
    therein humbled,
70   save him who repents, and believes, and
does righteous work—those, God will
change their evil deeds into good deeds,
for God is ever All-forgiving,
    All-compassionate;
and whosoever repents, and does
righteousness, he truly turns to God
    in repentance.
And those who bear not false witness
and, when they pass by idle talk, pass by
    with dignity;
who, when they are reminded of the signs
of their Lord, fall not down thereat
    deaf and blind;
who say, 'Our Lord, give us refreshment of
our wives and seed, and make us a model

to the godfearing.'
75 Those shall be recompensed with the highest
heaven, for that they endured patiently,
and they shall receive therein a greeting
and—'Peace!'
Therein they shall dwell forever;
fair it is as a lodging-place
and an abode.

Say: 'My Lord esteems you not at all
were it not for your prayer, for you
have cried lies, and it shall surely be
fastened.'

XXVI

THE POETS

In the Name of God, the Merciful, the Compassionate

Ta Sin Mim

Those are the signs of the Manifest Book.

> Perchance thou consumest thyself
>   that they are not believers.
> If We will, We shall send down on them
> out of heaven a sign, so their necks
>   will stay humbled to it.
> But never fresh remembrance comes to
> them from the All-merciful, except
>   they turn away from it.

5   So they have cried lies; therefore
> assuredly tidings will come to them
>   of that they mocked at.

What, have they not regarded the earth, how many therein
    We have caused to grow of every generous kind?

>   Surely in that is a sign,
> yet most of them are not believers.
>   Surely thy Lord, He is
> the All-mighty, the All-compassionate.

> And when thy Lord called to Moses,
> 'Go to the people of the evildoers, the

10   people of Pharaoh; will they not be godfearing?'
> He said, 'My Lord, I fear they will cry me
> lies, and my breast will be straitened,
> and my tongue will not be loosed; so
> send to Aaron. They also have a sin

against me, and I fear they will slay me.'
Said He, 'No indeed; but go, both of you,
with Our signs, and We assuredly
shall be with you, listening.
15   So go you to Pharaoh, and say,
"Verily, I am the Messenger
of the Lord of all Being; so send
forth with us the Children of Israel." '
He said, 'Did we not raise thee
amongst us as a child? Didst thou not
tarry among us years of thy life?
And thou didst the deed thou didst,   .
being one of the ungrateful!'
Said he, 'Indeed I did it then,
being one of those that stray;
20   so I fled from you, fearing you.
But my Lord gave me Judgment
and made me one of the Envoys.
That is a blessing thou reproachest me with,
having enslaved the Children of Israel.'
Pharaoh said, 'And what is the Lord
of all Being?' He said, 'The Lord
of the heavens and earth, and what
between them is, if you have faith.'
Said he to those about him,
25   'Do you not hear?' He said, 'Your Lord
and the Lord of your fathers, the ancients.'
Said he, 'Surely your Messenger
who was sent to you is possessed!'
He said, 'The Lord of the East and West,
and what between them is, if you
have understanding,' Said he, 'If thou
takest a god other than me,
I shall surely make thee one
of the imprisoned.' He said, 'What,
even though I brought thee something
30   manifest?' Said he, 'Bring it then,
if thou art of the truthful.' So he
cast his staff, and behold,

65

C

it was a serpent manifest.
And he drew forth his hand, and lo,
it was white to the beholders.
Said he to the Council about him,
'Surely this man is a cunning sorcerer
who desires to expel you from
your land by his sorcery; what
35   do you command?' They said, 'Put him
and his brother off a while, and
send among the cities musterers,
to bring thee every cunning sorcerer.'
So the sorcerers were assembled
for the appointed time of a fixed day.
The people were asked, 'Will you assemble?
Haply we shall follow the sorcerers
if it should be they are the victors.'
40   Then, when the sorcerers came, they said
to Pharaoh, 'Shall we indeed have a
wage, if we should be the victors?'
He said, 'Yes indeed; and you shall
then be among the near-stationed.'
Moses said to them, 'Cast you down
what you will cast.' So they cast
their ropes and their staffs, and said,
'By the might of Pharaoh we shall be
the victors.' Then Moses cast his staff
and lo, it forthwith swallowed up
45   their lying invention; so the sorcerers
were cast down, bowing themselves.
They said, 'We believe in the
Lord of all Being, the Lord of Moses
and Aaron.' Said Pharaoh, 'You have
believed him before I gave you leave.
Why, he is the chief of you, the same
that taught you sorcery; now you shall know!
I shall assuredly cut off
alternately your hands and feet,
then I shall crucify you all together.'
50   They said, 'There is no harm; surely

unto our Lord we are turning.
We are eager that our Lord should
forgive us our offences, for that
we are the first of the believers.'
Also We revealed unto Moses,
'Go with My servants by night; surely
you will be followed.' Then Pharaoh
sent among the cities musterers:
'Behold, these are a small troop,
55   and indeed they are enraging us;
and we are a host on our guard.'
So We expelled them from gardens
and fountains, and treasures and a
noble station; even so, and We
60   bequeathed them upon the Children of
Israel. Then they followed them
at the sunrise; and, when the two hosts
sighted each other, the companions
of Moses said, 'We are overtaken!'
Said he, 'No indeed; surely my
Lord is with me; He will guide me.'
Then We revealed to Moses,
'Strike with thy staff the sea'; and it clave,
and each part was as a mighty mount.
65   And there We brought the others on, and We
delivered Moses and those with him
all together; then We drowned the others.

Surely in that is a sign,
yet most of them are not believers.
Surely thy Lord, He is
the All-mighty, the All-compassionate.

And recite to them the tiding of Abraham
70   when he said to his father and his people,
'What do you serve?'
They said, 'We serve idols, and continue
cleaving to them.'

He said, 'Do they hear you when you call,
or do they profit you, or harm?'
They said, 'Nay, but we found our fathers
   so doing.'
75   He said, 'And have you considered what
     you have been serving,
you and your fathers, the elders?
They are an enemy to me, except the
   Lord of all Being
who created me, and Himself guides me,
and Himself gives me to eat and drink,
80   and, whenever I am sick, heals me,
who makes me to die, then gives me life,
and who I am eager shall forgive me
my offence on the Day of Doom.
My Lord, give me Judgment, and join me
   with the righteous,
and appoint me a tongue of truthfulness
   among the others.
85   Make me one of the inheritors of the
     Garden of Bliss.
and forgive my father, for he is one
   of those astray.
Degrade me not upon the day when they
   are raised up,
the day when neither wealth nor sons
   shall profit
except for him who comes to God with
   a pure heart.
90   And Paradise shall be brought forward
     for the godfearing,
and Hell advanced for the perverse.
It shall be said to them, 'Where is that
   you were serving
apart from God? Do they help you
   or help themselves?'
Then they shall be pitched into it,
   they and the perverse
95   and the hosts of Iblis, all together.

They shall say, as they dispute there
    one with another,
'By God, we were certainly in
    manifest error
when we made you equal with the
    Lord of all Being.
It was naught but the sinners that
    led us astray;
so now we have no intercessors,
    no loyal friend.
O that we might return again, and be
    among the believers!'

    Surely in that is a sign,
yet most of them are not believers.
    Surely thy Lord, He is
the All-mighty, the All-compassionate.

The people of Noah cried lies to the Envoys
when their brother Noah said to them,
    'Will you not be godfearing?
I am for you a faithful Messenger,
so serve you God, and obey you me.
I ask of you no wage for this;
my wage falls only upon the
    Lord of all Being;
so fear you God, and obey you me.'
They said, 'Shall we believe thee, whom
    the vilest follow?'
He said, 'What knowledge have I of that
    they have been doing?
Their account falls only upon my Lord,
    were you but aware.
I would not drive away the believers;
I am naught but a plain warner.'
They said, 'If thou givest not over,
Noah, thou shalt assuredly be
    one of the stoned.'
He said, 'My Lord, my people have

100

105

110

115

69

cried me lies,
so give true deliverance between me
and them, and deliver me and the believers
    that are with me.'
So We delivered him, and those with him,
    in the laden ship,
120   then afterwards We drowned the rest.

Surely in that is a sign,
yet most of them are not believers.
    Surely thy Lord, He is
the All-mighty, the All-compassionate.

Ad cried lies to the Envoys
when their brother Hood said to them,
    'Will you not be godfearing?
125   I am for you a faithful Messenger,
so fear you God, and obey you me.
I ask of you no wage for this;
my wage falls only upon the
    Lord of all Being.
What, do you build on every prominence
    a sign, sporting,
and do you take to you castles, haply
    to dwell forever?
130   When you assault, you assault
    like tyrants!
So fear you God, and obey you me;
and fear Him who has succoured you
    with what you know,
succoured you with flocks and sons,
    gardens and fountains.
135   Indeed, I fear for you the chastisement of
    a dreadful day.'
They said, 'Alike it is to us, whether
thou admonishest, or art not one of
    the admonishers;
this is nothing but the habit of
    the ancients,

and we shall not be chastised.'
So they cried him lies; then We destroyed them.

Surely in that is a sign,
yet most of them are not believers.
140   Surely thy Lord, He is
the All-mighty, the All-compassionate.

Thamood cried lies to the Envoys
when their brother Salih said to them,
'Will you not be godfearing?
I am for you a faithful Messenger,
so fear you God, and obey you me.
145   I ask of you no wage for this;
my wage falls only upon the
Lord of all Being.
Will you be left secure in this here, among
gardens and fountains,
sown fields, and palms with slender spathes?
Will you still skilfully hew houses
out of the mountains?
150   So fear you God, and obey you me,
and obey not the commandment
of the prodigal
who do corruption in the earth, and set
not things aright.'
They said, 'Thou art merely one of those
that are bewitched;
thou art naught but a mortal, like us;
then produce a sign, if thou art
one of the truthful.'
155   He said, 'This is a she-camel;
to her a draught and to you a draught, on
a day appointed,
and do not touch her with malice
so that there seize you the chastisement of
a dreadful day.'
But they hamstrung her, and in the morning
they were remorseful,

71

and the chastisement seized them.

Surely in that is a sign,
yet most of them are not believers.
Surely thy Lord, He is
the All-mighty, the All-compassionate.

160 The people of Lot cried lies to the Envoys
when their brother Lot said to them,
    'Will you not be godfearing?
I am for you a faithful Messenger,
so fear you God, and obey you me.
I ask of you no wage for this;
my wage falls only upon the
        Lord of all Being.
165 What, do you come to male beings,
leaving your wives that your Lord created
for you? Nay, but you are a people
        of transgressors.'
They said, 'If thou givest not over,
Lot, thou shalt assuredly be
        one of the expelled.'
He said, 'Truly I am a detester
        of what you do.
My Lord, deliver me and my people
        from that they do.'
170 So We delivered him and his people
        all together,
save an old woman among those that tarried;
then We destroyed the others, and We rained
on them a rain; and evil is the rain of
        them that are warned.

175 Surely in that is a sign,
yet most of them are not believers.
Surely thy Lord, He is
the All-mighty, the All-compassionate.

The men of the Thicket cried lies to the Envoys

when Shuaib said to them,
  'Will you not be godfearing?
I am for you a faithful Messenger,
so fear you God, and obey you me.

180   I ask of you no wage for this;
my wage falls only upon the
      Lord of all Being.
Fill up the measure, and be not cheaters,
and weigh with the straight balance,
and diminish not the goods of the people,
and do not mischief in the earth,
      working corruption.
Fear Him who created you, and the generations
      of the ancients.'

185   They said, 'Thou art merely one of those
      that are bewitched;
thou art naught but a mortal, like us;
indeed, we think that thou art
      one of the liars.
Then drop down on us lumps from heaven, if thou
      one of the truthful.'   [art
He said, 'My Lord knows very well
      what you are doing.'
But they cried him lies; then there seized them
the chastisement of the Day of Shadow;
assuredly it was the chastisement of
      a dreadful day.

190   Surely in that is a sign,
yet most of them are not believers.
      Surely thy Lord, He is
the All-mighty, the All-compassionate.

      Truly it is the revelation of
        the Lord of all Being,
      brought down by the Faithful Spirit
      upon thy heart, that thou mayest be
        one of the warners,
195   in a clear, Arabic tongue.

Truly it is in the Scriptures
of the ancients.

Was it not a sign for them, that it is known
to the learned of the Children of Israel?
If We had sent it down on a barbarian
and he had recited it to them, they would
not have believed in it.

200   Even so We have caused it to enter into
the hearts of the sinners,
who will not believe in it, until they
see the painful chastisement
so that it will come upon them suddenly,
while they are not aware,
and they will say, 'Shall we be respited?'
What, do they seek to hasten Our chastisement?

205   What thinkest thou? If We give them enjoyment
of days for many years,
then there comes on them that they were promised,
what will it then avail them, the enjoyment
of days they were given?

Never a city We destroyed, but it had warners
for a reminder; and never did We wrong.

210   Not by the Satans has it
been brought down;
it behoves them not, neither
are they able.
Truly, they are expelled
from hearing.

So call thou not upon another god
with God, lest thou shouldst be one of those
that are chastised.
And warn thy clan, thy nearest kin.

215   Lower thy wing to those who follow thee,
being believers;
then, if they disobey thee, say, 'I am quit

of that you do.'

Put thy trust in the All-mighty, the All-compassionate
who sees thee when thou standest
and when thou turnest about among those who bow.
220   Surely He is the All-hearing, the All-knowing.

Shall I tell you on whom the Satans come down?
They come down on every guilty impostor.
They give ear, but most of them are liars.
And the poets—the perverse follow them;
225   hast thou not seen how they wander in every valley
and how they say that which they do not?

Save those that believe, and do righteous deeds,
and remember God oft,
and help themselves after being wronged; and
those who do wrong shall surely know by what
overturning they will be overturned.

XXVII

THE ANT

In the Name of God, the Merciful, the Compassionate

Ta Sin

Those are the signs of the Koran
    and a Manifest Book,
a guidance, and good tidings
    unto the believers
who perform the prayer, and pay the alms,
and have sure faith in the Hereafter.

Those who believe not in the Hereafter,
We have decked out fair for them their
    works, and they wander blindly;
5   those are they whom an evil chastisement
awaits, and they will be the greatest losers
    in the Hereafter.

Thou receivest the Koran
from One All-wise, All-knowing.

When Moses said to his people
'I observe a fire, and will bring
you news of it, or I will bring
you a flaming brand, that haply
you shall warm yourselves.'
So, when he came to it, he
was called: 'Blessed is He
who is in the fire, and he
who is about it. Glory be to
God, the Lord of all Being!
Moses, behold, it is I, God,
the All-mighty, the All-wise.

10   Cast down thy staff.' And when he
saw it quivering like a serpent
he turned about, retreating,
and turned not back. 'Moses,
fear not; surely the Envoys
do not fear in My presence,
save him who has done evil,
then, after evil, has changed
into good; All-forgiving
am I, All-compassionate.
Thrust thy hand in thy bosom
and it will come forth white
without evil—among nine
signs to Pharaoh and his people;
they are an ungodly people.'
But when Our signs came to them
visibly, they said, 'This
is a manifest sorcery';
and they denied them, though
their souls acknowledged them,
wrongfully and out of pride.
Behold, how was the end of
the workers of corruption!

15   And We gave David and Solomon knowledge
and they said, 'Praise belongs to God
who has preferred us over many of His
       believing servants.'

And Solomon was David's heir,
and he said, 'Men, we have been
taught the speech of the birds, and we
have been given of everything; surely
this is indeed the manifest bounty.'
And his hosts were mustered to Solomon,
jinn, men and birds, duly disposed;
till, when they came on the Valley of Ants,
an ant said, 'Ants, enter your
dwelling-places, lest Solomon and

his hosts crush you, being unaware!'
But he smiled, laughing at its words,
and he said, 'My Lord, dispose me
that I may be thankful for Thy blessing
wherewith Thou hast blessed me and my
father and mother, and that I may do
righteousness well-pleasing to Thee;
and do Thou admit me, by Thy mercy,
amongst Thy righteous servants.'

20   And he reviewed the birds; then he said,
'How is it with me, that I do not see
the hoopoe? Or is he among the absent?
Assuredly I will chastise him with a
terrible chastisement, or I will slaughter
him, or he bring me a clear authority.'
But he tarried not long, and said,
'I have comprehended that which thou
hast not comprehended, and I have come
from Sheba to thee with a sure tiding.
I found a woman ruling over them,
and she has been given of everything,
and she possesses a mighty throne.
I found her and her people prostrating
to the sun, apart from God; Satan
has decked out fair their deeds to them
and he has barred them from the way,
and therefore they are not guided,

25   so that they prostrate not themselves
to God, who brings forth what is hidden
in the heavens and earth; and He knows
what you conceal and what you publish.
God: there is no god but He,
the Lord of the Mighty Throne.'
Said he, 'Now we will see whether
thou hast spoken truly, or whether
thou art amongst those that lie.
Take this letter of mine, and cast it
unto them, then turn back from them
and see what they shall return.'

She said, 'O Council, see, a letter
honourable has been cast unto me.
30   It is from Solomon, and it is "In the Name
of God, the Merciful, the Compassionate.
Rise not up against me, but come to me
in surrender." ' She said, 'O Council,
pronounce to me concerning my affair;
I am not used to decide an affair
until you bear me witness.' They said,
'We possess force and we possess great might.
The affair rests with thee; so consider
what thou wilt command.' She said, 'Kings,
when they enter a city, disorder it
and make the mighty ones of its inhabitants
abased. Even so they too will do.
35   Now I will send them a present, and see
what the envoys bring back.' But when he
came to Solomon he said, 'What, would you
succour me with wealth, and what God gave me
is better than what He has given you?
Nay, but instead you rejoice in your gift!
Return thou to them; we shall assuredly
come against them with hosts they have not
power to resist, and we shall expel them
from there, abased and utterly humbled.'
He said, 'O Council, which one of you will
bring me her throne, before they come to me
in surrender?' An efreet of the jinns
said, 'I will bring it to thee, before thou
risest from thy place; I have strength for it
40   and I am trusty.' Said he who possessed
knowledge of the Book, 'I will bring it to
thee, before ever thy glance returns to thee.'
Then, when he saw it settled before him,
he said, 'This is of my Lord's bounty
that He may try me, whether I am thankful
or ungrateful. Whosoever gives thanks
gives thanks only for his own soul's good,
and whosoever is ungrateful—my Lord

is surely All-sufficient, All-generous.'
He said, 'Disguise her throne for her,
and we shall behold whether she is guided
or if she is of those that are not guided.'
So, when she came, it was said, 'Is thy
throne like this?' She said, 'It seems
the same.' 'And we were given the knowledge
before her, and we were in surrender,
but that she served, apart from God, barred her,
for she was of a people of unbelievers.'
It was said to her, 'Enter the pavilion.'
But when she saw it, she supposed it was
a spreading water, and she bared her legs.
He said, 'It is a pavilion smoothed of
45   crystal.' She said, 'My Lord, indeed I
have wronged myself, and I surrender with
Solomon to God, the Lord of all Being.'

And We sent to Thamood their brother
Salih: 'Serve you God!' And behold,
they were two parties, that were disputing
            one with another.
He said, 'O my people, why do you seek
to hasten evil before good? Why do you
not ask forgiveness of God? Haply so
            you will find mercy.'
They said, 'We augur ill of thee and of
those that are with thee.' He said, 'Your augury
is with God; nay, but you are a people
            being proved.'
Now in the city there were nine persons
who did corruption in the land, and put
            not things right;
50   they said, 'Swear you, one to another, by
God, "We will attack him and his family
by night, then we will tell his protector,
We were not witnesses of the destruction
of his family; and assuredly we
            are truthful men." '

And they devised a device, and We
likewise devised a device, while they
   were not aware;
and behold, how was the end of their device!
For We destroyed them and their people
   all together.
Those are their houses, all fallen down
because of the evil they committed;
surely in that is a sign for a people
   who have knowledge.
And We delivered those who believed
   and were godfearing.

55 And Lot, when he said to his people,
  'What, do you commit indecency
    with your eyes open?
  What, do you approach men lustfully
  instead of women? No, you are a people
    that are ignorant.'
  And the only answer of his people
  was that they said, 'Expel the folk
  of Lot from your city; they are men that
    keep themselves clean!'
  So We delivered him and his family,
  except his wife; We decreed she should be
    of those that tarried.
  And We rained on them a rain;
  and evil indeed is the rain of
    them that are warned.

60 Say: 'Praise belongs to God,
  and peace be on His servants
   whom He has chosen.'
  What, is God better, or that
   they associate?

He who created the heavens and earth, and sent down for you
   out of heaven water;
and We caused to grow therewith gardens full of loveliness

81

whose trees you could never grow.
Is there a god with God?
Nay, but they are a people who assign to Him equals!

He who made the earth a fixed place
and set amidst it rivers
and appointed for it firm mountains
and placed a partition between the two seas.
Is there a god with God?
Nay, but the most of them have no knowledge.

He who answers the constrained, when he calls unto Him,
and removes the evil
and appoints you to be successors in the earth.
Is there a god with God?
Little indeed do you remember.

He who guides you in the shadows of the land and the sea
and looses the winds,
bearing good tidings before His mercy.
Is there a god with God?
High exalted be God, above that which they associate!

65 Who originates creation, then brings it back again,
and provides you out of heaven and earth.
Is there a god with God?
Say: 'Produce your proof, if you speak truly.'
Say: 'None knows the Unseen in the heavens and earth
except God.
And they are not aware
when they shall be raised;
nay, but their knowledge fails as to the Hereafter;
nay, they are in doubt of it;
nay, they are blind to it.

The unbelievers say, 'What, when we are
dust, and our fathers, shall we indeed
be brought forth?
70 We have been promised this, and our fathers

before; this is naught but the fairy-tales
of the ancients.'
Say: 'Journey in the land, then behold
how was the end of the sinners.'

Do not sorrow for them,
nor be thou straitened
for what they devise.

They say, 'When shall this promise come to
pass, if you speak the truth?'
Say: 'It may be that riding behind you
already is some part of that you seek
to hasten on.'

75   Surely thy Lord is bountiful to men; but most of them
are not thankful.
Surely thy Lord knows what their hearts conceal, and
what they publish.
And not a thing is
there hidden in heaven and earth
but it is in a Manifest Book.

Surely this Koran relates to the Children
of Israel most of that concerning which
they are at variance;
it is a guidance, and a mercy
unto the believers.
80   Surely thy Lord will decide between them
by His Judgment; He is the All-mighty,
the All-knowing.
So put thy trust in God;
thou art upon the manifest truth.

Thou shalt not make the dead to hear,
neither shalt thou make the deaf to hear the call
when they turn about, retreating.
Thou shalt not guide the blind out of their error

neither shalt thou make any to hear, save
such as believe in Our signs, and so surrender.
When the Word falls on them, We shall bring forth for them
out of the earth a beast that shall speak unto them:
'Mankind had no faith in Our signs.'

85 Upon the day when We shall muster out of every nation
a troop of those that cried lies to Our signs, duly disposed,
till, when they are come, He shall say, 'Did you cry lies to
My signs, not comprehending them in knowledge, or what
have you been doing?' And the Word shall fall upon them
because of the evil they committed, while they speak naught.

Have they not seen how We made the night
for them, to repose in it, and the day, to see?
Surely in that is a sign for a people who are believers.

On the day the Trumpet is blown, and terrified is whosoever
is in the heavens and earth, excepting whom God wills,
and every one shall come to Him, all utterly abject;

90 and thou shalt see the mountains, that thou supposest fixed,
passing by like clouds—God's handiwork, who has created
everything very well. He is aware of the things you do.
Whosoever comes with a good deed, he shall have better
than it; and they shall be secure from terror that day.
And whosoever comes with an evil deed, their faces shall be
thrust into the Fire: 'Are you recompensed but for what you
[did?'

I have only been commanded
to serve the Lord of this territory
which He has made sacred;
to Him belongs everything.
And I have been commanded
to be of those that surrender,
and to recite the Koran.
So whosoever is guided, is only guided
to his own gain; and whosoever goes
astray, say: 'I am naught but a warner.'

95 And say: 'Praise belongs to God.

He shall show you His signs
and you will recognise them.
Thy Lord is not heedless of the things you do.'

XXVIII

THE STORY

In the Name of God, the Merciful, the Compassionate

Ta Sin Mim

Those are the signs of the Manifest Book.

We will recite to thee something of the tiding
of Moses and Pharaoh truthfully, for a
    people who believe.
Now Pharaoh had exalted himself in the land
and had divided its inhabitants into sects,
abasing one party of them, slaughtering their
sons, and sparing their women; for he was of the
    workers of corruption.
Yet We desired to be gracious to those that were
abased in the land, and to make them leaders, and to
    make them the inheritors,
5   and to establish them in the land, and to show
Pharaoh and Haman, and their hosts, what they
    were dreading from them.
So We revealed to Moses' mother, 'Suckle him,
then, when thou fearest for him, cast him into
the sea, and do not fear, neither sorrow, for
We shall return him to thee, and shall appoint him
    one of the Envoys.'
So then the folk of Pharaoh picked him out
to be an enemy and a sorrow to them;
certainly Pharaoh and Haman, and their hosts,
    were of the sinners.
Said Pharaoh's wife, 'He will be a comfort
to me and thee. Slay him not; perchance he will
profit us, or we will take him for a son.' And
    they were not aware.

On the morrow the heart of Moses' mother
became empty, and she wellnigh disclosed him
had We not strengthened her heart, that she might be
    among the believers;

10   and she said to his sister, 'Follow him,'
and she perceived him from afar, even while
    they were not aware.
Now We had forbidden to him aforetime
to be suckled by any foster-mother; therefore
she said, 'Shall I direct you to the people of a
household who will take charge of him for you,
    and look after him?'
So We returned him to his mother, that she might be
comforted and not sorrow, and that she might know
that the promise of God is true; but most of
    them do not know.
And when he was fully grown and in the perfection
of his strength, We gave him judgment and
knowledge; even so do We recompense
    the good-doers.
And he entered the city, at a time when its people
were unheeding, and found there two men
fighting; the one was of his own party, and
the other was of his enemies. Then the one
that was of his party cried to him to aid him
against the other that was of his enemies; so
Moses struck him, and despatched him, and said,
'This is of Satan's doing; he is surely an enemy
    misleading, manifest.'

15   He said, 'My Lord, I have wronged myself. Forgive me!'
So God forgave him, for He is the All-forgiving,
    the All-compassionate.
He said, 'My Lord, forasmuch as Thou hast
blessed me, I will never be a partisan
    of the sinners.'
Now in the morning he was in the city,
fearful and vigilant; and behold, the man
who had sought his succour on the day before
cried out to him again. Moses said to him, 'Clearly

thou art a quarreller.'
But when he would have assaulted the man who
was an enemy to them both, the man said, 'Moses,
dost thou desire to slay me, even as thou slewest
a living soul yesterday? Thou only desirest to be
a tyrant in the land; thou desirest not to be of
    them that put things right.'
Then came a man from the furthest part of the
city, running; he said, 'Moses, the Council are
conspiring to slay thee. Depart; I am one of
    thy sincere advisers.'
20   So he departed therefrom, fearful and vigilant;
he said, 'My Lord, deliver me from the people
    of the evildoers.'
And when he turned his face towards Midian
he said, 'It may be that my Lord will guide me
    on the right way.'
And when he came to the waters of Midian
he found a company of the people there
    drawing water,
and he found, apart from them, two women
holding back their flocks. He said, 'What is
your business?' They said, 'We may not draw
water until the shepherds drive off, and our father
    is passing old.'
So he drew water for them; then he turned away
to the shade, and he said, 'O my Lord, surely
I have need of whatever good Thou shalt have
    sent down upon me.'
25   Then came one of the two women to him, walking
modestly, and said, 'My father invites thee,
that he may recompense thee with the wage of thy
drawing water for us.' So when he came to him
and had related to him the story, he said,
'Be not afraid; thou hast escaped from the people
    of the evildoers.'
Said one of the two women, 'Father, hire him;
surely the best man thou canst hire is the one
    strong and trusty.'

He said, 'I desire to marry thee to one of
these my two daughters, on condition that thou
hirest thyself to me for eight years. If thou
completest ten, that shall be of thy own accord;
I do not desire to press hard upon thee.
Thou shalt assuredly find me, if God wills,
    one of the righteous.'
Said he, 'So let it be between me and thee.
Whichever of the two terms I fulfil, it shall be
no injustice to me; and God is guardian
    of what we say.'
So when Moses had accomplished the term
and departed with his household, he observed
on the side of the Mount a fire. He said to his
household, 'Tarry you here; I observe a fire.
Perhaps I shall bring you news of it,
or a faggot from the fire, that haply
    you shall warm yourselves.'

30   When he came to it, a voice cried from the right bank
of the watercourse, in the sacred hollow,
coming from the tree: 'Moses, I am God, the
    Lord of all Being.
Cast down thy staff.' And when he saw it
quivering like a serpent, he turned about
retreating, and turned not back. 'Moses,
come forward, and fear not; for surely thou
    art in security.
Insert thy hand into thy bosom, and it will
come forth white without evil; and press to thee
thy arm, that thou be not afraid. So these
shall be two proofs from thy Lord to Pharaoh
and his Council; for surely they are an
    ungodly people.'
Said he, 'My Lord, I have indeed slain
a living soul among them, and I fear that
    they will slay me.
Moreover my brother Aaron is more eloquent
than I. Send him with me as a helper
and to confirm I speak truly, for I fear they

89

will cry me lies.'

35 Said He, 'We will strengthen thy arm by means
of thy brother, and We shall appoint to you
an authority, so that they shall not reach you
because of Our signs; you, and whoso follows you,
    shall be the victors.'
So when Moses came to them with Our signs,
clear signs, they said, 'This is nothing but a
forged sorcery. We never heard of this among
    our fathers, the ancients.'
But Moses said, 'My Lord knows very well
who comes with the guidance from Him, and shall
possess the Ultimate Abode; surely the evildoers
    will not prosper.'
And Pharaoh said, 'Council, I know not that you
have any god but me. Kindle me, Haman,
a fire upon the clay, and make me a tower, that I
may mount up to Moses' god; for I think that he is
    one of the liars.'
And he waxed proud in the land, he and his hosts,
wrongfully; and they thought they should not be
    returned to Us.

40 Therefore We seized him and his hosts, and cast them
into the sea; so behold how was the end
    of the evildoers!
And We appointed them leaders, calling to the
Fire; and on the Day of Resurrection they
    shall not be helped;
and We pursued them in this world with a curse,
and on the Day of Resurrection they shall be
    among the spurned.
And We gave Moses the Book, after that We had
destroyed the former generations, to be examples
and a guidance and a mercy, that haply so
    they might remember.

Thou wast not upon the western side
when We decreed to Moses the commandment,
nor wast thou of those witnessing;

45 but We raised up generations,
and long their lives continued.
Neither wast thou a dweller among
the Midianites, reciting to them Our
signs; but We were sending Messengers.
Thou wast not upon the side of the
Mount when We called; but for a mercy
from thy Lord, that thou mayest warn
a people to whom no warner came before
thee, and that haply they may remember.
Else, did an affliction visit them
for that their own hands have forwarded
then they might say, 'Our Lord, why
didst Thou not send a Messenger to us
that we might follow Thy signs
and so be among the believers?'
Yet when the truth came to them
from Ourselves, they said, 'Why
has he not been given the like of
that Moses was given?' But they,
did they not disbelieve also in
what Moses was given aforetime?
They said, 'A pair of sorceries
mutually supporting each other.'
They said, 'We disbelieve both.'

50 Say: 'Bring a Book from God that gives
better guidance than these, and follow it,
     if you speak truly.'
Then if they do not answer thee, know that
they are only following their caprices;
and who is further astray than he who
follows his caprice without guidance from
God? Surely God guides not the people
     of the evildoers.
Now We have brought them the Word; haply
     they may remember.
Those to whom We gave the Book before this
     believe in it

91

and, when it is recited to them, they say,
'We believe in it; surely it is the truth
from our Lord. Indeed, even before it
    we had surrendered.'
These shall be given their wage twice over
for that they patiently endured, and avert
evil with good, and expend of that
    We have provided them.

55   When they hear idle talk, they turn away
from it and say, 'We have our deeds, and you
your deeds. Peace be upon you! We desire
    not the ignorant.'
Thou guidest not whom thou likest, but God
guides whom He wills, and knows very well
    those that are guided.
They say, 'Should we follow the guidance
with thee, we shall be snatched from our land.'
Have We not established for them a sanctuary
secure, to which are collected the fruits of
everything, as a provision from Us? But
    most of them know not.
How many a city We have destroyed
that flourished in insolent ease! Those
are their dwelling-places, undwelt in
after them, except a little; Ourselves
    are the inheritors.
Yet thy Lord never destroyed the cities
until He sent in their mother-city
a Messenger, to recite Our signs
unto them; and We never destroyed
the cities, save that their inhabitants
    were evildoers.

60   Whatever thing you have been given
is the enjoyment of the present life
and its adornment; and what is with
God is better and more enduring.
    Will you not understand?
What, is he to whom We have promised
a fair promise, and he receives it,

like him to whom We have given the
enjoyment of the present life, then he
on the Resurrection Day shall be of those
that are arraigned?

Upon the day when He shall call to them, and He shall say,
'Where now are My associates whom you were asserting?'
Those against whom the Word is realized, they shall say,
'Our Lord, those whom we perverted, we perverted them
even as we ourselves erred. We declare our innocence
unto Thee; it was not us that they were serving.'
It shall be said, 'Call you now upon your associates!'
And they will call upon them, but they shall not answer them,
and they shall see the chastisement—ah, if they had been
[guided!
65 Upon the day when He shall call to them, and He shall say,
'What answer gave you to the Envoys?' Upon that day
the tidings will be darkened for them, nor will they ask
[each other.

But as for him who repents, and believes,
and works righteousness, haply he shall be
among the prosperers.
Thy Lord creates whatsoever He will
and He chooses; they have not the choice.
Glory be to God! High be He exalted above
that they associate!
And thy Lord knows what their breasts conceal
and what they publish.

70   And He is God;
there is no god but He.
His is the praise
in the former as in the latter;
His too is the Judgment,
and unto Him you shall be returned.

Say: 'What think you? If God should make
the night unceasing over you, until

the Day of Resurrection, what god other
than God shall bring you illumination?
	Will you not hear?'
Say: 'What think you? If God should make
the day unceasing over you, until
the Day of Resurrection, what god other
than God shall bring you night to repose in?
	Will you not see?
Of His mercy He has appointed for you
night and day, for you to repose in
and seek after His bounty, that haply
	you will be thankful.'

Upon the day when He shall call to them, and He shall say,
'Where now are My associates whom you were asserting?'
And We shall draw out from every nation a witness, and say,
75 'Produce your proof!' Then will they know that Truth is
	                                                  ⌈God's,
and there shall go astray from them that they were forging.

Now Korah was of the people of Moses; he
became insolent to them, for We had given him
treasures such that the very keys of them
were too heavy a burden for a company of
men endowed with strength. When his people
said to him, 'Do not exult; God loves not
	those that exult;
but seek, amidst that which God has given thee,
the Last Abode, and forget not thy portion
of the present world; and do good, as God has
been good to thee. And seek not to work
corruption in the earth; surely God loves not the
	workers of corruption.'
He said, 'What I have been given is only
because of a knowledge that is in me.' What,
did he not know that God had destroyed before
him generations of men stronger than he
in might, and more numerous in multitude?
And yet the sinners shall not be questioned

concerning their sins.
So he went forth unto his people in his
adornment. Those who desired the present life
said, 'Would that we possessed the like of that
Korah has been given! Surely he is a man
  of mighty fortune.'
80 But those to whom knowledge had been given
said, 'Woe upon you! The reward of God
is better for him who believes, and works
righteousness; and none shall receive it
  except the steadfast.'
So We made the earth to swallow him and his dwelling
and there was no host to help him, apart from God,
  and he was helpless;
and in the morning those who had longed to be
in his place the day before were saying,
'Ah, God outspreads and straitens His provision
to whomsoever He will of His servants. Had
God not been gracious to us, He would have made
us to be swallowed too. Ah, the unbelievers
  do not prosper.'

  That is the Last Abode;
We appoint it for those who desire not
exorbitance in the earth, nor corruption.
The issue ultimate is to the godfearing.
Whoso brings a good deed shall have better
than it; and whoso brings an evil deed—
those who have done evil deeds shall only
be recompensed for that they were doing.

85 He who imposed the Recitation upon thee
shall surely restore thee to a place of homing.
Say: 'My Lord knows very well who comes
with guidance, and who is in manifest error.'
Thou didst not hope that the Book should be
cast unto thee, except it be as a mercy
from thy Lord; so be thou not a partisan
of the unbelievers. Let them not bar thee

from the signs of God, after that they have been
sent down to thee. And call upon thy Lord,
and be thou not of the idolaters.

And call not upon another god with God;
    there is no god but He.
  All things perish, except His Face.
    His is the Judgment,
and unto Him you shall be returned.

XXIX

THE SPIDER

In the Name of God, the Merciful, the Compassionate

Alif Lam Mim

Do the people reckon that they will be left to say
    'We believe,' and will not be tried?
We certainly tried those that were before them,
and assuredly God knows those who speak truly,
    and assuredly He knows the liars.
Or do they reckon, those who do evil deeds, that
    they will outstrip Us? Ill they judge!
Whoso looks to encounter God, God's term is coming;
    He is the All-hearing, the All-knowing.

5   Whosoever struggles, struggles only to his
own gain; surely God is All-sufficient
    nor needs any being.
And those who believe, and do righteous deeds,
We shall surely acquit them of their evil
deeds, and shall recompense them the best of
    what they were doing.
We have charged man, that he be kind to his
parents; but if they strive with thee to make thee
associate with Me that whereof thou hast no
knowledge, then do not obey them; unto Me
you shall return, and I shall tell you
    what you were doing.
And those who believe, and do righteous deeds
assuredly We shall admit them
    among the righteous.

Some men there are who say, 'We believe
in God,' but when such a man is hurt

97

in God's cause, he makes the persecution
of men as it were God's chastisement;
then if help comes from thy Lord, he will say
'We were with you.' What, does not God
know very well what is in the breasts
　　　of all beings?
10　　　God surely knows the believers, and He knows
　　　　the hypocrites.

The unbelievers say to the believers,
'Follow our path, and let us carry
your offences'; yet they cannot carry
anything, even of their own offences;
　　　they are truly liars.
They shall certainly carry their loads,
and other loads along with their loads,
and upon the Day of Resurrection they
shall surely be questioned concerning
　　　that they were forging.

Indeed, We sent Noah to his people,
and he tarried among them a thousand years,
all but fifty; so the Flood seized them, while
　　　they were evildoers.
Yet We delivered him, and those who were
in the ship, and appointed it for a sign
　　　unto all beings.

15　　　And Abraham, when he said to his people,
'Serve God, and fear Him; that is better for
　　　you, did you know.
You only serve, apart from God, idols
and you create a calumny; those you serve,
apart from God, have no power to
provide for you. So seek after your
provision with God, and serve Him,
and be thankful to Him; unto Him
　　　you shall be returned.
But if you cry me lies, nations cried lies before

you; and it is only for the Messenger to deliver
    the Manifest Message.'
(Have they not seen how God originates
creation, then brings it back again? Surely
    that is an easy matter for God.
Say: 'Journey in the land, then behold how
He originated creation; then God causes
the second growth to grow; God is powerful
    over everything,

20   chastising whom He will, and having mercy
on whomsoever He will, and unto Him
    you shall be turned.
You are not able to frustrate Him
either in the earth or in heaven;
and you have not, apart from God, either
    protector or helper.
And those who disbelieve in God's signs
and the encounter with Him—they despair
of My mercy, and there awaits them
    a painful chastisement.)
But the only answer of his people was
that they said, 'Slay him, or burn him!'
Then God delivered him from the fire;
surely in that are signs for a people
    who believe.
And he said, 'You have only taken to
yourselves idols, apart from God, as
a mark of mutual love between you in
the present life; then upon the Day of
Resurrection you will deny one another,
and you will curse one another,
and your refuge will be the Fire, and you
    will have no helpers.'

25   But Lot believed him; and he said, 'I will
flee to my Lord; He is the All-mighty,
    the All-wise.'
And We gave him Isaac and Jacob, and We
appointed the Prophecy and the Book to be
among his seed; We gave him his wage in

this world, and in the world to come he shall be
    among the righteous.

And Lot, when he said to his people
'Surely you commit such indecency
as never any being in all the world
    committed before you.
What, do you approach men, and cut
the way, and commit in your assembly
dishonour?' But the only answer
of his people was that they said,
'Then bring us the chastisement of God, if
    thou speakest truly.'
He said, 'My Lord, help me against the people
    that work corruption.'

30   And when Our messengers came to Abraham
with the good tidings, they said, 'We shall
destroy the people of this city, for its people
    are evildoers.'
He said, 'Lot is in it.' They said, 'We
know very well who is in it; assuredly
We shall deliver him and his family,
except his wife; she has become
    of those that tarry.'
When that Our messengers came to Lot
he was troubled on their account
and distressed for them; but they said,
'Fear not, neither sorrow, for surely we
shall deliver thee and thy family,
except thy wife; she has become
    of those that tarry.
We shall send down upon the people
of this city wrath out of heaven
    for their ungodliness.'
And indeed, We have left thereof a
sign, a clear sign, unto a people
    who understand.

35   And to Midian their brother Shuaib;

he said, 'O my people, serve God,
and look you for the Last Day;
and do not mischief in the land,
    working corruption.'
But they cried lies to him; so
the earthquake seized them, and
morning found them in their habitation
    fallen prostrate.

And Ad, and Thamood—it has become
clear to you from their dwelling-places;
and Satan decked out fair to them
their works, and barred them from the way,
    though they saw clearly.

And Korah, and Pharaoh, and Haman;
Moses came to them with the clear signs, but
they waxed proud in the earth, yet they
    outstripped Us not.
Each We seized for his sin; and of them
against some We loosed a squall of pebbles
and some were seized by the Cry, and some
We made the earth to swallow, and some We
drowned; God would never wrong them, but
    they wronged themselves.

40   The likeness of those who have taken
to them protectors, apart from God,
is as the likeness of the spider that takes
to itself a house; and surely the frailest
of houses is the house of the spider,
    did they but know.
God knows whatever thing they call upon
apart from Him; He is the All-mighty,
    the All-wise.
And those similitudes—We strike them
for the people, but none understands them
    save those who know.
God created the heavens and the earth

with the truth; surely in that is a sign
    to the believers.

Recite what has been revealed to thee
of the Book, and perform the prayer;
prayer forbids indecency and dishonour.
God's remembrance is greater; and God knows
    the things you work.

45   Dispute not with the People of the Book
save in the fairer manner, except for
those of them that do wrong; and say,
'We believe in what has been sent down
to us, and what has been sent down to you;
our God and your God is One, and to Him
    we have surrendered.'

Even so We have sent down to thee
the Book. Those to whom We have given
the Book believe in it; and some of these
believe in it; and none denies Our signs but
    the unbelievers.
Not before this didst thou recite any
Book, or inscribe it with thy right hand,
for then those who follow falsehood
    would have doubted.
Nay; rather it is signs, clear signs
in the breasts of those who have been given
knowledge; and none denies Our signs but
    the evildoers.
They say, 'Why have signs not been sent
down upon him from his Lord?' Say:
'The signs are only with God, and I am only
    a plain warner.'
50   What, is it not sufficient for them that
We have sent down upon thee the Book
that is recited to them? Surely in that is
a mercy, and a reminder to a people
    who believe.

Say: 'God suffices as a witness between
    me and you.'
He knows whatsoever is in the heavens
and earth. Those who believe in vanity
and disbelieve in God—those,
    they are the losers.
And they demand of thee to hasten
the chastisement! But for a stated term
the chastisement would have come upon them;
but it shall come upon them suddenly, when
    they are not aware.
They demand of thee to hasten the
chastisement! Lo, Gehenna encompasses
    the unbelievers.

55 Upon the day the chastisement shall overwhelm them
from above them and from under their feet, and He shall say,
    'Taste now what you were doing!'

O My servants who believe, surely
My earth is wide; therefore Me
    do you serve!
Every soul shall taste of death; then unto Us
    you shall be returned.
And those who believe, and do righteous deeds,
We shall surely lodge them in lofty
chambers of Paradise, underneath which
rivers flow, therein dwelling forever;
and excellent is the wage of
    those who labour,
such men as are patient, and put their
    trust in their Lord.

60   How many a beast that bears not its own
provision, but God provides for it and you!
    He is the All-hearer, the All-knower.

If thou askest them,
'Who created the heavens and the earth

and subjected the sun and the moon?'
   they will say, 'God.'
  How then are they perverted?
God outspreads and straitens His provision
to whomsoever He will of His servants;
  God has knowledge of everything.

   If thou askest them,
'Who sends down out of heaven water, and
therewith revives the earth after it is dead?'
   they will say, 'God.'
  Say: 'Praise belongs to God.'
Nay, but most of them have no understanding.

This present life is naught but a diversion
and a sport; surely the Last Abode is Life,
   did they but know.

65   When they embark in the ships, they call on
God, making their religion sincerely His;
but when He has delivered them to the land,
    they associate others
with Him, that they may be ungrateful for what
We have given them, and take their enjoyment;
    they will soon know!
Have they not seen that We have appointed
a sanctuary secure, while all about them
the people are snatched away? What, do they
believe in vanity, and do they disbelieve
   in God's blessing?
And who does greater evil than he who
forges against God a lie, or cries lies
to the truth when it comes to him? What,
is there not in Gehenna a lodging
    for the unbelievers?

But those who struggle in Our cause, surely
We shall guide them in Our ways; and God is
   with the good-doers.

XXX

THE GREEKS

In the Name of God, the Merciful, the Compassionate

Alif Lam Mim

> The Greeks have been vanquished
> in the nearer part of the land;
> and, after their vanquishing,
> they shall be the victors
> in a few years.
> To God belongs the Command
> before and after,
> and on that day
> the believers shall rejoice in
> God's help; God
> helps whomsoever He will; and
> He is the All-mighty, the
> All-compassionate.

5   The promise of God! God fails not His promise,
> but most men do not know it.
> They know an outward part of the present life,
> but of the Hereafter they are heedless.
> What, have they not considered within themselves?
> God created not the heavens and the earth,
> and what between them is, save with the truth
> and a stated term; yet most men disbelieve
> in the encounter with their Lord.
> What, have they not journeyed in the land and
> beheld how was the end of those before them?
> They were stronger than themselves in might,
> and they ploughed up the earth and cultivated it
> more than they themselves have cultivated it;
> and their Messengers came to them with the clear

signs; and God would never wrong them, but
    themselves they wronged.
Then the end of those that did evil was evil,
    for that they cried lies to the signs of God
      and mocked at them.

10   God originates creation, then
            brings it back again,
      then unto Him you shall be returned.

Upon the day when the Hour is come, the sinners shall be
                        [confounded;
no intercessors shall they have amongst their associates, and
      shall disbelieve in their associates.   [they
Upon the day when the Hour is come, that day they shall be
                        [divided;
as for those who believed, and did deeds of righteousness,
      walk with joy in a green meadow,   [they shall
15 but as for those who disbelieved, and cried lies to Our signs
and the encounter of the Hereafter, they shall be arraigned
        into the chastisement.

        So glory be to God
        both in your evening hour
        and in your morning hour.
         His is the praise
        in the heavens and earth,
        alike at the setting sun
        and in your noontide hour.
He brings forth the living from the dead,
and brings forth the dead from the living,
and He revives the earth after it is dead;
      even so you shall be brought forth.

        And of His signs
is that He created you of dust; then lo,
you are mortals, all scattered abroad.
20   And of His signs
is that He created for you, of yourselves,

spouses, that you might repose in them,
and He has set between you love and mercy.
Surely in that are signs for a people who consider.
        And of His signs
is the creation of the heavens and earth
and the variety of your tongues and hues.
Surely in that are signs for all living beings.
        And of His signs
is your slumbering by night and day,
and your seeking after His bounty.
Surely in that are signs for a people who hear.
        And of His signs
He shows you lightning, for fear and hope,
and that He sends down out of heaven water
and He revives the earth after it is dead.
Surely in that are signs for a people who understand.
        And of His signs
is that the heaven and earth stand firm
by His command; then, when He calls you
once and suddenly, out of the earth, lo
        you shall come forth.

25 To Him belongs whosoever is in the heavens and the earth;
        all obey His will.
        And it is He who originates creation,
        then brings it back again,
        and it is very easy for Him.
His is the loftiest likeness in the heavens and the earth;
        He is the All-mighty, the All-wise.

        He has struck for you a similitude
from yourselves; do you have, among
that your right hands own, associates
in what We have provided for you
so that you are equal in regard to it,
you fearing them as you fear each other?
So We distinguish the signs for a people
        who understand.
Nay, but the evildoers follow their own

caprices, without knowledge; so who shall
guide those whom God has led astray?
They have no helpers.

So set thy face to the religion,
a man of pure faith—God's original
upon which He originated mankind.
There is no changing God's creation.
That is the right religion; but
      most men know it not—

30   turning to Him. And fear you Him,
and perform the prayer, and be not
      of the idolaters,
even of those who have divided up
their religion, and become sects,
each several party rejoicing in
      what is theirs.

When some affliction visits mankind, they
call unto their Lord, turning to Him; then,
when He lets them taste mercy from Him,
lo, a party of them assign associates
      to their Lord,
that they may be ungrateful for what We have
given them. 'Take your enjoyment; certainly
      you will soon know.'
Or have We sent down any authority
upon them, such as speaks of that they
      associate with Him?

35   And when We let men taste mercy, they
rejoice in it; but if some evil befalls them
for that their own hands have forwarded,
      behold, they despair.
Have they not seen that God outspreads and
straitens His provision to whom He will?
Surely in that are signs for a people
      who believe.

And give the kinsman his right,

and the needy, and the traveller;
that is better for those who desire
God's Face; those—they are
    the prosperers.
And what you give in usury,
that it may increase upon the
people's wealth, increases not
with God; but what you give in
alms, desiring God's Face,
those—they receive recompense
    manifold.

God is He that created you, then He provided for you,
then He shall make you dead, then He shall give you life;
is there any of your associates does aught of that?
Glory be to Him! High be He exalted above that
    they associate!

40   Corruption has appeared in the land and sea, for that
men's own hands have earned, that He may let them taste
some part of that which they have done, that haply so
    they may return.

Say: 'Journey in the land, then behold
how was the end of those that were before;
    most of them were idolaters.'

So set thy face to the true religion
before there comes a day from God that
cannot be turned back; on that day
    they shall be sundered apart.
Whoso disbelieves, his unbelief shall be
charged against him; and whosoever
does righteousness—for themselves
    they are making provision,
that He may recompense those who believe
and do righteous deeds of His bounty;
    He loves not the unbelievers.

45   And of His signs

is that He looses the winds, bearing good tidings
and that He may let you taste of His mercy,
and that the ships may run at His commandment,
and that you may seek His bounty; haply so
     you will be thankful.

Indeed, We sent before thee Messengers
unto their people, and they brought them
the clear signs; then We took vengeance
upon those who sinned; and it was
ever a duty incumbent upon Us, to
     help the believers.

God is He that looses the winds, that stir up clouds,
and He spreads them in heaven how He will, and shatters
                                 [them;
then thou seest the rain issuing out of the midst of them,
and when He smites with it whomsoever of His servants
     He will, lo, they rejoice,
although before it was sent down on them before that
     they had been in despair.

So behold the marks of God's mercy,
how He quickens the earth after it
was dead; surely He is the quickener
of the dead, and He is powerful
     over everything.

50   But if We loose a wind, and they see it growing yellow,
     they remain after that unbelievers.

Thou shalt not make the dead to hear,
neither shalt thou make the deaf to hear the call
     when they turn about, retreating.
Thou shalt not guide the blind out of their error
     neither shalt thou make any to hear
except for such as believe in Our signs, and so surrender.

God is He that created you of weakness, then He appointed
after weakness strength, then after strength He appointed

weakness and grey hairs; He creates what He will, and
He is the All-knowing, the All-powerful.

Upon the day when the Hour is come, the sinners shall swear
55   they have not tarried above an hour; so they were perverted.
But those who have been given knowledge and faith shall say,
'You have tarried in God's Book till the Day of the Upraising,
This is the Day of the Upraising, but you did not know.'
So that day their excuses will not profit the evildoers,
    nor will they be suffered to make amends.

    Indeed, We have struck for the people
    in this Koran every manner of
    similitude; and if thou bringest them
    a sign, those who are unbelievers
    will certainly say, 'You do nothing
      but follow falsehood.'
    Even so God seals the hearts of
      those that know not.

60   So be thou patient;
      surely God's promise is true;
    and let not those who have not sure faith
      make thee unsteady.

XXXI

LOKMAN

In the Name of God, the Merciful, the Compassionate

Alif Lam Mim

Those are the signs of the Wise Book
for a guidance and a mercy to the good-doers
who perform the prayer, and pay the alms,
and have sure faith in the Hereafter.
Those are upon guidance from their Lord;
    those are the prosperers.

5   Some men there are who buy diverting talk
to lead astray from the way of God
without knowledge, and to take it in
mockery; those—there awaits them
    a humbling chastisement.
And when Our signs are recited to such
a man he turns away, waxing proud, as
though he heard them not, and in his ears
were heaviness; so give him good tidings of
    a painful chastisement.
Surely those who believe, and do deeds
of righteousness, there awaits them
    Gardens of Bliss
therein to dwell forever—God's promise
in truth; and He is the All-mighty,
    the All-wise.
He created the heavens without pillars
you can see, and He cast on the earth
firm mountains, lest it shake with you,
and He scattered abroad in it all manner of
crawling thing. And We sent down out of
heaven water, and caused to grow in it of

every generous kind.
10   This is God's creation; now show me
what those have created that are apart
from Him! Nay, but the evildoers are in
    manifest error.

Indeed, We gave Lokman wisdom:
'Give thanks to God. Whosoever gives thanks
gives thanks only for his own soul's good,
and whosoever is ungrateful—surely God
is All-sufficient, All-laudable.'
And when Lokman said to his son,
admonishing him, 'O my son, do not
associate others with God; to associate
others with God is a mighty wrong.'
(And We have charged man concerning his
parents—his mother bore him in weakness
upon weakness, and his weaning was in
two years—'Be thankful to Me, and to
thy parents; to Me is the homecoming.
But if they strive with thee to make thee
associate with Me that whereof thou hast no
knowledge, then do not obey them. Keep them
company honourable in this world; but
follow the way of him who turns to Me.
Then unto Me you shall return, and
I shall tell you what you were doing.')
15   'O my son, if it should be but the
weight of one grain of mustard-seed, and
though it be in a rock, or in the heavens,
or in the earth, God shall bring it forth;
surely God is All-subtle, All-aware.
O my son, perform the prayer, and
bid unto honour, and forbid dishonour.
And bear patiently whatever may befall
thee; surely that is true constancy.
Turn not thy cheek away from men in
scorn, and walk not in the earth exultantly;
God loves not any man proud and boastful.

Be modest in thy walk, and lower thy voice;
the most hideous of voices is the ass's.'

Have you not seen how that God has subjected to you what-
        ·   is in the heavens and earth,   ⌈soever
and He has lavished on you His blessings, outward and
                                                  ⌈inward?

And among men there is such a one
that disputes concerning God without knowledge
or guidance, or an illuminating Book;
20   and when it is said to them, 'Follow
what God has sent down,' they say,
'No; but we will follow such things
as we found our fathers doing.'
What? Even though Satan were calling them
to the chastisement of the burning?

And whosoever submits his will to God,
being a good-doer, has laid hold
of the most firm handle; and unto God is
      the issue of all affairs.
And whoso disbelieves, let not his disbelief
grieve thee; unto Us they shall return,
and We shall tell them what they did.
Surely God knows all the thoughts
      within the breasts.
To them We give enjoyment a little, then
We compel them to a harsh chastisement.

        If thou askest them,
'Who created the heavens and the earth?'
     they will say, 'God.'
    Say: 'Praise belongs to God.'
Nay, but most of them have no knowledge.

25   To God belongs all that is in the heavens and the earth;
surely God—He is the All-sufficient, the All-laudable.

Though all the trees in the earth were
pens, and the sea—seven seas after it
    to replenish it,
yet would the Words of God not be spent.
    God is All-mighty, All-wise.

Your creation and your upraising are as
        but as a single soul.
    God is All-hearing, All-seeing.

Hast thou not seen how that God makes the night to enter
                                [into the day
    and makes the day to enter into the night.
and He has subjected the sun and the moon, each of them
        to a stated term,   [running
    and that God is aware of what you do?
That is because God—He is the Truth, and that they call
apart from Him—that is the false; and for that God is [upon
        the All-high, the All-great.
30 Hast thou not seen how that the ships run upon the sea by the
    blessing of God, that He may show you some of His signs?
        Surely in that are signs for every man
            enduring, thankful.
    And when the waves cover them like shadows
    they call upon God, making their religion
    sincerely His; but when He has delivered them
    to the land, some of them are lukewarm.
    And none denies Our signs, except every
        ungrateful traitor.

    O men, fear your Lord, and dread a day
    when no father shall give satisfaction
    for his child, and no child shall give
    satisfaction for his father whatever.
    Surely God's promise is true; so let not
    the present life delude you, and let not
    the Deluder delude you concerning God.

    Surely God—He has knowledge of the Hour;

He sends down the rain; He knows what is in the wombs.
No soul knows what it shall earn tomorrow, and
no soul knows in what land it shall die.
Surely God is All-knowing, All-aware.

XXXII

PROSTRATION

In the Name of God, the Merciful, the Compassionate

Alif Lam Mim

The sending down of the Book, wherein no doubt is,
  from the Lord of all Being.

  Or do they say, 'He has forged it'? Say:
  'Not so; it is the truth from thy Lord
  that thou mayest warn a people to whom no
  warner came before thee, that haply so
    they may be guided.

God is He that created the heavens and the earth,
  and what between them is, in six days,
  then seated Himself upon the Throne.
  Apart from Him, you have no protector
  neither mediator; will you not remember?
  He directs the affair from heaven to earth,
then it goes up to Him in one day, whose measure is
    a thousand years of your counting.
5 He is the knower of the Unseen and the Visible,
  the All-mighty, the All-compassionate,
    who has created all things well.
  And He originated the creation of man
    out of clay,
then He fashioned his progeny of an extraction of
    mean water,
then He shaped him, and breathed His spirit in him.
And He appointed for you hearing, and sight, and hearts;
    little thanks you show.

  They say, 'What, when we have gone astray

in the earth, shall we indeed be in a
    new creation?'
10   Nay, but they disbelieve in the encounter
    with their Lord.
Say: 'Death's angel, who has been charged
with you, shall gather you, then to your Lord
    you shall be returned.'

Ah, if thou couldst see the guilty hanging their heads before
                                    [their Lord!
'Our Lord, we have seen and heard; now return us, that we
    righteousness, for we have sure faith.'   [may do
'If We had so willed, We could have given every soul its
                                      [guidance;
but now My Word is realized—"Assuredly I shall fill
    with jinn and men all together."   [Gehenna
So now taste, for that you forgot the encounter of this your
                                      [day!
We indeed have forgotten you. Taste the chastisement of
    for that you were doing!'   [eternity

15   Only those believe in Our signs who, when
they are reminded of them, fall down prostrate
and proclaim the praise of their Lord,
    not waxing proud.
Their sides shun their couches as they call on their
Lord in fear and hope; and they expend of that
    We have provided them.
No soul knows what comfort is laid up
for them secretly, as a recompense for that
    they were doing.
What? Is he who has been a believer
like unto him who has been ungodly?
    They are not equal.
As for those who believe, and do deeds of
righteousness, there await them the Gardens
of the Refuge, in hospitality for that
    they were doing.
20   But as for the ungodly, their refuge

shall be the Fire; as often as they desire
to come forth from it, they shall be restored
into it, and it shall be said to them,
'Taste the chastisement of the Fire, which
          you cried lies to.'
And We shall surely let them taste the nearer
chastisement, before the greater; haply so
          they will return.
And who does greater evil than he who
is reminded of the signs of his Lord, then
turns away from them? We shall take vengeance
          upon the sinners.

Indeed, We gave Moses the Book; so be not
in doubt concerning the encounter with him;
and We appointed it for a guidance to the
          Children of Israel.
And We appointed from among them leaders
guiding by Our command, when they
endured patiently, and had sure faith
          in Our signs.
25   Surely thy Lord will distinguish between them
on the Resurrection Day, touching that whereon
          they were at variance.

Is it not a guidance to them, how many
generations We destroyed before them
in whose dwelling-places they walk?
Surely in that are signs; what,
          will they not hear?
Have they not seen how We drive the water
to the dry land and bring forth crops therewith
whereof their cattle and themselves eat? What,
          will they not see?

They also say, 'When shall be this Victory,
          if you speak truly?'
Say: 'On the Day of Victory their faith
shall not profit the unbelievers, nor shall

they be respited.'
So turn thou away from them, and wait;
they too are waiting.

XXXIII

THE CONFEDERATES

In the Name of God, the Merciful, the Compassionate

O Prophet, fear God,
  and obey not the unbelievers
and the hypocrites. God is All-knowing,
    All-wise.
And follow what is revealed to thee
from thy Lord; surely God is aware of
    the things you do.
And put thy trust in God; God suffices
    as a guardian.

God has not assigned to any man two hearts within
his breast; nor has He made your wives, when you
divorce, saying, 'Be as my mother's back,' truly
your mothers, neither has He made your adopted sons
your sons in fact. That is your own saying, the
words of your mouths; but God speaks the truth, and
    guides on the way.
5 Call them after their true fathers; that is more
equitable in the sight of God. If you know not
who their fathers were, then they are your brothers
in religion, and your clients. There is no fault
in you if you make mistakes, but only in what
your hearts premeditate. God is All-forgiving,
    All-compassionate.
The Prophet is nearer to the believers than their
selves; his wives are their mothers. Those who are
bound by blood are nearer to one another
in the Book of God than the believers and the
emigrants; nevertheless you should act towards
your friends honourably; that stands inscribed
    in the Book.

And when We took compact from the Prophets,
and from thee, and from Noah, and Abraham,
Moses, and Jesus, Mary's son; We took from them
      a solemn compact,
that He might question the truthful concerning their
truthfulness; and He has prepared for the unbelievers
      a painful chastisement.

O believers, remember God's blessing upon you
when hosts came against you, and We loosed
against them a wind, and hosts you saw not; and God sees
      the things you do.

10   When they came against you from above you
and from below you, and when your eyes swerved
and your hearts reached your throats, while you thought
      thoughts about God;
there it was that the believers were tried, and
      shaken most mightily.
And when the hypocrites, and those in whose hearts is
sickness, said, 'God and His Messenger promised us
      only delusion.'
And when a party of them said, 'O people of
Yathrib, there is no abiding here for you,
therefore return!' And a part of them were asking
leave of the Prophet, saying, 'Our houses are
exposed'; yet they were not exposed; they desired
      only to flee.
And if entrance had been forced against them
from those quarters, and then they had been asked to
apostatise, they would have done so, and but tarried
      about it briefly.

15   Yet they had made covenant with God before that, that
they would not turn their backs; and covenants with God
      shall be questioned of.
Say: 'Flight will not profit you, if you flee from
death or slaying; you will be given enjoyment of days
      then but little.'
Say: 'Who is he that shall defend you from God, if
He desires evil for you, or desires mercy for you?'

They shall find for themselves, apart from God,
      neither protector nor helper.
God would surely know those of you who hinder, and
those who say to their brothers, 'Come to us,' and come
      to battle but little,
being niggardly towards you. When fear comes
upon them, thou seest them looking at thee, their eyes
rolling like one who swoons of death; but when the
fear departs, they flay you with sharp tongues, being
niggardly to possess the good things. Those have never
believed; God has made their works to fail; and
      that is easy for God.

20   They think the Confederates have not departed;
and if the Confederates come, they will wish that
they were desert-dwellers among the Bedouins
asking for news of you. If they were among you, they
      would fight but little.
You have had a good example in God's Messenger
for whosoever hopes for God and the Last Day, and
      remembers God oft.
When the believers saw the Confederates
they said, 'This is what God and His Messenger
promised us, and God and His Messenger have
spoken truly.' And it only increased them in
      faith and surrender.
Among the believers are men who were true
to their covenant with God; some of them
have fulfilled their vow by death, and some
are still awaiting, and they have not
      changed in the least;
that God may recompense the truthful ones
for their truthfulness, and chastise the
hypocrites, if He will, or turn again
unto them. Surely God is All-forgiving,
      All-compassionate.

25   And God sent back those that were unbelievers
in their rage, and they attained no good; God
spared the believers of fighting. Surely God is

All-strong, All-mighty.
And He brought down those of the People of the
Book who supported them from their fortresses
and cast terror in their hearts; some you slew,
    some you made captive.
And He bequeathed upon you their lands,
their habitations, and their possessions,
and a land you never trod. God is powerful
    over everything.

O Prophet, say to thy wives: 'If you desire
the present life and its adornment, come now,
I will make you provision, and set you free
    with kindliness.
But if you desire God and His Messenger
and the Last Abode, surely God has prepared
for those amongst you such as do good
    a mighty wage.'

30 Wives of the Prophet, whosoever among you
commits a flagrant indecency, for her
the chastisement shall be doubled; that is
    easy for God.
But whosoever of you is obedient to God and His
Messenger, and does righteousness, We shall pay her
her wage twice over; We have prepared for her
    a generous provision.
Wives of the Prophet, you are not as other
women. If you are godfearing, be not
abject in your speech, so that he in whose
heart is sickness may be lustful; but speak
    honourable words.
Remain in your houses; and display not
your finery, as did the pagans of old.
And perform the prayer, and pay the alms,
and obey God and His Messenger.
People of the House, God only desires
to put away from you abomination
    and to cleanse you.
And remember that which is recited in your

124

houses of the signs of God and the Wisdom;
God is All-subtle, All-aware.

35   Men and women who have surrendered,
believing men and believing women,
obedient men and obedient women,
truthful men and truthful women,
enduring men and enduring women,
humble men and humble women,
men and women who give in charity,
men who fast and women who fast,
men and women who guard their private parts,
men and women who remember God oft—
for them God has prepared forgiveness
    and a mighty wage.

It is not for any believer, man or
woman, when God and His Messenger
have decreed a matter, to have the choice
in the affair. Whosoever disobeys
God and His Messenger has gone astray
    into manifest error.

When thou saidst to him whom God had blessed
and thou hadst favoured, 'Keep thy wife to thyself,
and fear God,' and thou wast concealing
within thyself what God should reveal,
fearing other men; and God has better right
for thee to fear Him. So when Zaid had accomplished
what he would of her, then We gave her in marriage
to thee, so that there should not be any fault
in the believers, touching the wives of their
adopted sons, when they have accomplished
what they would of them; and God's commandment
    must be performed.
There is no fault in the Prophet, touching what
God has ordained for him—God's wont with those
who passed away before; and God's commandment
    is doom decreed;

who were delivering the Messages of God,
and were fearing Him, and fearing not any one
except Him; and God suffices
  as a reckoner.

40   Muhammad is not the father of any one
of your men, but the Messenger of God,
and the Seal of the Prophets; God has knowledge
  of everything.

O believers, remember God oft,
and give Him glory at the dawn and in the evening.
It is He who blesses you, and His angels,
to bring you forth from the shadows into the light.
He is All-compassionate to the believers.
Their greeting, on the day when they shall meet Him,
will be 'Peace!' And He has prepared for them
  a generous wage.

O Prophet, We have sent thee as a
witness, and good tidings to bear
and warning, calling unto God by His
leave, and as a light-giving lamp.

45   Give good tidings to the believers that
there awaits them with God great bounty.
  And obey not the unbelievers
and the hypocrites; heed not their hurt,
but put thy trust in God; God suffices
  as a guardian.

O believers, when you marry believing women
and then divorce them before you touch them,
you have no period to reckon against them;
so make provision for them, and set them free
  with kindliness.

O Prophet, We have made lawful for thee
thy wives whom thou hast given their wages
and what thy right hand owns, spoils of war
that God has given thee, and the daughters of thy

uncles paternal and aunts paternal, thy
uncles maternal and aunts maternal, who
have emigrated with thee, and any woman
believer, if she give herself to the Prophet
and if the Prophet desire to take her in
marriage, for thee exclusively, apart
      from the believers—
50   We know what We have imposed upon them
touching their wives and what their right hands own—
that there may be no fault in thee; God is
      All-forgiving, All-compassionate.
Thou mayest put off whom thou wilt of them,
and whom thou wilt thou mayest take to thee;
and if thou seekest any thou hast set aside
there is no fault in thee. So it is likelier
they will be comforted, and not sorrow,
and every one of them will be well-pleased
with what thou givest her. God knows what
is in your hearts; God is All-knowing,
      All-clement.
Thereafter women are not lawful to thee,
neither for thee to take other wives in exchange
for them, though their beauty please thee, except
what thy right hand owns; God is watchful
      over everything.

O believers, enter not the houses of
the Prophet, except leave is given you
for a meal, without watching for its hour.
But when you are invited, then enter; and
when you have had the meal, disperse,
neither lingering for idle talk;
that is hurtful to the Prophet, and he
is ashamed before you; but God is not
ashamed before the truth. And when you
ask his wives for any object, ask them
from behind a curtain; that is cleaner
for your hearts and theirs. It is not
for you to hurt God's Messenger, neither

127

to marry his wives after him, ever;
surely that would be, in God's sight,
        a monstrous thing.
Whether you reveal anything, or whether
you conceal it, surely God has knowledge
        of everything.

55   There is no fault in the Prophet's wives
touching their fathers, their sons, their brothers,
their brothers' sons, their sisters' sons,
their women, and what their right hands own.
And fear you God; surely God is witness
        of everything.

God and His angels bless the Prophet.
O believers, do you also bless him, and
        pray him peace.
Those who hurt God and His Messenger—
them God has cursed in the present world and
the world to come, and has prepared for them
        a humbling chastisement.
And those who hurt believing men and
believing women, without that they have
earned it, have laid upon themselves calumny
        and manifest sin.

O Prophet, say to thy wives and daughters
and the believing women, that they draw
their veils close to them; so it is likelier
they will be known, and not hurt. God is
        All-forgiving, All-compassionate.

60   Now, if the hypocrites do not give over,
and those in whose hearts there is sickness
and they that make commotion in the city,
We shall assuredly urge thee against them
and then they will be thy neighbours there
        only a little;
cursed they shall be, and wheresoever

they are come upon they shall be seized
    and slaughtered all—
God's wont with those who passed away
before; and thou shalt find no changing
    the wont of God.

The people will question thee concerning
the Hour. Say: 'The knowledge of it is only
with God; what shall make thee know? Haply
    the Hour is nigh.'
God has cursed the unbelievers, and prepared
    for them a Blaze,
65   therein to dwell for ever; they shall find
    neither protector nor helper.

Upon the day when their faces are turned about in the Fire
they shall say, 'Ah, would we had obeyed God and the
                          [Messenger!'
They shall say, 'Our Lord, we obeyed our chiefs and great
                           [ones,
and they led us astray from the way. Our Lord, give them
chastisement twofold, and curse them with a mighty curse!'

O believers, be not as those who hurt
Moses, but God declared him quit of
what they said, and he was high honoured
    with God.
70   O believers, fear God, and speak words hitting
    the mark,
and He will set right your deeds for you
and will forgive you your sins. Whosoever
obeys God and His Messenger has won a mighty
    triumph.

We offered the trust to the heavens and the earth
and the mountains, but they refused to carry it
and were afraid of it; and man carried it. Surely
    he is sinful, very foolish.

E

That God may chastise the hypocrites,
men and women alike, and the idolaters,
men and women alike; and that God may
turn again unto the believers, men and
women alike. God is All-forgiving,
        All-compassionate.

XXXIV

SHEBA

In the Name of God, the Merciful, the Compassionate

Praise belongs to God
to whom belongs whatsoever is in the heavens
and whatsoever is in the earth.
To Him belongs praise also in the Hereafter;
He is the All-wise, the All-aware.
He knows what penetrates into the earth, and
what comes forth from it,
what comes down from heaven, and what goes up to it;
He is the All-compassionate, the All-forgiving.

The unbelievers say, 'The Hour will never
come to us.' Say: 'Yes indeed, by my Lord,
it shall come to you, by Him who knows
the Unseen; not so much as the weight of
an ant in heaven and earth escapes from Him,
neither is aught smaller than that, or greater,
but it is in a Manifest Book;
that He may recompense those who believe, and do
righteous deeds; theirs shall be forgiveness
and generous provision.
5   And those who strive against Our signs
to void them—theirs shall be a chastisement
of painful wrath.'
Those who have been given the knowledge see
that what has been sent down to thee from thy
Lord is the truth, and guides to the path of
the All-mighty, the All-laudable.

The unbelievers say, 'Shall we point you to a
man who will tell you, when you have been
utterly torn to pieces, then you shall be in

131

a new creation?'
What, has he forged against God a lie, or
is he possessed? Not so; but those who
believe not in the Hereafter are in chastisement
      and far error.
Have they not regarded what lies before them
and what lies behind them of heaven and earth?
Did We will, We would make the earth to
swallow them, or We would drop down on them
lumps from heaven. Surely in that is a sign to
      every penitent servant.

10   And We gave David bounty from Us:
'O you mountains, echo God's praises
with him, and you birds!' And We softened
for him iron: 'Fashion wide coats of mail,
and measure well the links.'—And do ye
righteousness, for surely I see
      the things you do.
And to Solomon the wind; its morning course
was a month's journey, and its evening course
was a month's journey. And We made
the Fount of Molten Brass to flow for him.
And of the jinn, some worked before him
by the leave of his Lord; and such of them
as swerved away from Our commandment,
We would let them taste the chastisement
      of the Blaze;
fashioning for him whatsoever he would—
places of worship, statues, porringers
like water-troughs, and anchored cooking-pots.
'Labour, O House of David, in thankfulness;
for few indeed are those that are thankful
      among My servants.'
And when We decreed that he should die,
naught indicated to them that he was dead
but the Beast of the Earth devouring his staff;
and when he fell down, the jinn saw clearly
that, had they only known the Unseen,

they would not have continued in the
    humbling chastisement.

For Sheba also there was a sign in
their dwelling-place—two gardens,
one on the right and one on the left:
'Eat of your Lord's provision, and give thanks
to Him; a good land, and a Lord
    All-forgiving.'
15   But they turned away; so We loosed on
them the Flood of Arim, and We gave them,
in exchange for their two gardens,
two gardens bearing bitter produce
and tamarisk-bushes, and here and there
    a few lote-trees.
Thus We recompensed them for their unbelief;
and do We ever recompense any but
    the unbeliever?
And We set, between them and the cities
that We have blessed, cities apparent
and well We measured the journey between them:
'Journey among them by night and day
    in security!'
But they said, 'Our Lord, prolong the
stages of our travel'; and they wronged
themselves, so We made them as but tales,
and We tore them utterly to pieces.
Surely in that are signs for every man
    enduring, thankful.
Iblis proved true his opinion of them,
and they followed him, except a party
    of the believers.
20   Yet he had no authority over them,
but that We might know him who believed
in the Hereafter from him who was in
doubt thereof. Thy Lord is Guardian
    over everything.

Say: 'Call on those you have asserted

apart from God; they possess not so much
as the weight of an ant in the heavens
nor in the earth; they have no partnership
in either of them, nor has He in them
      any supporter.'
Intercession will not avail with Him
save for him to whom He gives leave;
till, when terror is lifted from their hearts,
they will say, 'What said your Lord?'
They will say, 'The truth; and He is
      the All-high, the All-great.'

Say: 'Who provides for you out of the heavens and the
      Say: 'God.'   [earth?'
Surely, either we or you are upon right guidance, or in
      manifest error.

Say: 'You will not be questioned concerning our sins, neither
      shall we be questioned as to what you do.'
25   Say: 'Our Lord will bring us together, then make deliverance
      between us by the truth.
      He is the Deliverer, the All-knowing.'

Say: 'Show me those you have joined to Him as associates!
      No indeed; rather He is God,
      the All-mighty, the All-wise.'

We have sent thee not, except to mankind
entire, good tidings to bear, and warning;
      but most men do not know it.
They say, 'When shall this promise come to
      pass, if you speak the truth?'
Say: 'You have the tryst of a day that you
shall not put back by a single hour
      nor put it forward.'

30   The unbelievers say, 'We will not believe
      in this Koran, nor in that before it.'

Ah, if thou couldst see when the evildoers are stationed
                                          [before
their Lord, bandying argument the one against the other!
Those that were abased will say to those that waxed proud,
'Had it not been for you, we would have been believers.'
Those that waxed proud will say to those that were abased,
'What, did we bar you from the guidance after it came to
                    Nay, rather you were sinners.'   [you?
And those that were abased will say to those that waxed
                                         [proud,
'Nay, but devising night and day, when you were ordering us
to disbelieve in God, and to set up compeers to Him.'
They will be secretly remorseful when they see the chastise-
and We put fetters on the necks of the unbelievers; [ment
shall they be recompensed except for what they were doing?

We sent no warner into any city
except its men who lived at ease said,
'We disbelieve in the Message you
        have been sent with.'
They also said, 'We are more abundant
in wealth and children, and we shall not
        be chastised.'
35   Say: 'My Lord outspreads and straitens
His provision to whomsoever He will,
    but most men do not know it.'
It is not your wealth nor your children
that shall bring you nigh in nearness to Us,
except for him who believes, and does
righteousness; those—there awaits them
the double recompense for that they did,
and they shall be in the lofty chambers
        in security.
And those who strive against Our signs
to void them—those shall be arraigned
        into the chastisement.
Say: 'My Lord outspreads and straitens
His provision to whomsoever He will
of His servants; and whatever thing

you shall expend, He will replace it.
He is the best of providers.'

Upon the day when He shall muster them all together,
then He shall say to the angels, 'Was it you these were
⸢serving?'
40 They shall say, 'Glory be to Thee! Thou art our Protector,
apart from them; nay rather, they were serving the jinn;
most of them believed in them.'
'Therefore today none of you shall have power to profit
or hurt another.' And We shall say to the evildoers,
'Taste the chastisement of the Fire, which you cried lies to!'

And when Our signs are recited to them,
clear signs, they say, 'This is naught but
a man who desires to bar you from that
your fathers served'; and they say,
'This is nothing but a forged calumny.'
And the unbelievers say to the truth, when
it has come to them, 'This is nothing but
          manifest sorcery.'
We have not given them any Books to
study, nor have We sent them before thee
          any warner.
Those that were before them also cried lies,
yet they reached not a tenth of what We gave
them; they cried lies to My Messengers, and
          how was My horror!
45   Say: 'I give you but one admonition,
that you stand unto God, two by two
and one by one, and then reflect: no
madness is in your comrade. He is
naught but a warner unto you, before a
          terrible chastisement.'
Say: 'I have asked no wage of you;
that shall be yours. My wage falls
only upon God; and He is witness
          over everything.'
Say: 'My Lord hurls the truth—the Knower

of the Unseen.'
Say: 'Truth has come; falsehood originates not,
nor brings again.'
Say: 'If I go astray, I go astray
only to my own loss; if I am guided,
it is by what my Lord reveals to me.
He is All-hearing, Ever-nigh.'

50 Ah, if thou couldst see when they are terrified, and there is no
escape, and they are seized from a place near at hand,
and they say, 'We believe in it'; but how can they reach
from a place far away,
seeing they disbelieved in it before, guessing at the Unseen
from a place far away?
And a barrier is set between them and that they desire,
as was done with the likes of them aforetime; they were in
doubt disquieting.

XXXV

THE ANGELS

In the Name of God, the Merciful, the Compassionate

Praise belongs to God, Originator of the heavens and earth,
    who appointed the angels to be messengers
      having wings two, three and four,
      increasing creation as He wills.
    Surely God is powerful over everything.
Whatsoever mercy God opens to men, none can withhold and
    whatsoever He withholds, none can loose after Him.
      He is the All-mighty, the All-wise.

    O men, remember God's blessing upon you;
    is there any creator, apart from God, who
    provides for you out of heaven and earth?
      There is no god but He:
    how then are you perverted?

    If they cry lies to thee, Messengers before thee
    were cried lies to; and unto God all
      matters are returned.

5   O men, God's promise is true; so let not
    the present life delude you, and let not
    the Deluder delude you concerning God.
    Surely Satan is an enemy to you; so
    take him for an enemy. He calls his party
    only that they may be among the inhabitants
      of the Blaze.
    Those who disbelieve—there awaits them
      a terrible chastisement;
    but those who believe, and do deeds of
    righteousness—theirs shall be forgiveness
      and a great wage.

And what of him, the evil of whose deeds
has been decked out fair to him, so that he
thinks it is good? God leads astray
whomsoever He will, and whomsoever He will
He guides; so let not thy soul be wasted
in regrets for them; God has knowledge of
    the things they work.

10   God is He that looses the winds, that stir up cloud,
    then We drive it to a dead land
and therewith revive the earth, after it is dead.
    Even so is the Uprising.

    Whosoever desires glory,
the glory altogether belongs to God.
    To Him good words go up,
and the righteous deed—He uplifts it;
but those who devise evil deeds—theirs shall be
    a terrible chastisement,
and their devising shall come to naught.

    God created you of dust
    then of a sperm-drop,
    then He made you pairs.
No female bears or brings forth, save with His knowledge;
    and none is given long life who is given long life
neither is any diminished in his life, but it is in a Book.
    Surely that is easy for God.

Not equal are the two seas; this is sweet, grateful to taste,
    delicious to drink,
    and that is salt, bitter to the tongue.
    Yet of both you eat
fresh flesh, and bring forth out of it ornaments
    for you to wear;
and thou mayest see the ships cleaving through it,
    that you may seek
of His bounty, and so haply you will be thankful.
    He makes the night to enter into the day

and makes the day to enter into the night,
and He has subjected the sun and the moon, each of them
to a stated term.   ⌈running
That is God, your Lord; to Him belongs the Kingdom;
and those you call upon, apart from Him, possess
not so much as the skin of a date-stone.
15   If you call upon them, they will not hear your prayer,
and if they heard, they would not answer you; and
on the Day of Resurrection they will disown
your partnership.
None can tell thee like One who is aware.

O men, you are the ones that have need of God;
He is the All-sufficient, the All-laudable.
If He will, He can put you away
and bring a new creation; that
is surely no great matter for God.

No soul laden bears the load of another;
and if one heavy-burdened calls for its
load to be carried, not a thing of it
will be carried, though he be a near
kinsman. Thou warnest only those
who fear their Lord in the Unseen
and perform the prayer; and whosoever
purifies himself, purifies himself
only for his own soul's good. To God
is the homecoming.

20   Not equal are the blind and the seeing man,
the shadows and the light,
the shade and the torrid heat;
not equal are the living and the dead.
God makes to hear whomsoever He will;
thou canst not make those in their tombs to hear—
thou art naught but a warner.
Surely We have sent thee with the truth
good tidings to bear, and warning;
not a nation there is, but there has

passed away in it a warner.
If they cry thee lies, those before them
also cried lies; their Messengers
came to them with the clear signs,
the Psalms, the Illuminating Book;
then I seized the unbelievers, and
    how was My horror!

25 Hast thou not seen how that God sends down out of heaven
                                            ⌈water,
    and therewith We bring forth fruits of diverse hues?
And in the mountains are streaks white and red, of diverse
            and pitchy black;   ⌈hues,
    men too, and beasts and cattle—diverse are their hues.
    Even so only those of His servants
    fear God who have knowledge; surely God is
        All-mighty, All-forgiving.

    Surely those who recite the Book of God
    and perform the prayer, and expend of that
    We have provided them, secretly and in public,
    look for a commerce that comes not to naught,
    that He may pay them in full their wages
    and enrich them of His bounty; surely He is
        All-forgiving, All-thankful.
    And that We have revealed to thee of the
    Book is the truth, confirming what is before it;
    God is aware of and sees His servants.
    Then We bequeathed the Book on those of Our
    servants We chose; but of them some
    wrong themselves, some of them are lukewarm,
    and some are outstrippers in good works
    by the leave of God; that is the great bounty.
30 Gardens of Eden they shall enter; therein
    they shall be adorned with bracelets of gold
    and with pearls, and their apparel there
        shall be of silk.
    And they shall say, 'Praise belongs to God
    who has put away all sorrow from us. Surely

our Lord is All-forgiving, All-thankful,
who of His bounty has made us to dwell
in the abode of everlasting life
wherein no weariness assails us
      neither fatigue.'

As for the unbelievers, theirs shall be the fire of Gehenna;
they shall neither be done with and die, nor shall its chastise-
                                                        [ment
be lightened for them. Even so We recompense every
                                             [ungrateful one.
Therein they shall shout, 'Our Lord, bring us forth, and
we will do righteousness, other than what we have done.'
'What, did We not give you long life, enough to remember in
for him who would remember? To you the warner came;
so taste you now! The evildoers shall have no helper.'

God knows the Unseen in the heavens and the earth;
   He knows the thoughts within the breasts.
It is He who appointed you viceroys in the earth.
So whosoever disbelieves, his unbelief shall be
charged against him; their unbelief increases
the disbelievers only in hate in God's sight;
their unbelief increases the disbelievers only
         in loss.
Say: 'Have you considered your associates on whom
you call, apart from God? Show me what they have
created in the earth; or have they a partnership
in the heavens?' Or have We given them a Book,
so that they are upon a clear sign from it?
Nay, but the evildoers promise one another
        naught but delusion.

God holds the heavens and the earth, lest they remove;
did they remove, none would hold them after Him.
   Surely He is All-clement, All-forgiving.

40   They have sworn by God the most earnest oaths
        that if a warner came to them, they would be

more rightly guided than any one of the nations;
but when a warner came to them, it increased them
        only in aversion,
    waxing proud in the land, and devising
    evil; but evil devising encompasses
    only those who do it. So do they expect
    anything but the wont of the ancients?
    And thou shalt never find any changing
        the wont of God,
    and thou shalt never find any altering
        the wont of God.
    What, have they not journeyed in the land and
    beheld how was the end of those before them?
    They were stronger than themselves in might;
but God—there is naught in the heavens or the earth
    that can frustrate Him. Surely He is
        All-knowing, All-powerful.

If God should take men to task for what they have earned
He would not leave upon the face of the earth
one creature that crawls; but He is deferring them
        to a stated term.
    But when their term is come—surely God
        sees His servants.

XXXVI

YA SIN

In the Name of God, the Merciful, the Compassionate

Ya Sin

By the Wise Koran,
thou art truly among the Envoys
on a straight path;
the sending down of the All-mighty, the All-wise,
5   that thou mayest warn a people whose fathers were
never warned, so they are heedless.
The Word has been realised against most of them,
yet they do not believe.
Surely We have put on their necks fetters
up to the chin, so their heads are raised;
and We have put before them a barrier and
behind them a barrier; and We have covered
them, so they do not see.
Alike it is to them whether thou hast warned them
or thou hast not warned them, they do not believe.
10   Thou only warnest him who follows the Remembrance
and who fears the All-merciful in the Unseen; so
give him the good tidings of forgiveness
and a generous wage.
Surely it is We who bring the dead to life
and write down what they have forwarded
and what they have left behind; everything
We have numbered in a clear register.

Strike for them a similitude——
the inhabitants of the city, when
the Envoys came to it;
when We sent unto them two men,
but they cried them lies, so We

sent a third as reinforcement.
They said, 'We are assuredly
    Envoys unto you.'
They said, 'You are naught but
mortals like us; the All-merciful
has not sent down anything. You
    are speaking only lies.'
15 They said, 'Our Lord knows we are
    Envoys unto you;
and it is only for us to deliver
    the Manifest Message.'
They said, 'We augur ill of you. If
you give not over, we will stone you
and there shall visit you from us
    a painful chastisement.'
They said, 'Your augury is with you;
if you are reminded? But you are a
    prodigal people.'
Then came a man from the furthest part of
the city, running; he said, 'My people,
    follow the Envoys!
20 Follow such as ask no wage of you,
    that are right-guided.
And why should I not serve Him who
originated me, and unto whom
    you shall be returned?
What, shall I take, apart from Him, gods
whose intercession, if the All-merciful
desires affliction for me, shall not
avail me anything, and who will
    never deliver me?
Surely in that case I should be in
    manifest error.
Behold, I believe in your Lord;
    therefore hear me!'
25 It was said, 'Enter Paradise!'
He said, 'Ah, would that my people
    had knowledge
that my Lord has forgiven me

and that He has placed me
  among the honoured.'
And We sent not down upon his
people, after him, any host
out of heaven; neither would We
  send any down.
It was only one Cry and lo, they were
  silent and still.
Ah, woe for those servants! Never
comes unto them a Messenger, but
  they mock at him.

30   What, have they not seen how many
generations We have destroyed
  before them,
and that it is not unto them
  that they return?
They shall every one of them be arraigned
  before Us.

And a sign for them is the dead land, that We quickened
and brought forth from it grain, whereof they eat;
and We made therein gardens of palms and vines,
  and therein We caused fountains to gush forth,

35   that they might eat of its fruits and their hands' labour.
  What, will they not be thankful?
Glory be to Him, who created all the pairs
of what the earth produces, and of themselves,
  and of what they know not.
And a sign for them is the night; We strip it of the
  day and lo, they are in darkness.
And the sun—it runs to a fixed resting-place;
that is the ordaining of the All-mighty, the All-knowing.
And the moon—We have determined it by stations,
  till it returns like an aged palm-bough.

40   It behoves not the sun to overtake the moon, neither
  does the night outstrip the day,
    each swimming in a sky.
And a sign for them is that We carried their seed
    in the laden ship,

and We have created for them the like of it
      whereon they ride;
and if We will, We drown them,
then none have they to cry to,
neither are they delivered,
   save as a mercy from Us, and enjoyment
      for a while.

45   And when it is said to them, 'Fear what is before you
and what is behind you; haply you will find mercy'—
yet never any sign of the signs of their Lord
comes to them, but they are turning away from it.
And when it is said to them, 'Expend of that God has
provided you,' the unbelievers say to the believers,
'What, shall we feed such a one whom, if God willed,
He would feed? You are only in manifest error!'

They also say, 'When shall this promise come to
      pass, if you speak truly?'
They are awaiting only for one Cry to seize them
      while they are yet disputing,
50   then they will not be able to make any testament,
      nor will they return to their people.
And the Trumpet shall be blown; then behold, they are
      from their tombs unto their Lord.   [sliding down
They say, 'Alas for us! Who roused us out of our sleeping-
                     [place?
This is what the All-merciful promised, and the Envoys
                     [spoke truly.'
'It was only one Cry; then behold, they are all arraigned
                   [before Us.
So today no soul shall be wronged anything, and you shall
                     [not be
recompensed, except according to what you have been
                     [doing.
55 See, the inhabitants of Paradise today are busy in their
                    [rejoicing,
they and their spouses, reclining upon couches in the shade;
therein they have fruits, and they have all that they call for.

'Peace!'—such is the greeting, from a Lord All-
[compassionate.
'Now keep yourselves apart, you sinners, upon this day!
60 Made I not covenant with you, Children of Adam, that you
should not serve Satan—surely he is a manifest foe to you—
and that you should serve Me? This is a straight path.
He led astray many a throng of you; did you not understand?
This is Gehenna, then, the same that you were promised;
roast well in it today, for that you were unbelievers!'
65 Today We set a seal on their mouths, and their hands speak
[to Us,
and their feet bear witness as to what they have been earning.

Did We will, We would have obliterated
their eyes, then they would race to the path,
but how would they see?
Did We will, We would have changed them
where they were, then they could not go on,
nor could they return.
And to whomsoever We give long life,
We bend him over in His constitution; what,
do they not understand?

We have not taught him poetry; it is not
seemly for him. It is only a Remembrance
and a Clear Koran,
70 that he may warn whosoever is living,
and that the Word may be realized against
the unbelievers.

Have they not seen how that We have created for them
of that Our hands wrought cattle that they own?
We have subdued them to them, and some of them they
and some they eat;   [ride,
other uses also they have in them, and beverages.
What, will they not be thankful?
Yet they have taken, apart from God, gods;
haply they might be helped.
75 They cannot help them, though they be hosts

made ready for them.
So do not let their saying grieve thee;
assuredly We know what they keep secret
and what they publish.

Has not man regarded how that We created him
of a sperm-drop?
Then lo, he is a manifest adversary.
And he has struck for Us a similitude
and forgotten his creation;
he says, 'Who shall quicken the bones
when they are decayed?'
Say: 'He shall quicken them, who originated them
the first time; He knows all creation,
80   who has made for you out of the green tree
fire and lo, from it you kindle.'
Is not He, who created the heavens and earth,
able to create the like of them? Yes indeed;
He is the All-creator, the All-knowing.
His command, when He desires a thing, is to say to it
'Be,' and it is.
So glory be to Him, in whose hand is the dominion
of everything,
and unto whom you shall be returned.

XXXVII

THE RANGERS

In the Name of God, the Merciful, the Compassionate

By the rangers ranging
and the scarers scaring
and the reciters of a Remembrance,
surely your God is One,
5 Lord of the heavens and the earth, and of what between them
Lord of the Easts.   [is,
We have adorned the lower heaven with the adornment of
[the stars
and to preserve against every rebel Satan;
they listen not to the High Council.
for they are pelted from every side,
rejected, and theirs is an everlasting chastisement,
10 except such as snatches a fragment,
and he is pursued by a piercing flame.

So ask them for a pronouncement—
Are they stronger in constitution, or
those We created? We created them
of clinging clay.
Nay, thou marvellest; and they scoff
and, when reminded, do not remember
and, when they see a sign, would scoff;
15 and they say, 'This is nothing but
manifest sorcery.
What, when we are dead and become
dust and bones, shall we indeed
be raised up?
What, and our fathers, the ancients?'
Say: 'Yes, and in all lowliness.'

For it is only a single scaring, then behold, they are watching
150

20 and they say, 'Woe, alas for us! This is the Day of Doom.'
'This is the Day of Decision, even that you cried lies to.
Muster those who did evil, their wives, and that they were
[serving,
apart from God, and guide them unto the path of Hell!
25 And halt them, to be questioned: "Why help you not one
[another?" '
No indeed; but today they resign themselves in submission
and advance one upon another, asking each other questions.
These say, 'Why, you of old would come to us from the
[right hand.'
Those say, 'No; on the contrary, you were not believers;
we had no authority over you; no, you were an insolent
[people.
30 So our Lord's Word is realised against us; we are tasting it.
Therefore we perverted you, and we ourselves were
[perverts.'
So all of them on that day are sharers in the chastisement.
Even so We do with the sinners; for when it was said to
[them,
'There is no god but God,' they were ever waxing proud,
35 saying, 'What, shall we forsake our gods for a poet
[possessed?'
'No indeed; but he brought the truth, and confirmed the
[Envoys.
Now certainly you shall be tasting the painful chastisement,
and not be recompensed, except according to what you were
[doing.'

Except for God's sincere servants;
40   for them awaits a known provision,
fruits—and they high-honoured
in the Gardens of Bliss
upon couches, set face to face,
a cup from a spring being passed round to them,
45   white, a delight to the drinkers,
wherein no sickness is, neither intoxication;
and with them wide-eyed maidens
restraining their glances

151

as if they were hidden pearls.
They advance one upon another, asking each other questions.
One of them says, 'I had a comrade
50 who would say, "Are you a confirmer?
What, when we are dead and become
dust and bones, shall we indeed
  be requited?"'
He says, 'Are you looking down?'
Then he looks, and sees him in the midst of Hell.
He says, 'By God, wellnigh thou didst destroy me;
55 But for my Lord's blessing, I were one of the arraigned.
What, do we then not die
except for our first death, and are we not chastised?
This is indeed the mighty triumph,
and for the like of this let the workers work.'

60 Is that better as a hospitality,
    or the Tree of Ez-Zakkoum?
We have appointed it as a trial
    for the evildoers.
It is a tree that comes forth in
    the root of Hell;
its spathes are as the heads of Satans,
and they eat of it, and of it fill
    their bellies,
65 then on top of it they have a brew
    of boiling water,
then their return is unto Hell.
They found their fathers erring,
and they run in their footsteps.
Before them erred most of the ancients,
70 and We sent among them warners;
and behold, how was the end of
    them that were warned,
except for God's sincere servants.

Noah called to Us; and how excellent
    were the Answerers!
And We delivered him and his people

from the great distress,
75   and We made his seed the survivors,
and left for him among the later folk
'Peace be upon Noah among all beings!'
Even so We recompense the good-doers;
he was among Our believing servants.
80   Then afterwards We drowned the rest.

Of his party was also Abraham;
when he came unto his Lord with
    a pure heart,
when he said to his father and his folk,
    'What do you serve?
Is it a calumny, gods apart from God,
    that you desire?
85   What think you then of the Lord
    of all Being?'
And he cast a glance at the stars,
and he said, 'Surely I am sick.'
But they went away from him,
    turning their backs.
Then he turned to their gods, and said,
    'What do you eat?
90   What ails you, that you speak not?'
And he turned upon them smiting them
    with his right hand.
Then came the others to him hastening.
He said, 'Do you serve what you hew,
and God created you and what you make?'
95   They said, 'Build him a building, and cast him
    into the furnace!'
They desired to outwit him; so We made
    them the lower ones.
He said, 'I am going to my Lord;
    He will guide me.
My Lord, give me one of the righteous.'
Then We gave him the good tidings of
    a prudent boy;
100   and when he had reached the age of

running with him,
he said, 'My son, I see in a dream
that I shall sacrifice thee; consider,
    what thinkest thou?'
He said, 'My father, do as thou art
bidden; thou shalt find me, God willing,
    one of the steadfast.'
When they had surrendered, and he flung him
    upon his brow,
We called unto him, 'Abraham,

105   thou hast confirmed the vision;
even so We recompense the good-doers.
This is indeed the manifest trial.'
And We ransomed him with a mighty sacrifice,
and left for him among the later folk
    'Peace be upon Abraham!'

110   Even so We recompense the good-doers;
he was among Our believing servants.
Then We gave him the good tidings of
Isaac, a Prophet, one of the righteous.
And We blessed him, and Isaac;
and of their seed some are good-doers,
and some manifest self-wrongers.

We also favoured Moses and Aaron,

115   and We delivered them and their people
    from the great distress.
And We helped them, so that they
    were the victors;
and We gave them the Manifesting Book,
and guided them in the straight path,
and left for them among the later folk

120   'Peace be upon Moses and Aaron!'
Even so We recompense the good-doers;
they were among Our believing servants.

Elias too was one of the Envoys;
when he said to his people, 'Will you
    not be godfearing?

125 Do you call on Baal, and abandon the
          Best of creators?
God, your Lord, and the Lord of your
          fathers, the ancients?'
But they cried him lies; so they will be
          among the arraigned,
except for God's sincere servants;
and We left for him among the later folk
130   'Peace be upon Elias!'
Even so We recompense the good-doers;
he was among Our believing servants.

Lot too was one of the Envoys;
when We delivered him and his people
          all together,
135 save an old woman among those that tarried;
          then We destroyed the others,
and you pass by them in the morning and
in the night; will you not understand?

Jonah too was one of the Envoys;
140 when he ran away to the laden ship
and cast lots, and was of the rebutted,
then the whale swallowed him down,
          and he blameworthy.
Now had he not been of those that
          glorify God,
he would have tarried in its belly
until the day they shall be raised;
145 but We cast him upon the wilderness,
          and he was sick,
and We caused to grow over him
          a tree of gourds.
Then We sent him unto a hundred
          thousand, or more,
and they believed; so We gave them enjoyment
          for a while.

So ask them for a pronouncement—

Has thy Lord daughters, and they sons?
150　　Or did We create the angels
females, while they were witnesses?
Is it not of their own calumny
　　　that they say,
'God has begotten?' They are truly liars.
Has He chosen daughters above sons?
What ails you then, how you judge?
155　　What, and will you not remember?
Or have you a clear authority?
Bring your Book, if you speak truly!

They have set up a kinship between Him and the jinn;
and the jinn know that they shall be arraigned.
　　　Glory be to God
　　　above that they describe,
160　　except for God's sincere servants.
But as for you, and that you serve,
you shall not tempt any against Him
except him who shall roast in Hell.
None of us is there, but has a known station;
165　　　we are the rangers,
　　we are they that give glory.

What though they would say,
'If only we had had a Reminder from the ancients,
then were we God's sincere servants.'
170　　But they disbelieved in it; soon they shall know!
Already Our Word has preceded to Our servants, the Envoys;
　　assuredly they shall be helped,
　　and Our host—they are the victors.
So turn thou from them for a while,
175　　and see them; soon they shall see!
What, do they seek to hasten Our chastisement?
When it lights in their courtyard, how evil will be the
　　　　of them that are warned!　　　　[morning
So turn thou from them for a while,
and see; soon they shall see!
180　　Glory be to thy Lord, the Lord of Glory,

above that they describe!
And peace be upon the Envoys;
and praise belongs to God, the Lord of all Being.

XXXVIII

SAD

In the Name of God, the Merciful, the Compassionate

Sad

By the Koran, containing the Remembrance—
nay, but the unbelievers glory in their schism.
How many a generation We destroyed before them,
and they called, but time was none to escape.

Now they marvel that a warner has come to them
from among them; and the unbelievers say,
   'This is a lying sorcerer.
What, has he made the gods One God? This is
   indeed a marvellous thing.'
And the Council of them depart, saying
'Go! Be steadfast to your gods; this is
   a thing to be desired.
We have not heard of this in the last religion;
   this is surely an invention.
What, has the Remembrance been sent down on him
out of us all?' Nay, but they are in doubt
of My Remembrance; nay, they have not yet
   tasted My chastisement.
Or have they the treasuries of thy Lord's mercy,
   the All-mighty, the All-giving?
Or is theirs the kingdom of the heavens and earth
and of what between them is? Why, then let them
   ascend the cords!
A very host of parties is routed there!

Cried lies before them the people of Noah,
and Ad, and Pharaoh, he of the tent-pegs,
and Thamood, and the people of Lot, and
the men of the Thicket—those were the parties;

158

not one, that cried not lies to the Messengers,
    so My retribution was just.
These are only awaiting for a single Cry,
    to which there is no delay.

15   They say, 'Our Lord, hasten to us our share
        before the Day of Reckoning.'
Bear patiently what they say, and remember
Our servant David, the man of might;
    he was a penitent.
With him We subjected the mountains to give glory
    at evening and sunrise,
and the birds, duly mustered, every one
    to him reverting;
We strengthened his kingdom, and gave him wisdom
    and speech decisive.
20   Has the tiding of the dispute come to thee?
        When they scaled the Sanctuary,
when they entered upon David, and he took
fright at them; and they said, 'Fear not;
two disputants we are—one of us has
injured the other; so judge between us
justly, and transgress not, and guide us
    to the right path.'
'Behold, this my brother has ninety-nine
ewes, and I have one ewe. So he said,
"Give her into my charge"; and he overcame
    me in the argument.'
Said he, 'Assuredly he has wronged thee
in asking for thy ewe in addition to
his sheep; and indeed many intermixers
do injury one against the other,
save those who believe, and do deeds of
righteousness—and how few they are!'
And David thought that We had only
tried him; therefore he sought forgiveness
of his Lord, and he fell down, bowing,
    and he repented.
Accordingly We forgave him that,

159

and he has a near place in Our presence
and a fair resort.

25   'David, behold, We have appointed thee
a viceroy in the earth; therefore judge
between men justly, and follow not caprice,
lest it lead thee astray from the way of God.
Surely those who go astray from the way
of God—there awaits them a terrible
chastisement, for that they have forgotten
 the Day of Reckoning.'

We have not created the heavens and earth,
and what between them is, for vanity;
such is the thought of the unbelievers,
wherefore woe unto the unbelievers
 because of the Fire!
Or shall We make those who believe and do
righteous deeds as the workers of corruption
in the earth, or shall We make the godfearing
 as the transgressors?
A Book We have sent down to thee, Blessed,
that men possessed of minds may ponder its signs
 and so remember.

And We gave unto David Solomon;
how excellent a servant he was!
 He was a penitent.

30   When in the evening were presented to him
 the standing steeds,
he said, 'Lo, I have loved the love of
good things better than the remembrance
of my Lord, until the sun was hidden
 behind the veil.
Return them to me!' And he began to stroke
 their shanks and necks.
Certainly We tried Solomon, and We
cast upon his throne a mere body;
 then he repented.
He said, 'My Lord, forgive me, and

160

give me a kingdom such as may not
befall anyone after me; surely Thou
  art the All-giver.'
35 So We subjected to him the wind, that ran
at his commandment, softly, wherever
  he might light on,
and the Satans, every builder and diver
and others also, coupled in fetters:
'This is Our gift; bestow or withhold
  without reckoning.'
And he had a near place in Our presence
  and a fair resort.

40 Remember also Our servant Job;
when he called to his Lord, 'Behold,
Satan has visited me with weariness
  and chastisement.'
'Stamp thy foot! This is a laving-place
  cool, and a drink.'
And We gave to him his family, and
the like of them with them, as a mercy
from us, and a reminder unto men
  possessed of minds;
and, 'Take in thy hand a bundle of
rushes, and strike therewith, and do not
fail in thy oath.' Surely We found him
  a steadfast man.
How excellent a servant he was!
  He was a penitent.

45 Remember also Our servants Abraham,
Isaac and Jacob—men of might they
  and of vision.
Assuredly We purified them with a
quality most pure, the remembrance
  of the Abode,
and in Our sight they are of the chosen,
  the excellent.
Remember also Our servants Ishmael,

161

F

Elisha, and Dhul Kifl; each is among
    the excellent.

This is a Remembrance; and for the godfearing
    is a fair resort,
50   Gardens of Eden, whereof the gates
    are open to them,
wherein they recline, and wherein
they call for fruits abundant, and
    sweet potions,
and with them maidens restraining their glances
    of equal age.
'This is what you were promised for the
    Day of Reckoning;
this is Our provision, unto which
    there is no end.'
55   All this; but for the insolent awaits
    an ill resort,
Gehenna, wherein they are roasted—
    an evil cradling!
All this; so let them taste it—boiling
    water and pus,
and other torments of the like kind
    coupled together.

'This is a troop rushing in with you; there is no Welcome
    they shall roast in the Fire.'   [for them;
60   They say, 'No, it is you have no Welcome; you forwarded it
    how evil a stablishment!'   [for us;
They say, 'Our Lord, whoso forwarded this for us, give him
    chastisement in the Fire!'   [a double
They say, 'How is it with us, that we do not see men here
    counted among the wicked?   [that we
What, did we take them for a laughing-stock? Or have our
    swerved away from them?'   [eyes

Surely that is true—the disputing of
    the inhabitants of the Fire.

65   Say: 'I am only a warner.
There is not any god but God,
the One, the Omnipotent,
Lord of the heavens and earth, and of what between them is,
the All-mighty, the All-forgiving.'
Say: 'It is a mighty tiding
from which you are turning away.
I had no knowledge of the High Council
when they disputed.
70 This alone is revealed to me, that I am only a clear warner.'

When thy Lord said to the angels,
'See, I am creating a mortal
of a clay.
When I have shaped him, and breathed
My spirit in him, fall you down,
bowing before him!'
Then the angels bowed themselves
all together,
save Iblis; he waxed proud, and was
one of the unbelievers.
75   Said He, 'Iblis, what prevented thee
to bow thyself before that I created
with My own hands?
Hast thou waxed proud, or art thou
of the lofty ones?'
Said he, 'I am better than he;
Thou createdst me of fire, and him Thou
createdst of clay.'
Said He, 'Then go thou forth hence;
thou art accursed.
Upon thee shall rest My curse, till
the Day of Doom.'
80   Said he, 'My Lord, respite me till
the day they shall be raised.'
Said He, 'Thou art among the ones
that are respited
until the day of the known time.'
Said he, 'Now, by Thy glory,

I shall pervert them all together,
excepting those Thy servants among them
    that are sincere.'
85   Said He, 'This is the truth, and the
truth I say; I shall assuredly
fill Gehenna with thee, and with
whosoever of them follows thee,
    all together.'

Say: 'I ask of you no wage for it,
neither am I of those who take things
    upon themselves.
It is nothing but a reminder
    unto all beings,
and you shall surely know its tiding
    after a while.'

XXXIX

THE COMPANIES

In the Name of God, the Merciful, the Compassionate

The sending down of the Book is from God
    the All-mighty, the All-wise.
We have sent down to thee the Book with the truth;
    so worship God, making thy religion
        His sincerely.
Belongs not sincere religion to God?
And those who take protectors, apart from Him—
    'We only serve them that they may bring
    us nigh in nearness to God'—surely God
shall judge between them touching that whereon
        they are at variance.
5   Surely God guides not him who is a liar,
        unthankful.
Had God desired to take to Him a son,
He would have chosen whatever He willed of that
He has created. Glory be to Him! He is God,
        the One, the Omnipotent.

He created the heavens and the earth in truth,
    wrapping night about the day, and
    wrapping the day about the night;
and He has subjected the sun and the moon, each of them
        to a stated term.   [running
Is not He the All-mighty, the All-forgiving?
He created you of a single soul, then
    from it He appointed its mate;
and He sent down to you of the cattle eight couples.
He creates you in your mothers' wombs
    creation after creation
    in threefold shadows.
That then is God, your Lord;

to Him belongs the Kingdom;
there is no god but He;
so how are you turned about?
If you are unthankful, God is independent of you,
yet He approves not unthankfulness in His servants;
but if you are thankful, He will approve it in you.
And no soul laden bears the load of another. Then
to your Lord shall you return, and He will tell you
what you have been doing.

10   He knows the thoughts within the breasts.

When some affliction visits a man, he
calls upon his Lord, turning to him; then
when He confers on him a blessing from Him
he forgets that he was calling to before
and sets up compeers to God, to lead
astray from His way. Say: 'Enjoy thy
unbelief a little; thou shalt be among
    the inhabitants of the Fire.'
Or is he who is obedient in the watches
of the night, bowing himself and standing,
he being afraid of the world to come
and hoping for the mercy of his Lord . . .?
Say: 'Are they equal—those who know and
those who know not?' Only men possessed
    of minds remember.
Say: 'My servants who believe, fear your
Lord. For those who do good in this world
good, and God's earth is wide. Surely the
patient will be paid their wages in full
    without reckoning.'
Say: 'I have been commanded to serve God
making my religion His sincerely; and
I have been commanded to be the first of
    those that surrender.'

15   Say: 'Truly I fear, if I should rebel
against my Lord, the chastisement
    of a dreadful day.'
Say: 'God I serve, making my religion

His sincerely;
so serve what you will apart from Him.'
Say: 'Surely the losers are they who
lose themselves and their families
on the Day of Resurrection; is not that
      the manifest loss?
Above them they shall have overshadowings
of the Fire, and underneath them
overshadowings; that it is wherewith God
frightens His servants: "O My servants,
      so fear you Me!" '
Those who eschew the serving of idols
and turn penitent to God, for them is
good tidings! So give thou good tidings
to My servants who give ear to the Word
and follow the fairest of it. Those are they
whom God has guided; those—they are men
      possessed of minds.

20   He against whom the word of chastisement
is realized—shalt thou deliver him
      out of the Fire?
But those who fear their Lord—for them
await lofty chambers, above which are
built lofty chambers, underneath which
rivers flow—God's promise; God fails
      not the tryst.

Hast thou not seen how that God has sent down out of heaven
      and threaded it as springs in the earth,   [water
then He brings forth therewith crops of diverse hues,
then they wither, and thou seest them turning yellow,
      then He makes them broken orts?
Surely in that is a reminder for men
      possessed of minds.

Is he whose breast God has expanded
unto Islam, so he walks in a light
from his Lord . . .? But woe to those
whose hearts are hardened against

the remembrance of God! Those are
in manifest error.
God has sent down the fairest discourse as
a Book, consimilar in its oft-repeated,
whereat shiver the skins of those who fear
their Lord; then their skins and their hearts
soften to the remembrance of God.
That is God's guidance, whereby
He guides whomsoever He will;
and whomsoever God leads astray,
no guide has he.

25   Is he who guards himself with his face
against the evil of the chastisement
on the Day of Resurrection . . .? And it
is said to the evildoers, 'Taste now
that you were earning!'
Those that were before them cried lies, then
the chastisement came upon them from whence
they were not aware;
so God let them taste degradation
in this present life; and the chastisement
of the world to come is assuredly greater,
did they but know.

Indeed We have struck for the people
in this Koran every manner of similitude;
haply they will remember;
an Arabic Koran, wherein there is no crookedness;
haply they will be godfearing.

30   God has struck a similitude—a man
in whom partners disagreeing share,
and a man the property of one man.
Are the two equal in likeness? Praise
belongs to God! Nay, but most of them
do not know.

Thou art mortal, and they are mortal;
then on the Day of Resurrection before your Lord

you shall dispute.

But who does greater evil than he who
lies against God and cries lies to the
very truth, when it comes to him?
Is there not in Gehenna a lodging
    for the unbelievers?
And he who has come with the very
truth and confirms it, those—they
    are the godfearing.
35   They shall have whatsoever they will
with their Lord; that is the recompense
    of the good-doers,
that God may acquit them of the worst
of what they did, and recompense them
with the wages of the fairest of
    what they were doing.
Shall not God suffice His servant, though
they frighten thee with those apart from
Him? And whomsoever God leads astray,
    no guide has he.
But whomso God guides, none shall lead
him astray; is not God All-mighty,
    All-vengeful?

    If thou askest them,
'Who created the heavens and the earth?'
    they will say, 'God.'
Say: 'What think you? That you call upon
apart from God—if God desires
affliction for me, shall they remove
His affliction? Or if He desires
mercy for me, shall they withhold His
mercy?' Say: 'God is enough for me;
in Him all those put their trust
    who put their trust.'
40   Say: 'My people, act according to
your station; I am acting; and
    soon you will know

169

to whom will come a chastisement
degrading him, and upon whom lights
   a lasting chastisement.'

Surely We have sent down upon thee
the Book for mankind with the truth.
Whosoever is guided, is only guided
to his own gain, and whosoever goes
astray, it is only to his own loss;
thou art not a guardian over them.

   God takes the souls at the time of their death,
   and that which has not died, in its sleep;
He withholds that against which He has decreed death,
   but looses the other till a stated term.
Surely in that are signs for a people who reflect.
Or have they taken intercessors apart from God?
Say: 'What, even though they have no power whatever
       and no understanding?'
45   Say: 'To God belongs intercession altogether.
His is the kingdom of the heavens and the earth;
   then unto Him you will be returned.'

   When God is mentioned alone, then shudder
the hearts of those who believe not in the Hereafter,
   but when those apart from Him are mentioned
      behold, they rejoice.
Say: 'O God, Thou originator of the heavens and the earth
   who knowest the Unseen and the Visible,
Thou shalt judge between Thy servants touching that
      they are at variance.'   ⌈whereon

   If the evildoers possessed all that is in the earth,
and the like of it with it, they would offer it to
ransom themselves from the evil of the chastisement
on the Day of Resurrection; yet there would appear
to them from God that they never reckoned with, and
there would appear to them the evils of that they
have earned, and they would be encompassed by

that they mocked at.

50   When some affliction visits a man, he
     calls unto Us; then, when We confer on
     him a blessing from Us, he says, 'I was
     given it only because of a knowledge.'
     Nay, it is a trial, but most of them
            do not know it.
     So said those that were before them; but
     that they earned did not avail them,
     in that the evils of that they earned
     smote them. The evildoers of these men,
     they too shall be smitten by the evils
     of that they earned; they will not be able
            to frustrate it.

Do they know that God outspreads and straitens
     His provision to whomsoever He will?
Surely in that are signs for a people who believe.

     Say: 'O my people who have been prodigal
     against yourselves, do not despair of
     God's mercy; surely God forgives sins
     altogether; surely He is the All-forgiving,
            the All-compassionate.
55   Turn unto your Lord and surrender to Him,
     ere the chastisement comes upon you, then
            you will not be helped.
     And follow the fairest of what has been
     sent down to you from your Lord, ere the
     chastisement comes upon you suddenly
            while you are unaware.'
     Lest any soul should say, 'Alas for me,
     in that I neglected my duty to God,
            and was a scoffer,'
     or lest it should say, 'If only God
     had guided me, I should have been
            among the godfearing,'
     or lest it should say, when it sees

the chastisement, 'O that I might
return again, and be among
    the good-doers.'
60   'Yes indeed! My signs did come to thee,
but thou hast cried them lies, and thou
hast waxed proud, and become one of
    the unbelievers.'

And upon the Day of Resurrection thou shalt see those who
                                                    ⌈lied
against God, their faces blackened; is there not in Gehenna
    a lodging for those that are proud?

But God shall deliver those that were godfearing
in their security; evil shall not visit them,
    neither shall they sorrow.

God is the Creator of every thing;
He is Guardian over every thing;
unto Him belong the keys of the heavens and the earth.
And those who disbelieve in the signs of God,
    those—they are the losers.

65   Say: 'Is it other than God you bid me serve,
        you ignorant ones?'
It has been revealed to thee, and to those before thee,
    'If thou associatest other gods with God,
    thy work shall surely fail and thou wilt be
        among the losers.'
Nay, but God do thou serve; and be thou
    among the thankful.

They measure not God with His true measure.
The earth altogether shall be His handful
on the Day of Resurrection, and the heavens
    shall be rolled up in His right hand.
Glory be to Him! High be He exalted above
    that they associate!

For the Trumpet shall be blown, and whosoever is in the
[heavens
and whosoever is in the earth shall swoon, save whom God
[wills.
Then it shall be blown again, and lo, they shall stand,
[beholding.
And the earth shall shine with the light of its Lord, and the
[Book
shall be set in place, and the Prophets and witnesses shall be
[brought,
and justly the issue be decided between them, and they not
[wronged.

70   Every soul shall be paid in full for what it has wrought; and
knows very well what they do.   [He
Then the unbelievers shall be driven in companies into
[Gehenna
till, when they have come thither, then its gates will be
[opened
and its keepers will say to them, 'Did not Messengers come
[to you
from among yourselves, reciting to you the signs of your
[Lord
and warning you against the encounter of this your day?'
They shall say, 'Yes indeed; but the word of the chastisement
has been realized against the unbelievers.'
It shall be said, 'Enter the gates of Gehenna, to dwell therein
forever.' How evil is the lodging of those that are proud!
Then those that feared their Lord shall be driven in com-
[panies
into Paradise, till, when they have come thither, and its gates
are opened, and its keepers will say to them, 'Peace be upon
Well you have fared; enter in, to dwell forever.' [you!
And they shall say, 'Praise belongs to God, who has been
[true
in His promise to us, and has bequeathed upon us the earth,
for us to make our dwelling wheresoever we will in Para-
How excellent is the wage of those that labour! [dise.'

75   And thou shalt see the angels encircling about the Throne
proclaiming the praise of their Lord; and justly the issue

shall be decided between them; and it shall be said,
'Praise belongs to God, the Lord of all Being.'

XL

THE BELIEVERS

In the Name of God, the Merciful, the Compassionate

Ha Mim

The sending down of the Book is from God
   the All-mighty, the All-knowing,
Forgiver of sins, Accepter of penitence,
      Terrible in retribution,
         the Bountiful;
            there is no god but He,
and unto Him is the homecoming.

None but the unbelievers dispute concerning
the signs of God; so let not their going
      to and fro in the land delude thee.
The people of Noah before them also cried
lies, and the parties after them; every
nation purposed against their Messenger
to seize him, and disputed with falsehood
that they might rebut thereby the truth.
Then I seized them; and how was My retribution!
Even so the Word of thy Lord was realised
against the unbelievers, that they are the inhabitants of
            the Fire.

Those who bear the Throne, and those round about it
proclaim the praise of their Lord, and believe in Him,
   and they ask forgiveness for those who believe:
   'Our Lord, Thou embracest every thing in mercy
   and knowledge; therefore forgive those who have
repented, and follow Thy way, and guard them against
            the chastisement of Hell.
Our Lord, and admit them to the Gardens of Eden

that Thou hast promised them and those who were
                                                  [righteous
of their fathers, and their wives, and their seed; surely
      Thou art the All-mighty, the All-wise.
And guard them against evil deeds; whomsoever
Thou guardest against evil deeds on that day,
  on him Thou hast had mercy; and that is indeed
        the mighty triumph.

10   It shall be proclaimed to the unbelievers, 'Surely God's
                                         [hatred
is greater than your hatred one of another, when you were
        unto belief, and disbelieved.'   [called
They shall say, 'Our Lord, Thou hast caused us to die two
                                       [deaths
and Thou hast given us twice to live; now we confess our
        Is there any way to go forth?'   [sins.

       That is because, when God was called to alone,
       you disbelieved; but if others are associated
       with Him, then you believe. Judgment belongs to
          God, the All-high, the All-great.

        It is He who shows you His signs
       and sends down to you out of heaven provision;
         yet none remembers but he who repents.
         So call unto God, making your religion
       His sincerely, though the unbelievers be averse.

15   Exalter of ranks is He, Possessor of the Throne,
       casting the Spirit of His bidding upon
        whomever He will of His servants,
    that he may warn them of the Day of Encounter,
the day they sally forth, and naught of theirs is hidden from
                                     [God.
'Whose is the Kingdom today?' 'God's, the One, the Omni-
                                      [potent.
Today each soul shall be recompensed for that it has earned;
         no wrong today.

Surely God is swift at the reckoning.'

And warn them against the Day of the Imminent
when, choking with anguish, the hearts are in the throats
and the evildoers have not one loyal friend,
     no intercessor to be heeded.

20   He knows the treachery of the eyes
        and what the breasts conceal.

God shall decide justly, and those they call on,
apart from Him, shall not decide by any means.
surely God is the All-hearing, the All-seeing.

What, have they not journeyed in the land and
beheld how was the end of those before them?
They were stronger than themselves in might
and left firmer traces in the earth; yet God
seized them in their sins, and they had none
     to defend them from God.
That was because their Messengers came to them
with the clear signs; but they disbelieved,
so God seized them. Surely He is All-strong,
     terrible in retribution.

We also sent Moses with Our signs and
     a clear authority,
25   to Pharaoh, Haman and Korah; they said,
     'A lying sorcerer!'
And when he brought them the truth from
Us, they said, 'Slay the sons of those
who believe with him, and spare their
women.' But the guile of the unbelievers
     is ever in error.
And Pharaoh said, 'Let me slay Moses,
and let him call to his Lord. I fear
that he may change your religion, or
that he may cause corruption to appear
     in the land.'

And Moses said, 'I take refuge in
my Lord and your Lord from every man
who is proud, and believes not in the
            Day of Reckoning.'
Then said a certain man, a believer
of Pharaoh's folk that kept hidden
his belief, 'What, will you slay a man
because he says, "My Lord is God,"
yet he has brought you the clear signs
from your Lord? If he is a liar,
his lying is upon his own head; but
if he is truthful, somewhat of that he
promises you will smite you. Surely
God guides not him who is prodigal
            and a liar.

30   O my people, today the kingdom is
yours, who are masters in the land.
But who will help us against the might
of God, if it comes upon us?' Said
Pharaoh, 'I only let you see what
I see; I only guide you in the way
            of rectitude.'
Then said he who believed, 'My people,
truly I fear for you the like of the
            day of the parties,
the like of the case of Noah's people,
            Ad, Thamood,
and those after them; and God desires not
            wrong for His servants.

35   O my people, I fear for you the Day
            of Invocation,
the day you turn about, retreating,
having none to defend you from God;
and whomsoever God leads astray,
            no guide has he.
Joseph brought you the clear signs before,
yet you continued in doubt concerning
that he brought you until, when he
perished, you said, "God will never

178

send forth a Messenger after him."
Even so God leads astray the prodigal
      and the doubter.'
(Those who dispute concerning the signs
of God, without any authority
come to them, very hateful is that
in the sight of God and the believers;
so God sets a seal on every heart
      proud, arrogant.)
Pharaoh said, 'Haman, build for me
a tower, that haply so I may reach
      the cords,
the cords of the heavens, and look upon
Moses' God; for I think that he is
      a liar.'
40 So the evil of his deeds was decked out
fair to Pharaoh, and he was barred from
the way, and Pharaoh's guile came only
      to ruin.
Then said he who believed, 'My people,
follow me, and I will guide you in the way
      of rectitude.
O my people, surely this present life
is but a passing enjoyment; surely
the world to come is the abode of
      stability.
Whosoever does an evil deed shall be
recompensed only with the like of it,
but whosoever does a righteous deed,
be it male or female, believing—those shall
enter Paradise, therein provided
      without reckoning.
O my people, how is it with me, that
I call you to salvation, and you call
      me to the Fire?
45 You call me to disbelieve in God, and
to associate with Him that whereof I
have no knowledge, while I call you to
    the All-mighty, the All-forgiving.

No doubt that what you call me to has
no call heard, in this world or in the
world to come, that to God we return,
and that the prodigal are the inhabitants
of the Fire.
You will remember what I say to you.
I commit my affair to God; surely God
sees His servants.'
So God guarded him against the evil
things of their devising, and there
encompassed the folk of Pharaoh the evil
chastisement,
the Fire, to which they shall be exposed
morning and evening; and on the day
when the Hour is come: 'Admit the folk
of Pharaoh into the most terrible
chastisement!'

50   And when they argue one with the other in the Fire, and the
[weak
say unto those who waxed proud, 'Why, we were your
[followers;
will you avail us now against any part of the Fire?' Then
those who waxed proud shall say, 'Every one of us is in it;
indeed, God already has passed judgment between His ser-
[vants.'
And those who are in the Fire will say to the keepers of
[Gehenna,
'Call on your Lord, to lighten for us one day of the chastise-
[ment!'
They shall say, 'Did not your Messengers bring you the
[clear signs?'
They shall say, 'Yes indeed.' They shall say, 'Then do you
[call!'
But the calling of the unbelievers is only in error.

Surely We shall help Our Messengers
and those who have believed, in the
present life, and upon the day when

the witnesses arise,
55   upon the day when their excuses
shall not profit the evildoers,
and theirs shall be the curse, and
theirs the evil abode.

We also gave Moses the guidance,
and We bequeathed upon the Children
of Israel the Book for a guidance
and for a reminder to men possessed
of minds.
So be thou patient;
surely God's promise is true.
And ask forgiveness for thy sin, and
proclaim the praise of thy Lord at evening and dawn.

Those who dispute concerning the signs
of God, without any authority
come to them, in their breasts is only
pride, that they shall never attain.
So seek thou refuge in God;
surely He is the All-hearing, the All-seeing.

Certainly the creation of the heavens and earth is greater
than the creation of men;
but most men know it not.

60   Not equal are the blind and the seeing man,
those who believe and do deeds of righteousness,
and the wrongdoer.
Little do you reflect.
The Hour is coming, no doubt of it, but most men
do not believe.

Your Lord has said, 'Call upon Me
and I will answer you. Surely those
who wax too proud to do Me service
shall enter Gehenna utterly abject.'

181

It is God who made for you the night, to repose in it,
and the day, to see.
Surely God is bountiful to men, but most men
are not thankful.
That then is God, your Lord, the Creator of everything;
there is no god but He.
How then are you perverted?

65   Even so perverted are they who deny
the signs of God.

It is God who made for you the earth a fixed place
and heaven for an edifice;
And He shaped you, and shaped you well,
and provided you with the good things.
That then is God, your Lord, so blessed be God,
the Lord of all Being.

He is the Living One;
there is no god but He.
So call upon Him, making your religion
His sincerely. Praise belongs to God,
the Lord of all Being.

Say: 'I am forbidden to serve those you call on
apart from God
since the clear signs came to me from my Lord;
and I am commanded to surrender to
the Lord of all Being.'

It is He who created you of dust
then of a sperm-drop,
then of a blood-clot,
then He delivers you as infants,
then that you may come of age,
then that you may be old men—
though some of you there are who die before it—
and that you may reach a stated term;
haply you will understand.

70   It is He who gives life, and makes to die;

and when He decrees a thing, He but says to it
    'Be,' and it is.

    Hast thou not regarded those who dispute
    concerning the signs of God, how they
        are turned about?
    Those who cry lies to the Book and that
    wherewith We sent Our Messengers—
        soon they will know!

When the fetters and chains are on their necks, and they
                        ⌈dragged
into the boiling water, then into the Fire they are poured;
then it is said to them, 'Where are those you associated,
apart from God?' They shall say, 'They have gone astray
                        ⌈from us;
nay, but it was nothing at all that we called upon aforetime.'
    Even so God leads astray the unbelievers.
75 'That is because you rejoiced in the earth without right, and
were exultant. Enter the gates of Gehenna, to dwell therein
forever.' How evil is the lodging of those that are proud!

        So be thou patient;
         surely God's promise is true.
    Whether We show thee a part of that We
    promise them, or We call thee unto Us,
        to Us they shall be returned.

    We sent Messengers before thee; of some
    We have related to thee, and some We
    have not related to thee. It was not for
    any Messenger to bring a sign, save by
    God's leave. When God's command comes,
    justly the issue shall be decided; then
        the vain-doers shall be lost.

    It is God who appointed for you the cattle,
        some of them to ride
        and of some you eat;

80   other uses also you have in them;
and that on them you may attain a need in your breasts,
    and upon them and on the ships you are carried.
And He shows you His signs; then which of God's signs
            do you reject?

        What, have they not journeyed in the land and
        beheld how was the end of those before them?
        They were stronger than themselves in might
        and left firmer traces in the earth; yet
        that they earned did not avail them.
        So, when their Messengers brought them
        the clear signs, they rejoiced in what
        knowledge they had, and were encompassed by
                that they mocked at.
        Then, when they saw Our might, they said,
        'We believe in God alone, and we disbelieve
        in that we were associating with Him.'
85   But their belief when they saw Our might
        did not profit them—the wont of God, as
        in the past, touching His servants; then
            the unbelievers shall be lost.

XLI

DISTINGUISHED

In the Name of God, the Merciful, the Compassionate

Ha Mim

A sending down from the Merciful, the Compassionate.
A Book whose signs have been distinguished as
an Arabic Koran for a people having knowledge,
 good tidings to bear, and warning, but
most of them have turned away, and do not give ear.
They say, 'Our hearts are veiled from what thou callest us to,
 and in our ears is a heaviness,
 and between us and thee there is a veil;
 so act; we are acting!'
5 Say: 'I am only a mortal, like you are.
To me it has been revealed that your God is One God; so go
straight with Him, and ask for His forgiveness;
 and woe to the idolaters
who pay not the alms, and disbelieve in the world to come.
Surely those who believe, and do righteous deeds
 shall have a wage unfailing.'

Say: 'What, do you disbelieve in Him who
created the earth in two days, and do you
set up compeers to Him? That is the
 Lord of all Being.
And He set therein firm mountains over it,
and He blessed it, and He ordained therein
its diverse sustenance in four days, equal
 to those who ask.
10 Then He lifted Himself to heaven when it was
smoke, and said to it and to the earth, "Come
willingly, or unwillingly!" They said,
 "We come willingly."
So He determined them as seven heavens

in two days, and revealed its commandment
in every heaven.'
And We adorned the lower heaven with lamps, and to
[preserve;
that is the ordaining of the All-mighty, the All-knowing.
But if they turn away, then say, 'I warn you
of a thunderbolt like to the thunderbolt of
Ad and Thamood.'
When the Messengers came unto them from
before them and from behind them, saying,
'Serve none but God,' they said, 'Had our
Lord willed, surely He would have sent down
angels; so we disbelieve in the Message
you were sent with.'
As for Ad, they waxed proud in the earth
without right, and they said, 'Who is
stronger than we in might?' What, did they
not see that God, who created them, was
stronger than they in might? And they
denied Our signs.
15   Then We loosed against them a wind
clamorous in days of ill fortune, that
We might let them taste the chastisement
of degradation in the present life;
and the chastisement of the world to
come is even more degrading, and they
shall not be helped.
As for Thamood, We guided them, but
they preferred blindness above guidance,
so the thunderbolt of the chastisement
of humiliation seized them for that
they were earning.
And We delivered those who believed and
were godfearing.

Upon the day when God's enemies are mustered to the Fire,
[duly disposed,
till when they are come to it, their hearing, their eyes and
[their skins

bear witness against them concerning what they have been
[doing,
20   and they will say to their skins, 'Why bore you witness
[against us?'
They shall say, 'God gave us speech, as He gave everything
[speech.
He created you the first time, and unto Him you shall be
[returned.
Not so did you cover yourselves, that your hearing, your
[eyes
and your skins should not bear witness against you; but you
[thought
that God would never know much of the things that you were
[working.
That then, the thought you thought about your Lord, has
[destroyed you,
and therefore you find yourselves this morning among the
[losers.'

Then if they persist, the Fire shall be a
lodging for them; and if they ask amends
yet no amends shall be made to them.
We have allotted them comrades, and
they have decked out fair to them that
which is before them and behind them.
So against them has been realized the
Word concerning nations that passed away
before them, men and jinn alike; surely
they were losers.

25   The unbelievers say, 'Do not give ear
to this Koran, and talk idly about it;
haply you will overcome.'
So We shall let the unbelievers taste
a terrible chastisement,
and shall recompense them with the worst
of what they were working.
That is the recompense of God's enemies—
the Fire, wherein they shall have the Abode

of Eternity as a recompense, for that
    they denied Our signs.
And the unbelievers shall say, 'Our Lord,
show us those that led us astray, both
jinn and men, and we shall set them
underneath our feet, that they may be
    among the lower ones.'

30   Those who have said, 'Our Lord is God.'
then have gone straight, upon them the
angels descend, saying, 'Fear not,
neither sorrow; rejoice in Paradise
    that you were promised.
We are your friends in the present life
and in the world to come; therein you
shall have all that your souls desire,
    all that you call for,
as hospitality from One All-forgiving,
    One All-compassionate.'
And who speaks fairer than he who
calls unto God and does righteousness
and says, 'Surely I am of them
    that surrender'?

Not equal are the good deed and the evil deed.
    Repel with that which is fairer
and behold, he between whom and thee
there is enmity shall be as if he were
    a loyal friend.

35   Yet none shall receive it, except the
steadfast; none shall receive it, except a man
    of mighty fortune.

    If a provocation
from Satan should provoke thee,
    seek refuge in God;
He is the All-hearing, the All-knowing.

    And of His signs
are the night and the day, the sun and the moon.

Bow not yourselves to the sun and moon,
but bow yourselves to God who created them,
    if Him you serve.

And if they wax proud,
yet those who are with thy Lord do glorify Him
by night and day, and grow not weary.

And of His signs
is that thou seest the earth humble;
then, when We send down water upon it,
    it quivers, and swells.
Surely He who quickens it is He who
quickens the dead; surely He is powerful
    over everything.

40   Those who blaspheme Our signs are not hidden from Us.
What, is he who shall be cast into the Fire better, or
he who comes on the Day of Resurrection in security?
    Do what you will; surely He sees
    the things you do.

Those who disbelieve in the Remembrance
when it comes to them—and surely it is
    a Book Sublime;
falsehood comes not to it from before it
nor from behind it; a sending down from
    One All-wise, All-laudable.
Naught is said to thee but what already
was said to the Messengers before thee.
Surely thy Lord is a Lord of forgiveness
    and of painful retribution.
If We had made it a barbarous Koran,
they would have said, 'Why are its signs
not distinguished? What, barbarous
and Arabic?' Say: 'To the believers
it is a guidance, and a healing;
but those who believe not, in their ears
is a heaviness, and to them it is a

blindness; those—they are called
from a far place.'

45   And We gave Moses the Book; and there was
difference concerning it, and but for a Word
that preceded from thy Lord, it had been
decided between them; and they are in doubt
of it disquieting.

Whoso does righteousness, it is to his own gain,
and whoso does evil, it is to his own loss.
Thy Lord wrongs not His servants.
To Him is referred the knowledge of the Hour.
Not a fruit comes forth from its sheath,
no female bears or brings forth, save with His knowledge.

Upon the day when He shall call to them, 'Where now are
[My associates?'
they shall say, 'We proclaim to Thee, there is not a witness
[among us.'
Then that they called upon before will go astray from
and they will think that they have no asylum.   [them,

Man wearies not of praying for good; but
when evil visits him, then he is cast down
and desperate.

50   And if We let him taste mercy from Us
after hardship that has visited him, he
surely says, 'This is mine; I think not
the Hour is coming. If I am returned
to my Lord, surely the reward most fair
with Him will be mine.' Then We shall tell
the unbelievers the things they have done,
and assuredly We shall let them taste
a harsh chastisement.
And when We bless man, he turns away
and withdraws aside; but when evil
visits him, he is full of endless prayers.

Say: 'What think you? If it is from God,
then you disbelieve in it, who is further
astray than he who is in wide schism?'

We shall show them Our signs in the horizons and
in themselves, till it is clear to them
that it is the truth. Suffices it not
as to thy Lord, that He is witness over
         everything?
Are they not in doubt touching the encounter
with their Lord? Does He not encompass
         everything?

XLII

COUNSEL

In the Name of God, the Merciful, the Compassionate

Ha Mim
Ain Sin Qaf

So reveals to thee, and to those before thee,
    God, the All-mighty, the All-wise.
To Him belongs whatsoever is in the heavens
and whatsoever is in the earth; and He is
    the All-high, the All-glorious.
The heavens wellnigh are rent above them,
when the angels proclaim the praise of their
Lord, and ask forgiveness for those on earth.
Surely God—He is the All-forgiving, the All-compassionate.
And those who have taken to them protectors
apart from Him—God is Warden over them;
    thou art not a guardian over them.

5   And so We have revealed to thee an
    Arabic Koran, that thou mayest warn
    the Mother of Cities and those who
    dwell about it, and that thou mayest
    warn of the Day of Gathering, wherein
    is no doubt—a party in Paradise,
        and a party in the Blaze.

If God had willed, He would have made them
one nation; but He admits whomsoever He will
into His mercy, and the evildoers shall have
    neither protector nor helper.
Or have they taken to them protectors apart
from Him? But God—He is the Protector;
He quickens the dead, and He is powerful
    over everything.

192

And whatever you are at variance on,
the judgment thereof belongs to God.
That then is God, my Lord;
in Him I have put my trust, and to Him
I turn, penitent.
The Originator of the heavens and the earth;
He has appointed for you, of yourselves, pairs,
and pairs also of the cattle,
therein multiplying you. Like Him there is naught;
He is the All-hearing, the All-seeing.
10   To Him belong the keys of the heavens and the earth.
He outspreads and straitens His provision to whom He will;
surely He has knowledge of everything.

He has laid down for you as religion
that He charged Noah with, and that
We have revealed to thee, and that We
charged Abraham with, Moses and Jesus:
'Perform the religion, and scatter not
regarding it.' Very hateful is that
for the idolaters,
that thou callest them to. God chooses
unto Himself whomsoever He will,
and He guides to Himself whosoever
turns, penitent.
They scattered not, save after knowledge
had come to them, being insolent
one to another; and but for a Word
that preceded from thy Lord until a
stated term, it had been decided
between them. But those to whom the Book
has been given as an inheritance
after them, behold, they are in doubt
of it disquieting.
Therefore call thou, and go straight as
thou hast been commanded; do not follow
their caprices. And say: 'I believe
in whatever Book God has sent down; I
have been commanded to be just between

193

G

you. God is our Lord and your Lord.
We have our deeds, and you have your deeds;
there is no argument between us and you;
God shall bring us together, and unto Him
　　is the homecoming.'

15　And those who argue concerning God
after that answer has been made to Him,
their argument is null and void in the
sight of their Lord; anger shall rest
upon them, and there awaits them a
　　terrible chastisement.
God it is who has sent down the Book
with the truth, and also the Balance.
And what shall make thee know? Haply
　　the Hour is nigh.
Those that believe not therein seek to
hasten it; but those who believe in it
go in fear of it, knowing that it is
the truth. Why, surely those who are
in doubt concerning the Hour are indeed
　　in far error.

God is All-gentle to His servants,
providing for whomsoever He will.
He is the All-strong, the All-mighty.

Whoso desires the tillage of the world
to come, We shall give him increase
in his tillage; and whoso desires the
tillage of this world, We shall give him
of it, but in the world to come he
　　will have no share.

20　Or have they associates who have laid
down for them as religion that for which
God gave not leave? But for the Word of
Decision, it had been decided between
them. For the evildoers there awaits a
　　painful chastisement.

194

Thou seest the evildoers going in fear
of that they have earned, that is about
to fall on them; but those who believe
and do righteous deeds are in Meadows
of the Gardens; whatsoever they will
they shall have with their Lord; that is
      the great bounty.
That is the good tidings God gives to His
servants who believe and do righteous
deeds. Say: 'I do not ask of you
a wage for this, except love for the
kinsfolk; and whosoever gains a good
deed, We shall give him increase of good
in respect of it. Surely God is
      All-forgiving, All-thankful.'
Or do they say, 'He has forged against
God a lie?' But if God wills, He
will set a seal on thy heart; and God
blots out falsehood and verifies the
truth by His words; He knows the thoughts
      within the breasts.
It is He who accepts repentance from His
servants, and pardons evil deeds; He knows
      the things you do.
And He answers those who believe
and do righteous deeds, and He
gives them increase of His bounty.
And the unbelievers—for them awaits a
      terrible chastisement.
Had God expanded His provision to His
servants, they would have been insolent
in the earth; but He sends down
in measure whatsoever He will;
surely He is aware of and sees
      His servants.

And it is He who sends down the rain
   after they have despaired,
   and He unfolds His mercy;

25

He is the Protector, the All-laudable.
And of His signs
is the creation of the heavens and earth
and the crawling things He has scattered abroad in them;
and He is able to gather them whenever He will.

Whatever affliction may visit you is for
what you own hands have earned; and He
pardons much.
30   You are not able to frustrate Him in the
earth; and, apart from God, you have
neither protector nor helper.

And of His signs
are the ships that run on the sea like landmarks;
and if He wills, He stills the wind, and
they remain motionless on its back.
Surely in that are signs for every man
enduring, thankful.
Or He wrecks them for what they have earned; and He
pardons much;
and that those who dispute concerning Our signs may know
they have no asylum.

Whatever thing you have been given is
the enjoyment of the present life; but
what is with God is better and more
enduring for those who believe and put
their trust in their Lord.
35   And those who avoid the heinous sins
and indecencies and when they are angry
forgive,
and those who answer their Lord, and
perform the prayer, their affair being
counsel between them, and they expend of
that We have provided them,
and who, when insolence visits them,
do help themselves—
and the recompense of evil is evil

the like of it; but whoso pardons
and puts things right, his wage falls
upon God; surely He loves not
    the evildoers.
And whosoever helps himself after he
has been wronged—against them
    there is no way.

40   The way is only open against those who do
wrong to the people, and are insolent in
the earth wrongfully; there awaits them a
    painful chastisement.
But surely he who bears patiently
and is forgiving—surely that is
    true constancy.

Whomsoever God leads astray, he has no protector
after him; and thou shalt see the evildoers,
when they see the chastisement, saying, 'Is there
    any way to be sent back?'
And thou shalt see them, as they are exposed to it,
abject in humbleness, looking with furtive glance;
and the believers shall say, 'Surely the losers
are they who lose themselves and their families
on the Day of Resurrection; surely the evildoers
    are in lasting chastisement.

45   They have no protectors to help them, apart from God,
and whomsoever God leads astray, no way has he.'

Answer your Lord, before there comes a
day from God that cannot be turned
back; upon that day you shall have
    no shelter, no denial.

But if they turn away, We sent thee
not to be a guardian over them. It is
for thee only to deliver the Message.

And when We let man taste mercy from
Us, he rejoices in it; but if some

evil befalls him for that his own hands
have forwarded, then surely man is
    unthankful.

To God belongs the Kingdom of the heavens and the earth;
    He creates what He will;
    He gives to whom He will females,
    and He gives to whom He will males
or He couples them, both males and females;
    and He makes whom He will barren.
Surely He is All-knowing, All-powerful.

50   It belongs not to any mortal that
    God should speak to him, except
    by revelation, or from behind
        a veil,
    or that He should send a messenger
    and he reveal whatsoever He will,
    by His leave; surely He is
        All-high, All-wise.
    Even so We have revealed to thee a
    Spirit of Our bidding. Thou knewest
    not what the Book was, nor belief;
    but We made it a light, whereby We
    guide whom We will of Our servants. And thou,
    surely thou shalt guide unto a
        straight path—
the path of God, to whom belongs whatsoever is in
the heavens, and whatsoever is in the earth. Surely
    unto God all things come home.

XLIII

ORNAMENTS

In the Name of God, the Merciful, the Compassionate

Ha Mim

By the Clear Book,
behold, We have made it an Arabic Koran;
haply you will understand;
and behold, it is in the Essence of the Book, with Us;
sublime indeed, wise.
Shall We turn away the Remembrance from you, for
that you are a prodigal people?

5　　　How many a Prophet We sent among
the ancients,
but not a Prophet came to them,
without they mocked at him;
so We destroyed men stronger in
valour than they, and the example
of the ancients passed away.

If thou askest them, 'Who created
the heavens and earth?' they will say,
'The All-mighty, the All-knowing
created them.'
He who appointed the earth to be
a cradle for you, and appointed
ways for you therein, that haply
you may be guided;
10　　　and who sent down out of heaven water
in measure; and We revived thereby
a land that was dead; even so you
shall be brought forth;
and who created the pairs, all of them,

and appointed for you ships and cattle
    such as you ride,
that you may be seated on their backs
and then remember your Lord's blessing
when you are seated on them, and say,
'Glory be to Him, who has subjected
this to us, and we ourselves were not
    equal to it;
surely unto our Lord we are turning.'

Yet they have assigned to Him a part
of His own servants! Man is clearly
    unthankful.

15   Or has He taken to Himself, from that
He creates, daughters, and favoured you
    with sons?
And when any of them is given the good
tidings of that he has likened to the
All-merciful, his face is darkened, and
    he chokes inwardly.
What, one who is reared amid ornaments
and, when the time of altercation comes,
    is not to be seen?
And they have made the angels, who are
themselves servants of the All-merciful,
females. What, did they witness their
creation? Their witness shall be written
    down, and they shall be questioned.
They say, 'Had the All-merciful so
willed, we would not have served them.'
They have no knowledge of that; they are
    only conjecturing.

20   Or did We bring them a Book aforetime
    to which they hold?
Nay, but they say, 'We found our fathers
upon a community, and we are guided
    upon their traces.'
Even so We sent never before thee
any warner into any city, except that

its men who lived at ease said, 'We
indeed found our fathers upon a
community, and we are following
    upon their traces.'
Say: 'What, though I should bring you a
better guidance than you found your
fathers upon?' They say, 'We disbelieve
    in that you were sent with.'
So We took vengeance upon them;
and behold how was the end of them
    that cried lies.

25   And when Abraham said to his father
and his people, 'Surely I am quit of
    that you serve,
except Him who originated me;
    and He will guide me.'
And he made it a word enduring
among his posterity; haply so
    they would return.
Nay, but I gave these and their fathers
enjoyment of days, until the truth
came unto them, and a manifest
    Messenger.
And when the truth came to them, they
said, 'This is a sorcery, and in it
    we are unbelievers.'
30   They say, 'Why was this Koran not sent
down upon some man of moment in the
    two cities?'
What, is it they who divide the mercy
of thy Lord? We have divided between
them their livelihood in the present
life, and raised some of them above
others in rank, that some of them may
take others in servitude; and the
mercy of thy Lord is better than that
    they amass.
And were it not that mankind would be

one nation, We would have appointed for
those who disbelieve in the All-merciful
roofs of silver to their houses, and stairs
      whereon to mount,
and doors to their houses, and couches
      whereon to recline,
and ornaments; surely all this is but
the enjoyment of the present life,
and the world to come with thy Lord is
      for the godfearing.

35   Whoso blinds himself to the Remembrance
of the All-merciful, to him We assign a
      Satan for comrade;
and they bar them from the way, and they
      think they are guided,
till, when he comes to Us, he says,
'Would there had been between me and
thee the distance of the two Easts!'
      An evil comrade!
It shall not profit you today, since
you did evil, that you are partners in
      the chastisement.

What, shalt thou make the deaf to hear,
      or shalt thou guide the blind
and him who is in manifest error?

40   Whether We take thee away,
We shall take vengeance upon them,
      or We show thee a part
of that We promised them, surely
      We have power over them.
So hold thou fast unto that which has
      been revealed unto thee;
surely thou art upon a straight path.
      Surely it is a Reminder
to thee and to thy people; and assuredly
      you will be questioned.
Ask those of Our Messengers We sent
      before thee: Have We

appointed, apart from the All-merciful,
   gods to be served?

45   We also sent Moses with Our signs to
Pharaoh and his Council, and he said,
'Surely I am the Messenger of the
      Lord of all Being.'
But when he brought them Our signs, lo,
   they laughed at them.
And not a sign We showed them, but
it was greater than its sister sign;
and We seized them with chastisement,
   that haply they should return.
And they said, 'Sorcerer, pray to thy
Lord for us by the covenant He has
made with thee, and surely we shall
     be right-guided.'
But when We removed from them the
chastisement, behold, they broke
   their troth.

50   And Pharaoh proclaimed among his
people: 'O my people, do I not
possess the kingdom of Egypt, and
these rivers flowing beneath me? What,
   do you not see?
Or am I better than this man, who is
   contemptible
and scarcely makes things clear?
Why then have bracelets of gold not
been cast on him, or angels not come
   with him conjoined?'
So he made his people unsteady, and
they obeyed him; surely they were an
   ungodly people.

55   So, when they had angered Us, We took
vengeance on them, and We drowned them
   all together;
and We made them a thing past, and
We appointed them for an example

to later folk.

And when the son of Mary is
cited as an example, behold,
thy people turn away from it
and say, 'What, are our gods
better, or he?' They cite not
him to thee, save to dispute;
nay, but they are a people
contentious. He is only a
servant We blessed, and We
made him to be an example
to the Children of Israel.

60 Had We willed, We would have appointed
angels among you to be successors in
   the earth.
It is knowledge of the Hour; doubt not
concerning it, and follow me. This is
   a straight path.
Let not Satan bar you; he is for you
   a manifest foe.

And when Jesus came with the
clear signs he said, 'I have
come to you with wisdom, and
that I may make clear to you
some of that whereon you are
at variance; so fear you God
and obey you me. Assuredly
God is my Lord and your Lord;
therefore serve Him; this is
   a straight path.'

65 But the parties among them fell into
variance; so woe unto those who did
evil, because of the chastisement of
   a painful day.
Are they looking for aught but the Hour,

that it shall come upon them suddenly,
        when they are not aware?

Friends on that day shall be foes to one another, but the god-
                        [fearing—
'O My servants, today no fear is on you, neither do you
                        [sorrow'—
even those who believed in Our signs, and had surrendered
                        [themselves:
70 'Enter Paradise, you and your wives, walking with joy!'
There shall be passed around them platters of gold, and cups,
therein being whatever the souls desire, and the eyes delight
        'And therein you shall dwell forever.   [in.
This is the Paradise that you have been given for an in-
        for the things that you were doing.   [heritance
Therein you have abundant fruits, whereof you may eat.'
But the evildoers dwell forever in the chastisement of
                        [Gehenna
75 that is not abated for them and therein they are sore con-
                        [founded.
We never wronged them, but they themselves did the wrong.
And they shall call, 'O Malik, let thy Lord have done with
        He will say, 'You will surely tarry.'   [us!'
'We brought you the truth, but most of you were averse to
                        [the truth.'

        Or have they contrived some matter? We
            too are contriving.
80   Or do they think We hear not their secret
        and what they conspire together? Yes indeed,
        and Our messengers are present with them
            writing it down.

        Say: 'If the All-merciful has a son,
        then I am the first to serve him.
        Glory be to the Lord of the heavens
        and the earth, the Lord of the Throne,
            above that they describe.'
        Then leave them alone to plunge and play,

until they encounter that day of theirs
    which they are promised.
And it is He who in heaven is God
and in earth is God; He is the All-wise,
    the All-knowing.
85   Glory be to Him, to whom belongs the
Kingdom of the heavens and the earth
and all that between them is; with Him
is the knowledge of the Hour, and to Him
    you shall be returned.
Those they call upon, apart from Him,
have no power of intercession, save
such as have testified to the truth,
    and that knowingly.
If thou askest them, 'Who created you?'
    they will say, 'God.'
    How then are they perverted?

And for his saying, 'My Lord, surely
these are a people who believe not'—
yet pardon them, and say, 'Peace!'
    Soon they will know.

XLIV

SMOKE

In the Name of God, the Merciful, the Compassionate

Ha Mim

By the Clear Book.
We have sent it down in a blessed night
(We are ever warning)
therein every wise bidding determined
as a bidding from Us,
(We are ever sending)
5   as a mercy from thy Lord
(surely He is the All-hearing, the All-knowing)
Lord of the heavens and earth, and all that between them is,
if you have faith.
There is no god but He;
He gives life and makes to die;
your Lord and the Lord of your fathers, the ancients.

Nay, but they are in doubt, playing.
So be on the watch for a day when heaven shall bring
a manifest smoke
10   covering the people; this is a painful chastisement.
'O our Lord, remove Thou from us the chastisement;
we are believers.'
How should they have the Reminder,
seeing a clear Messenger already came to them, then
they turned away from him
and said, 'A man tutored, possessed!'
'Behold, We are removing the chastisement a little;
behold, you revert!'
15   Upon the day when We shall assault most mightily,
then We shall take Our vengeance.

Already before them We tried the people

207

of Pharaoh, and a noble Messenger
  came unto them,
saying, 'Deliver to me God's servants;
I am for you a faithful Messenger,'
and, 'Rise not up against God; behold,
I come to you with a clear authority,
and I take refuge in my Lord and
your Lord, lest you should stone me.
20 But if so be that you believe me not,
  go you apart from me!'
And he called to his Lord, saying,
  'These are a sinful people.'
'Then set thou forth with My servants
in a watch of the night; surely you
  will be followed.
And leave the sea becalmed; they are
  a drowned host.'
They left how many gardens and fountains,
25 sown fields, and how noble a station,
and what prosperity they had rejoiced in!
Even so; and We bequeathed them upon
  another people.
Neither heaven nor earth wept for them,
  nor were they respited;
and We delivered the Children of Israel
  from the humbling chastisement,
30 from Pharaoh; surely he was a high one,
  of the prodigals;
and We chose them, out of a knowledge,
  above all beings.
and gave them signs wherein there was a
  manifest trial.

   These men do say,
'There is nothing but our first death;
  we shall not be revived.
35 Bring us our fathers, if you speak truly!'
Are they better, or the people of Tubba'
and those before them whom We destroyed?

They were surely sinners.

We created not the heavens and earth,
and all that between them is, in play;
We created them not save in truth; but
  most of them know it not.

40 Surely the Day of Decision shall be
  their appointed time, all together,
the day a master shall avail nothing
a client, and they shall not be helped,
save him upon whom God has mercy; He is
  the All-mighty, the All-compassionate.

  Lo, the Tree of Ez-Zakkoum
  is the food of the guilty,
45 like molten copper, bubbling in the belly
  as boiling water bubbles.
'Take him, and thrust him into the midst of Hell,
then pour over his head the chastisement of
    boiling water!'
'Taste! Surely thou art the mighty, the noble.
50 This is that concerning which you were doubting.'

Surely the godfearing shall be in a station secure
    among gardens and fountains,
robed in silk and brocade, set face to face.
  Even so; and We shall espouse them
    to wide-eyed houris,
55 therein calling for every fruit, secure.
They shall not taste therein of death,
    save the first death,
And He shall guard them against the chastisement of Hell—
a bounty from thy Lord; that is the mighty triumph.

Now We have made it easy by thy tongue,
  that haply they may remember.
So be on the watch; they too are on the watch.

XLV

HOBBLING

In the Name of God, the Merciful, the Compassionate

Ha Mim

The sending down of the Book is from God,
the All-mighty, the All-wise.

Surely in the heavens and earth there are signs
for the believers;
and in your creation,
and the crawling things He scatters abroad, there are signs
for a people having sure faith,
and in the alternation of night and day,
and the provision God sends down from heaven,
and therewith revives the earth after it is dead,
and the turning about of the winds, there are signs
for a people who understand.

5 Those are the signs of God that We recite to thee in truth;
in what manner of discourse then, after God and His signs,
will they believe?

Woe to every guilty impostor
who hears the signs of God being recited to him,
then perseveres in waxing proud, as if he has
not heard them; so give him the good tidings of
a painful chastisement.
And when he knows anything of Our signs, he
takes them in mockery; those—for them awaits
a humbling chastisement.
Behind them Gehenna; and that they have earned
shall not avail them aught, nor those they took
as protectors, apart from God; for them awaits

a mighty chastisement.

10   This is guidance;
and those who disbelieve in the signs of their
Lord, there awaits them a painful chastisement
            of wrath.

God is He who has subjected to you the sea, that
the ships may run on it at His commandment, and
    that you may seek His bounty; haply so
        you will be thankful.
And He has subjected to you what is in the heavens
and what is in the earth, all together, from Him.
    Surely in that are signs for a people
            who reflect.

Say unto those who believe, that they forgive
those who do not look for the days of God,
    that He may recompense a people for that
            they have been earning.

Whoso does righteousness, it is to his own gain,
and whoso does evil, it is to his own loss; then
        to your Lord you shall be returned.

15   Indeed, We gave the Children of Israel
the Book, the Judgment, and the Prophethood,
and We provided them with good things,
and We preferred them above all beings.
We gave them clear signs of the Command;
so they differed not, except after the
knowledge had come to them, being
insolent one to another. Surely
thy Lord will decide between them
on the Day of Resurrection touching
        their differences.
Then We set thee upon an open way
of the Command; therefore follow it,
and follow not the caprices of those

who do not know.
Surely they will not avail thee aught
against God. Surely the evildoers are
friends one of the other; God is the friend
    of the godfearing.

This is clear proofs for men,
and a guidance, and a mercy
to a people having sure faith.

20   Or do those who commit evil deeds
think that We shall make them as those
who believe and do righteous deeds,
equal their living and their dying?
    How ill they judge!
God created the heavens and the earth
in truth, and that every soul may be
recompensed for what it has earned;
    they shall not be wronged.

Hast thou seen him who has taken
his caprice to be his god, and God
has led him astray out of a knowledge,
and set a seal upon his hearing
and his heart, and laid a covering
on his eyes? Who shall guide him
after God? What, will you not remember?

        They say,
'There is nothing but our present life;
we die, and we live, and nothing but
Time destroys us.' Of that they have
no knowledge; they merely conjecture.
And when Our signs are recited to them,
clear signs, their only argument is
that they say, 'Bring us our fathers,
        if you speak truly.'
25   Say:
'God gives you life, then makes you die,

212

then He shall gather you to the Day
of Resurrection, wherein is no doubt,
    but most men do not know.'

To God belongs the Kingdom of the heavens and the earth.

And on the day when the Hour is come,
upon that day the vain-doers shall lose.
And thou shalt see every nation hobbling on their knees,
every nation being summoned unto its Book: 'Today
you shall be recompensed for that you were doing.
This is Our Book, that speaks against you the truth;
We have been registering all that you were doing.'

And as for those who have believed
and done deeds of righteousness,
their Lord shall admit them into
His mercy; that is the manifest
        triumph.

30   But as for those who have disbelieved:
'Were not My signs recited to you, and
you waxed proud, and were a sinful
        people?
And when it was said, "God's promise
is true, and the Hour, there is no
doubt of it," you said, "We know not
what the Hour may be; we have only
a surmise, and are by no means
        certain." '
And the evil deeds that they have done shall appear to
                          [them,
and they shall be encompassed by that they mocked at.
And it shall be said, 'Today We do forget you, even
as you forgot the encounter of this your day; and your
refuge is the Fire, and you shall have no helpers.
That is for that you took God's signs in mockery,
    and the present life deluded you.'
So today they shall not be brought forth from it,
    nor will they be suffered to make amends.

35   So to God belongs praise,
the Lord of the heavens and the Lord of the earth,
Lord of all Being.
His is the Domination in the heavens and the earth;
He is the All-mighty, the All-wise.

XLVI

THE SAND-DUNES

In the Name of God, the Merciful, the Compassionate

Ha Mim

The sending down of the Book is from God,
the All-mighty, the All-wise.

We have not created the heavens and the earth,
and what between them is, save with the truth
and a stated term; but the unbelievers are
turning away from that they were warned of.
Say: 'Have you considered that you call upon
apart from God? Show me what they have
created of the earth; or have they a partnership
in the heavens? Bring me a Book before
this, or some remnant of a knowledge,
                if you speak truly.'
And who is further astray than he who calls,
apart from God, upon such a one as shall not
answer him till the Day of Resurrection?
5   Such as are heedless of their calling, and when
mankind are mustered, shall be enemies to them,
                and shall deny their service.

And when Our signs are recited to them,
clear signs, the unbelievers say to the
truth when it has come to them, 'This is
                manifest sorcery.'
Or do they say, 'He has forged it'?
Say: 'If I have forged it, you have no
power to help me against God. He knows
very well what you are pressing upon;
He suffices as a witness between me
and you; He is the All-forgiving,

the All-compassionate.'
Say: 'I am not an innovation among
the Messengers, and I know not what
shall be done with me or with you.
I only follow what is revealed to me;
   I am only a clear warner.'
Say: 'Have you considered? If it be from
God, and you disbelieve in it, and a
witness from among the Children of Israel
bears witness to its like, and believes,
and you wax proud, God guides not the people
      of the evildoers.'

10   The unbelievers say, as regards the
believers, 'If it had been aught good,
they had not outstripped us to it.'
And since they are not guided by it,
certainly they will say, 'This is an
      old calumny!'
Yet before it was the Book of Moses
for a model and a mercy; and this is
a Book confirming, in Arabic tongue,
to warn the evildoers, and good tidings
      to the good-doers.

Surely those who say, 'Our Lord is God'
     and then go straight,
no fear shall be on them, neither shall they sorrow.
Those are the inhabitants of Paradise,
therein dwelling forever, as a recompense for that
     they have been doing.

We have charged man, that he be kind to his
parents; his mother bore him painfully, and
painfully she gave birth to him; his bearing
and his weaning are thirty months. Until,
when he is fully grown, and reaches forty
years, he says, 'O my Lord, dispose me
that I may be thankful for Thy blessing

wherewith Thou hast blessed me and my
father and mother, and that I may do
righteousness well-pleasing to Thee;
and make me righteous also in my seed.
Behold, I repent to Thee, and am among
       those that surrender.'

15   Those are they from whom We shall accept
the best of what they have done, and We
shall pass over their evil deeds. They are
among the inhabitants of Paradise—
the promise of the very truth, which
       they were promised.
But he who says to his father and his
mother, 'Fie upon you! Do you promise me
that I shall be brought forth, when already
generations have passed away before me?'
while they call upon God for succour—
'Woe upon thee! Believe; surely God's
promise is true'; then he says, 'This is
naught but the fairy-tales of the ancients'—
such men are they against whom has been
realized the Word concerning nations that
passed away before them, men and jinn alike;
       they were losers.
All shall have their degrees, according to
what they have wrought, and that He may
pay them in full for their works, and they
       not being wronged.

Upon the day when the unbelievers are exposed to the Fire:
'You dissipated your good things in your present life,
and you took your enjoyment in them; therefore today you
shall be recompensed with the chastisement of humiliation
for that you waxed proud in the earth without right, and
       for your ungodliness.'

20   And remember the brother of Ad, when he
warned his people beside the sand-dunes—
and already warners had passed away

alike before him and behind him—
saying, 'Serve none but God! Truly
I fear for you the chastisement of
    a dreadful day.'
They said, 'What, hast thou come to
pervert us from our gods? Then bring us
that thou promisest us, if indeed
    thou speakest truly.'
He said, 'Knowledge is only with God,
and I deliver to you the Message with
which I was sent; but I see you are
    an ignorant people.'
Then, when they saw it as a sudden cloud
coming towards their valleys, they said,
'This is a cloud, that shall give us
rain!' 'Not so; rather it is that you
sought to hasten—a wind, wherein is a
    painful chastisement,
destroying everything by the commandment
of its Lord.' So in the morning there was
naught to be seen but their dwelling-places.
Even so do We recompense the people
    of the sinners.

25   And We had established them in that
wherein We have not established you,
and We appointed for them hearing, and
sight, and hearts; and yet their hearing,
their sight and their hearts availed them
nothing, since they denied the signs
of God, and they were encompassed by
    that they mocked at.
And We destroyed the cities about you,
and We turned about the signs, that haply
    they would return.
Then why did those not help them
that they had taken to themselves
as mediators, gods apart from God?
Not so; but they went astray from them,
and that was their calumny, and what

they had been forging.

And when We turned to thee a company of jinn
giving ear to the Koran; and when they were
in its presence they said, 'Be silent!'
Then, when it was finished, they turned back
        to their people, warning.
They said, 'Our people, we have heard a Book
that was sent down after Moses, confirming
what was before it, guiding to the truth and
        to a straight path.
30   O our people, answer God's summoner, and
believe in Him, and He will forgive you
some of your sins, and protect you from a
        painful chastisement.
Whosoever answers not God's summoner
cannot frustrate God in the earth, and he
has no protectors apart from Him; those are
        in manifest error.'

What, have they not seen that God
who created the heavens and earth,
not being wearied by creating them,
is able to give life to the dead?
Yes indeed; He is powerful over
        everything.

Upon the day when the unbelievers are exposed to the Fire:
'Is not this the truth?' They shall say, 'Yes, by our Lord!'
He shall say, 'Then taste the chastisement of your unbelief!'

        So be thou patient,
as the Messengers possessed of constancy were also patient.
        Seek not to hasten it for them—
it shall be as if, on the day they see that they are promised,
35   they had not tarried but for an hour of a single day.
        A Message to be delivered !
And shall any be destroyed but the people of the ungodly?

XLVII

MUHAMMAD

In the Name of God, the Merciful, the Compassionate

Those who disbelieve and bar from God's way,
    God will send their works astray.
But those who believe and do righteous deeds
and believe in what is sent down to Muhammad —
    and it is the truth from their Lord—
    He will acquit them of their evil deeds,
      and dispose their minds aright.
That is because those who disbelieve follow falsehood,
and those who believe follow the truth from their Lord.
Even so God strikes their similitudes for men.

When you meet the unbelievers, smite their necks,
then, when you have made wide slaughter among them,
    tie fast the bonds;
5   then set them free, either by grace or ransom,
    till the war lays down its loads.
    So it shall be; and if God had willed,
    He would have avenged Himself upon them;
but that He may try some of you by means of others.
And those who are slain in the way of God, He
    will not send their works astray.
He will guide them, and dispose their minds aright,
    and He will admit them to Paradise,
    that He has made known to them.

O believers, if you help God, He will help
you, and confirm your feet. But as for the
unbelievers, ill chance shall befall them!
    He will send their works astray.
10   That is because they have been averse to
what God has sent down, so He has made

their works to fail.
What, have they not journeyed in the land and
beheld how was the end of those before them?
God destroyed them; the unbelievers shall have
the likes thereof.
That is because God is the Protector
of the believers, and that the unbelievers
have no protector.
God shall surely admit those who believe
and do righteous deeds into gardens
underneath which rivers flow. As for the
unbelievers, they take their enjoyment
and eat as cattle eat; and the Fire shall
be their lodging.
How many a city that was stronger in might
than thy city which has expelled thee
have We destroyed! And there was no
helper for them.

15   What, is he who is upon a clear sign
from his Lord like unto such a one
unto whom his evil deeds have been
decked out fair, and they have followed
their caprices?
This is the similitude of Paradise
which the godfearing have been promised:
therein are rivers of water unstaling,
rivers of milk unchanging in flavour,
and rivers of wine—a delight
to the drinkers,
rivers, too, of honey purified;
and therein for them is every fruit,
and forgiveness from their Lord—
Are they as he who dwells forever
in the Fire, such as are given to
drink boiling water, that tears their
bowels asunder?

And some of them there are give ear to

thee, till, when they go forth from thee,
they say to those who have been given
knowledge, 'What said he just now?'
Those are they upon whose hearts God
has set a seal, and they have followed
        their caprices.
But those who are guided aright, them
He increases in guidance, and gives them
        their godfearing.

20   Are they looking for aught but the Hour,
that it shall come upon them suddenly?
Already its tokens have come; so, when
it has come to them, how shall they have
        their Reminder?

      Know thou therefore that
      there is no god but God,
and ask forgiveness for thy sin, and
for the believers, men and women. God
knows your going to and fro, and
        your lodging.

Those who believe say, 'Why has a sura
not been sent down?' Then, when a clear
sura is sent down, and therein fighting
is mentioned, thou seest those in whose
hearts is sickness looking at thee as
one who swoons of death; but better
for them would be obedience, and words
        honourable.
Then, when the matter is resolved, if
they were true to God, it would be
      better for them.
If you turned away, would you then haply
work corruption in the land, and break your
        bonds of kin?
25   Those are they whom God has cursed,
and so made them deaf, and blinded
        their eyes.

What, do they not ponder the Koran?
Or is it that there are locks upon
       their hearts?

Those who have turned back in their traces
after the guidance has become clear to them,
Satan it was that tempted them, and God
       respited them.
That is because they said to those who were
averse to what God sent down, 'We will
obey you in some of the affair'; and God
       knows their secrets.
How shall it be, when the angels
take them, beating their faces and
       their backs?
30   That is because they have followed what
angers God, and have been averse to
His good pleasure, so He has made
       their works to fail.
Or did those in whose hearts is sickness
think that God would not bring to light
       their rancour?
Did We will, We would show them to thee,
then thou wouldst know them by their mark;
and thou shalt certainly know them in
the twisting of their speech; and God
       knows your deeds.
And We shall assuredly try you
until We know those of you who
struggle and are steadfast, and try
       your tidings.

Those who disbelieve and bar from God's way
and make a breach with the Messenger
after the guidance has become clear to them,
they will nothing hurt God, and He will make
       their works to fail.

35   O believers, obey God, and obey

the Messenger, and do not make your
own works vain.
Those who disbelieve and bar from God's way
and then die disbelieving, them God
will not forgive.
So do not faint and call for peace;
you shall be the upper ones, and God
is with you, and will not deprive you
of your works.
The present life is naught but a sport
and a diversion; and if you believe
and are godfearing, He will give you
your wages, and will not ask of you
your goods.
If He asks you for them, and presses you,
you are niggardly, and He brings to light
your rancour.

40   Ha, there you are; you are called upon
to expend in God's way, and some of
you are niggardly. Whoso is niggardly
is niggardly only to his own soul. God is
the All-sufficient; you are the needy ones.
If you turn away, He will substitute
another people instead of you, then they will
not be your likes.

XLVIII

VICTORY

In the Name of God, the Merciful, the Compassionate

Surely We have given thee
a manifest victory,
that God may forgive thee thy former and thy latter sins,
and complete His blessing upon thee, and guide thee
on a straight path,
and that God may help thee
with mighty help.

It is He who sent down the Shechina
into the hearts of the believers, that
they might add faith to their faith—
to God belong the hosts of the heavens and the earth;
God is All-knowing, All-wise—
5   and that He may admit the believers,
men and women alike, into gardens
underneath which rivers flow, therein
to dwell forever, and acquit them of
their evil deeds; that is in God's sight
a mighty triumph;
and that He may chastise the hypocrites,
men and women alike, and the idolaters,
men and women alike, and those who think
evil thoughts of God; against them
shall be the evil turn of fortune. God
is wroth with them, and has cursed them,
and has prepared for them Gehenna—
an evil homecoming!
To God belong the hosts of the heavens and the earth;
God is All-mighty, All-wise.

Surely We have sent thee

H

as a witness,
good tidings to bear, and warning, that
you may believe in God and His Messenger
and succour Him, and reverence Him, and
that you may give Him glory at the dawn
and in the evening.

10   Those who swear fealty to thee
swear fealty in truth to God;
God's hand is over their hands.
Then whosoever breaks his oath
breaks it but to his own hurt;
and whoso fulfils his covenant
made with God, God will give him
a mighty wage.

The Bedouins who were left behind
will say to thee, 'We were occupied
by our possessions and our families;
so ask forgiveness for us!' They say
with their tongues what is not in their
hearts. Say: 'Who can avail you
aught against God, if He desires
hurt for you, or desires profit for
you? Nay, but God is ever aware of
the things you do.
Nay, but you thought that the Messenger
and the believers would never return to
their families, and that was decked out
fair in your hearts, and you thought
evil thoughts, and you were a
people corrupt.'

Whoso believes not in God and His Messenger,
We have prepared for the unbelievers
a Blaze.
To God belongs the kingdom of the heavens
and of the earth; whomsoever He will

He forgives, and whomsoever He will
He chastises; God is All-forgiving,
    All-compassionate.

15   The Bedouins who were left behind
will say, when you set forth after
spoils, to take them, 'Let us follow
you,' desiring to change God's words.
Say: 'You shall not follow us; so
God said before.' Then they will say,
'Nay, but you are jealous of us.'
Nay, but they have not understood
    except a little.
Say to the Bedouins who were left
behind: 'You shall be called against
a people possessed of great might
to fight them, or they surrender.
If you obey, God will give you a
goodly wage; but if you turn your
backs, as you turned your backs
before, He will chastise you with a
    painful chastisement.'

There is no fault in the blind, and there is
no fault in the lame, and there is no fault
in the sick. And whosoever obeys
God and His Messenger, He will admit
him into gardens underneath which
rivers flow; but whosoever turns his
back, him He will chastise with a
    painful chastisement.
God was well pleased with the believers
when they were swearing fealty to thee
under the tree, and He knew what was
in their hearts, so He sent down the
Shechina upon them, and rewarded them with
    a nigh victory
and many spoils to take; and God is ever
    All-mighty, All-wise.

20 God has promised you many spoils
to take; these He has hastened to
you, and has restrained the hands of
men from you, and that it may be a
sign to the believers, and to guide you
    on a straight path,
and other spoils you were not able
to take; God had encompassed
them already. God is powerful
    over everything.
If the unbelievers had fought you, they
would have turned their backs, and then found
    neither protector nor helper;
the wont of God, as in the past before,
and thou shalt never find any changing
    the wont of God.
It is He who restrained their hands
from you, and your hands from them, in
the hollow of Mecca, after that He
made you victors over them. God sees
    the things you do.
25 They are the ones who disbelieved,
and barred you from the Holy Mosque
and the offering, detained so as
not to reach its place of sacrifice.
If it had not been for certain men
believers and certain women believers
whom you knew not, lest you should
trample them, and there befall you
guilt unwittingly on their account
(that God may admit into His mercy
whom He will), had they been separated
clearly, then We would have chastised
the unbelievers among them with a
    painful chastisement.
When the unbelievers set in their hearts
fierceness, the fierceness of pagandom,
then God sent down His Shechina upon
His Messenger and the believers, and

fastened to them the word of godfearing
to which they have better right and are
worthy of; and God has knowledge
of everything.
God has indeed fulfilled the vision He
vouchsafed to His Messenger truly:
'You shall enter the Holy Mosque,
if God wills, in security, your
heads shaved, your hair cut short,
not fearing.' He knew what you
knew not, and appointed ere that a
nigh victory.

It is He who has sent His Messenger with
the guidance and the religion of truth, that
He may uplift it above every religion.
God suffices as a witness.

Muhammad is the Messenger of God,
and those who are with him are hard
against the unbelievers, merciful
one to another. Thou seest them
bowing, prostrating, seeking bounty
from God and good pleasure. Their
mark is on their faces, the trace of
prostration. That is their likeness
in the Torah, and their likeness
in the Gospel: as a seed that puts
forth its shoot, and strengthens it,
and it grows stout and rises straight
upon its stalk, pleasing the sowers,
that through them He may enrage
the unbelievers. God has promised
those of them who believe and do deeds
of righteousness forgiveness and
a mighty wage.

XLIX

APARTMENTS

In the Name of God, the Merciful, the Compassionate

O believers, advance not before God
and His Messenger; and fear God. God is
    All-hearing, All-knowing.

O believers, raise not your voices above
the Prophet's voice, and be not loud
in your speech to him, as you are loud
one to another, lest your works fail
    while you are not aware.
Surely those who lower their voices in
the presence of God's Messenger, those
are they whose hearts God has tested for
godfearing; they shall have forgiveness
    and a mighty wage.
Surely those who call unto thee from
behind the apartments, the most of them
    do not understand.
5   And if they had patience, until thou
comest out to them, that would be better
for them; and God is All-forgiving,
    All-compassionate.

O believers, if an ungodly man
comes to you with a tiding, make
clear, lest you afflict a people
unwittingly, and then repent of
    what you have done.
And know that the Messenger of God
is among you. If he obeyed you
in much of the affair, you would
suffer; but God has endeared to you
belief, decking it fair in your hearts,

230

and He has made detestable to you
unbelief and ungodliness and
disobedience. Those—they are
    the right-minded,
by God's favour and blessing; God is
   All-knowing, All-wise.

If two parties of the believers fight,
put things right between them; then,
if one of them is insolent against
the other, fight the insolent one
till it reverts to God's commandment.
If it reverts, set things right between
them equitably, and be just. Surely
    God loves the just.
10   The believers indeed are brothers;
so set things right between your
two brothers, and fear God; haply so
    you will find mercy.

O believers, let not any people
scoff at another people who may be
better than they; neither let women
scoff at women who may be better
than themselves. And find not fault
with one another, neither revile one
another by nicknames. An evil name
is ungodliness after belief. And
whoso repents not, those—they are
    the evildoers.

O believers, eschew much suspicion;
some suspicion is a sin. And do not
spy, neither backbite one another;
would any of you like to eat the
flesh of his brother dead? You would
abominate it. And fear you God;
assuredly God turns, and He is
    All-compassionate.

O mankind, We have created you
male and female, and appointed you
races and tribes, that you may know
one another. Surely the noblest
among you in the sight of God is
the most godfearing of you. God is
     All-knowing, All-aware.

The Bedouins say, 'We believe.'
Say: 'You do not believe; rather
say, "We surrender"; for belief
has not yet entered your hearts.
If you obey God and His Messenger,
He will not diminish you anything
of your works. God is All-forgiving,
     All-compassionate.'
15   The believers are those who believe
in God and His Messenger, then have
not doubted, and have struggled
with their possessions and their selves
in the way of God; those—they are
     the truthful ones.
Say: 'What, would you teach God
what your religion is, and God knows
what is in the heavens and what is
in the earth? And God has knowledge
     of everything.'
They count it as a favour to thee
that they have surrendered! Say:
'Do not count your surrendering
as a favour to me; nay, but
rather God confers a favour
upon you, in that He has guided
you to belief, if it be that
     you are truthful.
God knows the Unseen of the heavens
and of the earth; and God sees
     the things you do.'

L

QAF

In the Name of God, the Merciful, the Compassionate

Qaf

By the glorious Koran!

Nay, but they marvel that a warner has come to
them from among them; and the unbelievers say,
    'This is a marvellous thing!
What, when we are dead and become dust? That
    is a far returning!'
We know what the earth diminishes of them;
    with Us is a book recording.
5   Nay, but they cried lies to the truth
    when it came to them, and so they are
      in a case confused.
What, have they not beheld heaven above them,
how We have built it, and decked it out fair,
    and it has no cracks?
And the earth—We stretched it forth, and cast on it
    firm mountains,
and We caused to grow therein of every joyous kind
    for an insight
and a reminder to every penitent servant.
    And We sent down out of heaven
      water blessed,
    and caused to grow thereby gardens
      and grain of harvest
10   and tall palm-trees with spathes compact,
    a provision for the servants,
and thereby We revived a land that was dead.
    Even so is the coming forth.

Cried lies before them the people of Noah

and the men of Er-Rass, and Thamood, and
Ad and Pharaoh, the brothers of Lot, the
men of the Thicket, the people of Tubba'.
Every one cried lies to the Messengers,
and My threat came true.

What, were We wearied by the first creation?
No indeed; but they are in uncertainty
as to the new creation.

15   We indeed created man; and We know
what his soul whispers within him,
and We are nearer to him than the
jugular vein.

When the two angels meet together,
sitting one on the right, and one
on the left,
not a word he utters, but by him
is an observer ready.
And death's agony comes in truth; that is what thou wast
[shunning!
And the Trumpet shall be blown; that is the Day of the
[Threat.
20   And every soul shall come, and with it a driver and a witness.
'Thou wast heedless of this; therefore We have now removed
from thee thy covering, and so thy sight today is piercing.'
And his comrade shall say, 'This is what I have, made ready.'
'Cast, you twain, into Gehenna every froward unbeliever,
every hinderer of the good, transgressor, disquieter,
25   who set up with God another god; therefore, you twain, cast
[him
into the terrible chastisement.' And his comrade shall say,
'Our Lord, I made him not insolent, but he was in far error.'
He shall say, 'Dispute not before Me! For I sent you before-
[hand
the threat. The Word is not changed with Me; I wrong not
[My servants.'

Upon the day We shall say unto Gehenna, 'Art thou filled?'
30 And it shall say, 'Are there any more to come?' And Paradise
shall be brought forward to the godfearing, not afar: 'This is
that you were promised; it is for every mindful penitent.'

Whosoever fears the All-merciful
in the Unseen, and comes with a
    penitent heart:
'Enter it in peace! This is the
    Day of Eternity.'
Therein they shall have whatever
they will; and with Us there is
    yet more.

35 How many a generation We destroyed before them
that was stronger in valour than they, then
they searched about in the land; was there
    any asylum?
Surely in that there is a reminder to him
who has a heart, or will give ear with a
    present mind.

We created the heavens and the earth, and
what between them is, in six days, and no
    weariness touched Us.

So be thou patient under what they say, and
    proclaim thy Lord's praise
before the rising of the sun, and before its setting, and
    proclaim thy Lord's praise
in the night, and at the ends of the prostrations.

40   And listen thou for the day
when the caller shall call from a near place.
        On the day they hear
the Cry in truth, that is the day of coming forth.
It is We who give life, and make to die,
    and to Us is the homecoming.

235

Upon the day when the earth is split asunder from about them
as they hasten forth; that is a mustering easy for Us.

We know very well what they say;
thou art not a tyrant over them.
45   Therefore remind by the Koran him
who fears My threat.

LI

THE SCATTERERS

In the Name of God, the Merciful, the Compassionate

By the swift scatterers
and the burden-bearers
and the smooth runners
and the partitioners,
5   surely that you are promised is true, and
surely the Doom is about to fall!

By heaven with all its tracks
surely you speak at variance, and
perverted therefrom are some.

10   Perish the conjecturers
who are dazed in perplexity
asking, 'When shall be the Day of Doom?'
Upon the day when they shall be tried at the Fire:
'Taste your trial! This is that you were seeking to hasten.'

15 Surely the godfearing shall be among gardens and fountains
taking whatsoever their Lord has given them;
they were good-doers before that.
Little of the night would they slumber,
and in the mornings they would ask for forgiveness;
and the beggar and the outcast had a share in their wealth.

20   In the earth are signs for those having sure faith;
and in your selves; what, do you not see?
And in heaven is your provision, and that you are promised.
So by the Lord of heaven and earth, it is as surely true
as that you have speech.

Hast thou received the story of

the honoured guests of Abraham?
25   When they entered unto him, saying
'Peace!' he said 'Peace! You
are a people unknown to me.'
Then he turned to his household
and brought a fattened calf,
and he laid it before them
saying, 'Will you not eat?'
Then he conceived a fear of them.
They said, 'Be not afraid!'
And they gave him good tidings
of a cunning boy. Then came
forward his wife, clamouring,
and she smote her face, and
said, 'An old woman, barren!'
30   They said, 'So says thy Lord; He
is the All-wise, the All-knowing.'
Said he, 'And what is your business,
envoys?' They said, 'We have been
sent to a people of sinners, to
loose upon them stones of clay
marked with thy Lord for the prodigal.'
So We brought forth such believers
35   as were in it, but We found not
therein except one house of those
that have surrendered themselves.
And therein We left a sign to those
who fear the painful chastisement.

And also in Moses, when We sent him
unto Pharaoh, with a clear authority,
but he turned his back, with his court,
saying, 'A sorcerer, or a man possessed!'
40   So We seized him and his hosts, and We
cast them into the sea, and he blameworthy.

And also in Ad, when We loosed against them
        the withering wind
that left nothing it came upon, but made it

as stuff decayed.

And also in Thamood, when it was said to them,
    'Take your enjoyment for a while!'
Then they turned in disdain from the commandment
of their Lord, and the thunderbolt took them
    and they themselves beholding
45   and they were not able to stand upright, and
    were not helped.

    And the people of Noah before; surely
    they were an ungodly people.

    And heaven—We built it with might,
    and We extend it wide.
And the earth—We spread it forth;
    O excellent Smoothers!
And of everything created We two kinds;
    haply you will remember.

50   Therefore flee unto God!
I am a clear warner from Him to you.
And set not up with God another god;
I am a clear warner from Him to you.

Even so not a Messenger came to those before them
but they said, 'A sorcerer, or a man possessed!'
What, have they bequeathed it one to another?
    Nay, but they are an insolent people.

    So turn thou from them;
    thou wilt not be reproached.
55   And remind;
    the Reminder profits the believers.

I have not created jinn and mankind
    except to serve Me.
I desire of them no provision,
neither do I desire that they should feed Me.

Surely God is the All-provider,
the Possessor of Strength, the Ever-Sure

The evildoers shall have their portion,
like the portion of their fellows; so
let them not hasten Me!
60 So woe to the unbelievers, for that day of theirs
that they are promised.

LII

THE MOUNT

In the Name of God, the Merciful, the Compassionate

By the Mount
and a Book inscribed
in a parchment unrolled,
by the House inhabited
5   and the roof uplifted
and the sea swarming,
surely thy Lord's chastisement is about to fall;
there is none to avert it.

Upon the day when heaven spins dizzily
10   and the mountains are in motion,
woe that day unto those that cry lies,
such as play at plunging,
the day when they shall be pitched into the fire of Gehenna:
'This is the fire that you cried lies to!
15   What, is this magic, or is it you that do not see?
Roast in it! And bear you patiently, or bear not patiently,
equal it is to you; you are only being recompensed for
that you were working.'

Surely the godfearing shall be in gardens and bliss,
rejoicing in that their Lord has given them;
and their Lord shall guard them against the chastisement of
'Eat and drink, with wholesome appetite, for [Hell.
that you were working.'
20   Reclining upon couches ranged in rows;
and We shall espouse them to wide-eyed houris.
And those who believed, and their seed followed them
in belief, We shall join their seed with them, and We
shall not defraud them of aught of their work;
every man shall be pledged for what he earned.

And We shall succour them with fruits and flesh
    such as they desire
while they pass therein a cup one to another
wherein is no idle talk, no cause of sin,
and there go round them youths, their own,
    as if they were hidden pearls.
25   They advance one upon another, asking each other questions.
    They say, 'We were before among our people, ever
        going in fear,
and God was gracious to us, and guarded us
against the chastisement of the burning wind;
we were before ever calling upon Him; surely
He is the All-benign, the All-compassionate.'

        Therefore remind!
by thy Lord's blessing thou art not a soothsayer
    neither possessed.

30   Or do they say, 'He is a poet for whom
    we await Fate's uncertainty'? Say:
    'Await! I shall be awaiting with you.'

        Or do their intellects bid them do this?
    Or are they an insolent people?
Or do they say, 'He has invented it?'
    Nay, but they do not believe.
Then let them bring a discourse like it,
    if they speak truly.

35   Or were they created out of nothing?
    Or are they the creators?
Or did they create the heavens and earth?
    Nay, but they have not sure faith.
Or are thy Lord's treasuries in their keeping?
    Or are they the registrars?
Or have they a ladder whereon they listen?
Then let any of them that has listened bring
    a clear authority.

Or has He daughters, and they sons?

40   Or askest thou them for a wage, and so they
        are weighed down with debt?
Or is the Unseen in their keeping, and so
    they are writing it down?
Or desire they to outwit? The unbelievers,
    they are the outwitted.
Or have they a god, other than God?
Glory be to God, above that which
        they associate!

Even if they saw lumps falling from heaven,
    they would say, 'A massed cloud!'
45   Then leave them, till they encounter their day
        wherein they shall be thunderstruck,
the day when their guile shall avail them naught,
    and they shall not be helped.
And there surely awaits the evildoers a
chastisement beyond even that, but
        most of them know it not.

And be thou patient under the judgment of thy Lord;
        surely thou art before Our eyes.
And proclaim the praise of thy Lord
        when thou arisest,
and proclaim the praise of thy Lord
in the night, and at the declining of the stars.

LIII

THE STAR

In the Name of God, the Merciful, the Compassionate

By the Star when it plunges,
your comrade is not astray, neither errs,
nor speaks he out of caprice.
This is naught but a revelation revealed,
5   taught him by one terrible in power,
very strong; he stood poised,
being on the higher horizon,
then drew near and suspended hung,
two bows'-length away, or nearer,
10   then revealed to his servant that he revealed.
His heart lies not of what he saw;
what, will you dispute with him what he sees?

Indeed, he saw him another time
by the Lote-Tree of the Boundary
15   nigh which is the Garden of the Refuge,
when there covered the Lote-Tree that which covered;
his eye swerved not, nor swept astray.
Indeed, he saw one of the greatest signs of his Lord.

Have you considered El-Lat and El-'Uzza
20   and Manat the third, the other?
What, have you males, and He females?
That were indeed an unjust division.
They are naught but names yourselves
have named, and your fathers; God has
sent down no authority touching them.
They follow only surmise, and what the
souls desire; and yet guidance has
come to them from their Lord.
Or shall man have whatever he fancies?

25   And to God belongs the First and the Last.

How many an angel there is in the heavens whose
intercession avails not anything, save after
that God gives leave to whomsoever He wills
            and is well-pleased.
Those who do not believe in the world to come
name the angels with the names of females.
They have not any knowledge thereof; they follow
only surmise, and surmise avails naught against truth.

30   So turn thou from him who turns away
from Our Remembrance, and desires only
            the present life.
That is their attainment of knowledge.
    Surely thy Lord knows very well
    those who have gone astray from
    His way, and He knows very well
        those who are guided.

To God belongs whatsoever is in the heavens
and whatsoever is in the earth, that He may
recompense those who do evil for what they
have done, and recompense those who have done
        good with the reward most fair.

    Those who avoid the heinous sins and
    indecencies, save lesser offences—
surely thy Lord is wide in His forgiveness.

Very well He knows you, when He produced you
from the earth, and when you were yet unborn
in your mothers' wombs; therefore hold not
yourselves purified; God knows very well
        him who is godfearing.

Hast thou considered him who turns his back
35   and gives a little, and then grudgingly?
Does he possess the knowledge of the Unseen,
        and therefore he sees?

Or has he not been told of what is in the
      scrolls of Moses,
and Abraham, he who paid his debt in full?
That no soul laden bears the load of another,
40   and that a man shall have to his account only
      as he has laboured,
and that his labouring shall surely be seen,
then he shall be recompensed for it with the
      fullest recompense,
and that the final end is unto thy Lord,
and that it is He who makes to laugh, and
      that makes to weep,
45   and that it is He who makes to die, and
      that makes to live,
and that He Himself created the two kinds,
      male and female,
of a sperm-drop, when it was cast forth,
and that upon Him rests the second growth,
and that it is He who gives wealth and riches,
50   and that it is He who is the Lord of Sirius,
and that He destroyed Ad, the ancient,
and Thamood, and He did not spare them,
and the people of Noah before—certainly
they did exceeding evil, and were insolent—
55   and the Subverted City He also overthrew,
so that there covered it that which covered.
Then which of thy Lord's bounties disputest thou?

This is a warner, of the warners of old.
The Imminent is imminent; apart from God
      none can disclose it.
Do you then marvel at this discourse,
60   and do you laugh, and do you not weep,
      while you make merry?

So bow yourselves before God, and serve Him!

LIV

THE MOON

In the Name of God, the Merciful, the Compassionate

The Hour has drawn nigh: the moon is split.

Yet if they see a sign they turn away, and they say
    'A continuous sorcery!'
They have cried lies, and followed their caprices;
    but every matter is settled.
And there have come to them such tidings as contain
    a deterrent—
a Wisdom far-reaching; yet warnings do not avail.
5   So turn thou away from them.

Upon the day when the Caller shall call unto a horrible thing,
abasing their eyes, they shall come forth from the tombs as if
    they were scattered grasshoppers,
running with outstretched necks to the Caller. The unbelievers
    shall say, 'This is a hard day!'

The people of Noah cried lies before them;
they cried lies to Our servant, and said,
'A man possessed!' And he was rejected.
10   And so he called unto his Lord, saying,
'I am vanquished; do Thou succour me!'
Then We opened the gates of heaven unto
    water torrential,
and made the earth to gush with fountains,
and the waters met for a matter decreed.
And We bore him upon a well-planked vessel
    well-caulked
running before Our eyes—a recompense for
    him denied.
15   And We left it for a sign.

Is there any that will remember?
How then were My chastisement and My warnings?
Now We have made the Koran easy for Remembrance.
Is there any that will remember?

Ad cried lies.
How then were My chastisement and My warnings?
We loosed against them a wind
clamorous in a day of ill fortune continuous,
20   plucking up men as if they were stumps of
uprooted palm-trees.
How then were My chastisement and My warnings?
Now We have made the Koran easy for Remembrance.
Is there any that will remember?

Thamood cried lies to the warnings
and said, 'What, shall we follow
a mortal, one out of ourselves?
Then indeed we should be in error
and insanity!
25   Has the Reminder been cast upon him
alone among us? Nay, rather he is
an impudent liar.'
'They shall surely know tomorrow
who is the impudent liar.
We shall send the She-camel as a
trial for them; so watch thou them
and keep patience.
And tell them that the water is to
be divided between them, each drink
for each in turn.'
Then they called their comrade, and
he took in hand, and hamstrung her.
30 How then were My chastisement and My warnings?
We loosed against them one Cry,
and they were as the wattles of a
pen-builder.
Now We have made the Koran easy for Remembrance.
Is there any that will remember?

The people of Lot cried lies to the warnings.
We loosed against them a squall of pebbles
except the folk of Lot; We delivered them
    at the dawn--
35   a blessing from Us; even so We recompense
    him who is thankful.
He had warned them of Our assault, but
    they disputed the warnings.
Even his guests they had solicited of him;
so We obliterated their eyes, saying,
'Taste now My chastisement and My warnings!'
In the morning early there came upon them
    a settled chastisement:
'Taste now My chastisement and My warnings!'
40 Now We have made the Koran easy for Remembrance.
    Is there any that will remember?

The warnings came also to Pharaoh's folk.
They cried lies to Our signs, all of them,
so We seized them with the seizing of One
    mighty, omnipotent.

What, are your unbelievers better than those?
Or have you an immunity in the Scrolls? Or
do they say, 'We are a congregation that
    shall be succoured?'
45   Certainly the host shall be routed, and
    turn their backs.

    Nay, but the Hour is their tryst,
    and the Hour is very calamitous
    and bitter.
    Surely the sinners are in error
    and insanity!

The day when they are dragged on their faces into the Fire:
    'Taste now the touch of Sakar!'

    Surely We have created everything

in measure.

50   Our commandment is but one word,
            as the twinkling of an eye.

        We have destroyed the likes of you;
        is there any that will remember?

        Every thing that they have done
            is in the Scrolls,
        and everything, great and small,
            is inscribed.

    Surely the godfearing shall dwell amid gardens
            and a river
55   in a sure abode, in the presence of
            a King Omnipotent.

LV

THE ALL-MERCIFUL

In the Name of God, the Merciful, the Compassionate

The All-merciful has taught the Koran.
He created man
and He has taught him the Explanation.

The sun and the moon to a reckoning,
5   and the stars and the trees bow themselves;
and heaven—He raised it up, and set
the Balance.
(Transgress not in the Balance,
and weigh with justice, and skimp not in the Balance.)
And earth—He set it down for all beings,
10   therein fruits, and palm-trees with sheaths,
and grain in the blade, and fragrant herbs.
O which of your Lord's bounties will you and you deny?

He created man of a clay
like the potter's,
and He created the jinn
of a smokeless fire.
15   O which of your Lord's bounties will you and you deny?

Lord of the Two Easts,
Lord of the Two Wests,
O which of your Lord's bounties will you and you deny?

He let forth the two seas that meet together,
20   between them a barrier they do not overpass.
O which of your Lord's bounties will you and you deny?
From them come forth the pearl and the coral.
O which of your Lord's bounties will you and you deny?
His too are the ships that run, raised up in the sea like land-
[marks.

251

25   O which of your Lord's bounties will you and you deny?

All that dwells upon the earth is perishing, yet still
    abides the Face of thy Lord, majestic, splendid.
O which of your Lord's bounties will you and you deny?
Whatsoever is in the heavens and the earth implore Him;
    every day He is upon some labour.
30   O which of your Lord's bounties will you and you deny?

We shall surely attend to you at leisure,
    you weight and you weight!
O which of your Lord's bounties will you and you deny?
O tribe of jinn and of men, if you are able to
pass through the confines of heaven and earth,
pass through them! You shall not pass through
        except with an authority.
O which of your Lord's bounties will you and you deny?
35   Against you shall be loosed
    a flame of fire, and molten
    brass; and you shall not be helped.
O which of your Lord's bounties will you and you deny?
    And when heaven is split asunder,
    and turns crimson like red leather—
O which of your Lord's bounties will you and you deny?
    on that day none shall be questioned
    about his sin, neither man nor jinn.
40   O which of your Lord's bounties will you and you deny?
    The sinners shall be known by their mark,
and they shall be seized by their forelocks and their feet.
O which of your Lord's bounties will you and you deny?
    This is Gehenna, that sinners cried lies to;
    they shall go round between it and between
        hot, boiling water.
45   O which of your Lord's bounties will you and you deny?

But such as fears the Station of his Lord,
    for them shall be two gardens—
O which of your Lord's bounties will you and you deny?
    abounding in branches—

O which of your Lord's bounties will you and you deny?
50   therein two fountains of running water—
O which of your Lord's bounties will you and you deny?
     therein of every fruit two kinds—
O which of your Lord's bounties will you and you deny?
     reclining upon couches lined with brocade,
     the fruits of the gardens nigh to gather—
55 O which of your Lord's bounties will you and you deny?
     therein maidens restraining their glances,
     untouched before them by any man or jinn—
O which of your Lord's bounties will you and you deny?
     lovely as rubies, beautiful as coral—
O which of your Lord's bounties will you and you deny?
60 Shall the recompense of goodness be other than goodness?
O which of your Lord's bounties will you and you deny?

     And besides these shall be two gardens—
O which of your Lord's bounties will you and you deny?
     green, green pastures—
65 O which of your Lord's bounties will you and you deny?
     therein two fountains of gushing water—
O which of your Lord's bounties will you and you deny?
     therein fruits,
     and palm-trees, and pomegranates—
O which of your Lord's bounties will you and you deny?
70   therein maidens good and comely—
O which of your Lord's bounties will you and you deny?
     houris, cloistered in cool pavilions—
O which of your Lord's bounties will you and you deny?
     untouched before them by any man or jinn—
75 O which of your Lord's bounties will you and you deny?
reclining upon green cushions and lovely druggets—
O which of your Lord's bounties will you and you deny?

Blessed be the Name of thy Lord, majestic, splendid.

LVI

THE TERROR

In the Name of God, the Merciful, the Compassionate

When the Terror descends
(and none denies its descending)
abasing, exalting,
when the earth shall be rocked
5   and the mountains crumbled
and become a dust scattered,
and you shall be three bands—

Companions of the Right (O Companions of the Right!)
Companions of the Left (O Companions of the Left!)
10   and the Outstrippers: the Outstrippers
those are they brought nigh the Throne,
in the Gardens of Delight
(a throng of the ancients
and how few of the later folk)
15   upon close-wrought couches
reclining upon them, set face to face,
immortal youths going round about them
with goblets, and ewers, and a cup from a spring
(no brows throbbing, no intoxication)
20   and such fruits as they shall choose,
and such flesh of fowl as they desire,
and wide-eyed houris
as the likeness of hidden pearls,
a recompense for that they laboured.
Therein they shall hear no idle talk, no cause of sin,
25   only the saying 'Peace, Peace!'

The Companions of the Right (O Companions of the Right!)
mid thornless lote-trees and serried acacias,
30   and spreading shade and outpoured waters,

and fruits abounding
unfailing, unforbidden,
and upraised couches.
Perfectly We formed them, perfect,
35 and We made them spotless virgins,
chastely amorous, like of age
for the Companions of the Right.
A throng of the ancients
and a throng of the later folk.

40 The Companions of the Left (O Companions of the Left!)
mid burning winds and boiling waters
and the shadow of a smoking blaze
neither cool, neither goodly;
and before that they lived at ease,
45 and persisted in the Great Sin,
ever saying,
'What, when we are dead and become
dust and bones, shall we indeed
be raised up?
What, and our fathers, the ancients?'

Say: 'The ancients, and the later folk
shall be gathered to the appointed time
of a known day.
50 Then you erring ones, you that cried lies,
you shall eat of a tree called Zakkoum,
and you shall fill therewith your bellies
and drink on top of that boiling water
55 lapping it down like thirsty camels.'
This shall be their hospitality on the
Day of Doom.

We created you; therefore why will you
not believe?

Have you considered the seed you spill?
Do you yourselves create it, or are We
the Creators?

60 We have decreed among you Death; We shall
   not be outstripped;
that We may exchange the likes of you,
and make you to grow again in a fashion
   you know not.
You have known the first growth; so why
   will you not remember?

Have you considered the soil you till?
Do you yourselves sow it, or are We
   the Sowers?
65 Did We will, We would make it broken
orts, and you would remain bitterly
   jesting—
'We are debt-loaded; nay, we have been
   robbed!'

Have you considered the water you drink?
Did you send it down from the clouds, or
   did We send it?
Did We will, We would make it bitter; so
   why are you not thankful?

70 Have you considered the fire you kindle?
Did you make its timber to grow, or
   did We make it?
We Ourselves made it for a reminder, and
   a boon to the desert-dwellers.

Then magnify the Name of thy Lord, the All-mighty.

No! I swear by the fallings of the stars
75 (and that is indeed a mighty oath, did
   you but know it)
it is surely a noble Koran
in a hidden Book
none but the purified shall touch,
a sending down from the Lord of all Being.
80 What, do you hold this discourse in disdain, and

do you make it your living to cry lies?

Why, but when the soul leaps to the throat of the dying
and that hour you are watching
(And We are nigher him than you, but you do not see Us)
85   why, if you are not at Our disposal,
do you not bring back his soul, if you speak truly?

Then, if he be of those brought nigh the Throne,
there shall be repose and ease, and a Garden of Delight;
90   and if he be a Companion of the Right:
'Peace be upon thee, Companion of the Right!' ,
But if he be of them that cried lies, and went astray,
there shall be a hospitality of boiling water
and the roasting in Hell.

95   Surely this is the truth of certainty.
Then magnify the Name of thy Lord, the All-mighty.

I

LVII

IRON

In the Name of God, the Merciful, the Compassionate

All that is in the heavens and the earth magnifies God;
        He is the All-mighty, the All-wise.
To Him belongs the Kingdom of the heavens and the earth;
He gives life, and He makes to die, and He is powerful
                over everything.
He is the First and the Last, the Outward and the Inward;
        He has knowledge of everything.
    It is He that created the heavens and the earth
                in six days
        then seated Himself upon the Throne.
    He knows what penetrates into the earth,
            and what comes forth from it,
what comes down from heaven, and what goes up unto it.
    He is with you wherever you are; and God sees
                the things you do.
5   To Him belongs the Kingdom of the heavens and the earth;
        and unto Him all matters are returned.
        He makes the night to enter into the day
        and makes the day to enter into the night.
        He knows the thoughts within the breasts.

    Believe in God and His Messenger, and expend of
    that unto which He has made you successors. And
    those of you who believe and expend shall have
                a mighty wage.
    How is it with you, that you believe not in God
    seeing that the Messenger is calling you to
    believe in your Lord, and He has taken compact
        with you, if you are believers?
    It is He who sends down upon His servant signs,
    clear signs, that He may bring you forth from

the shadows into the light. Surely God is to you
    All-gentle, All-compassionate.
10   How is it with you, that you expend not in the
way of God, and to God belongs the inheritance
of the heavens and the earth? Not equal is he
among you who spent, and who fought before the
victory; those are mightier in rank than they
who spent and fought afterwards; and unto each
God has promised the reward most fair; and God
        is aware of the things you do.
Who is he that will lend to God a good loan,
and He will multiply it for him, and his shall be
        a generous wage?

Upon the day when thou seest the believers, men and women,
their light running before them, and on their right hands.
'Good tidings for you today! Gardens underneath which
rivers flow, therein to dwell for ever; that is indeed
        the mighty triumph.'
Upon the day when the hypocrites, men and women, shall say
to those who have believed, 'Wait for us, so that we may
borrow your light!' It shall be said, 'Return you back
behind, and seek for a light!' And a wall shall be set up
between them, having a door in the inward whereof is
mercy, and against the outward thereof is chastisement.
They shall be calling unto them, 'Were we not with you?'
They shall say, 'Yes indeed; but you tempted yourselves,
and you awaited, and you were in doubt, and fancies
deluded you, until God's commandment came, and the
Deluder deluded you concerning God. Therefore today
no ransom shall be taken from you, neither from those who
disbelieved. Your refuge is the Fire, that is your master—
        an evil homecoming!'

15   Is it not time that the hearts of those
who believe should be humbled to the
Remembrance of God and the Truth which
He has sent down, and that they should
not be as those to whom the Book was

given aforetime, and the term seemed
over long to them, so that their hearts
have become hard, and many of them
            are ungodly?
Know that God revives the earth after
it was dead. We have indeed made clear
for you the signs, that haply you will
            understand.
Surely those, the men and the women,
who make freewill offerings and have
lent to God a good loan, it shall be
multiplied for them, and theirs shall be
            a generous wage.
And those who believe in God and His
Messengers—they are the just men
and the martyrs in their Lord's sight;
they have their wage, and their light.
But the unbelievers, who have cried lies
to Our signs, they are the inhabitants
            of Hell.
Know that the present life is but a
sport and a diversion, an adornment
and a cause for boasting among you,
and a rivalry in wealth and children.
It is as a rain whose vegetation
pleases the unbelievers; then it
withers, and thou seest it turning
yellow, then it becomes broken orts.
And in the world to come there is a
            terrible chastisement,
20   and forgiveness from God and good pleasure;
and the present life is but the joy
            of delusion.
Race to forgiveness from your Lord,
and a Garden the breadth whereof is
as the breadth of heaven and earth,
made ready for those who believe in
God and His Messengers. That is the
bounty of God; He gives it unto

whomsoever He will; and God is of
 bounty abounding.
No affliction befalls in the earth
or in yourselves, but it is in a
Book, before We create it; that is
  easy for God;
that you may not grieve for what
escapes you, nor rejoice in what has
come to you; God loves not any man
 proud and boastful,
such as are niggardly, and bid men
to be niggardly. And whosoever
turns away, God is the All-sufficient,
 the All-laudable.

25 Indeed, We sent Our Messengers with
the clear signs, and We sent down
with them the Book and the Balance
so that men might uphold justice.
And We sent down iron, wherein is
great might, and many uses for men,
and so that God might know who
helps Him, and His Messengers,
in the Unseen. Surely God is
 All-strong, All-mighty.
And We sent Noah, and Abraham,
and We appointed the Prophecy and
the Book to be among their seed; and
some of them are guided, and many of
 them are ungodly.

 Then We sent, following
 in their footsteps, Our
 Messengers; and We sent,
 following, Jesus son of
 Mary, and gave unto him
  the Gospel.
And We set in the hearts of those who
followed him tenderness and mercy.

And monasticism they invented—We
did not prescribe it for them—only
seeking the good pleasure of God; but
they observed it not as it should be
observed. So We gave those of them
who believed their wage; and many of
   them are ungodly.

O believers, fear God, and believe
in His Messenger, and He will give you
a twofold portion of His mercy, and
He will appoint for you a light whereby
you shall walk, and forgive you; God is
  All-forgiving, All-compassionate;
that the People of the Book may know
that they have no power over anything
of God's bounty, and that bounty is in
the hand of God; He gives it unto
whomsoever He will; and God is of
   bounty abounding.

LVIII

THE DISPUTER

In the Name of God, the Merciful, the Compassionate

God has heard the words of her that disputes with thee
concerning her husband, and makes complaint unto God.
God hears the two of you conversing together; surely
God is All-hearing, All-seeing.

Those of you who say, regarding their wives, 'Be as
my mother's back,' they are not truly their mothers;
their mothers are only those who gave them birth, and
they are surely saying a dishonourable saying, and a
falsehood.
Yet surely God is All-pardoning, All-forgiving.
And those who say, regarding their wives, 'Be as my
mother's back,' and then retract what they have said,
they shall set free a slave, before the two of them
touch one another. By that you are admonished; and
God is aware of the things you do.
5 But whosoever finds not the means, then let him fast
two successive months, before the two of them touch
one another. And if any man is not able to, then
let him feed sixty poor persons—that, that you may
believe in God and His Messenger. Those are God's
bounds; and for the unbelievers there awaits yet
a painful chastisement.

Surely those who oppose God and His Messenger
shall be frustrated as those before them were
frustrated. Now We have sent down signs,
clear signs; and for the unbelievers awaits
a humbling chastisement,
upon the day when God shall raise them up all
together, then He shall tell them what they did.

God has numbered it, and they have forgotten it.
God is witness over everything.

Hast thou not seen that God knows whatsoever is in
the heavens, and whatsoever is in the earth? Three
men conspire not secretly together, but He is the
fourth of them, neither five men, but He is the
sixth of them, neither fewer than that, neither
more, but He is with them, wherever they may be;
then He shall tell them what they have done, on the
Day of Resurrection. Surely God has knowledge
of everything.

Hast thou not regarded those who were forbidden
to converse secretly together, then they return
to that they were forbidden, and they converse
secretly together in sin and enmity, and in
disobedience to the Messenger? Then, when they
come to thee, they greet thee with a greeting
God never greeted thee withal; and they say
within themselves, 'Why does God not chastise
us for what we say?' Sufficient for them shall
be Gehenna, at which they shall be roasted—
an evil homecoming!

10 O believers, when you conspire secretly, then
conspire not together in sin and enmity and
disobedience to the Messenger, but conspire
in piety and godfearing. Fear God, unto whom
you shall be mustered.
Conspiring secretly together is of Satan,
that the believers may sorrow; but he will
not hurt them anything, except by the leave
of God. And in God let the believers
put all their trust.

O believers, when it is said to you
'Make room in the assemblies', then
make room, and God will make room for
you; and when it is said, 'Move up',

move up, and God will raise up in rank
those of you who believe and have been
given knowledge. And God is aware of
    the things you do.
O believers, when you conspire with
the Messenger, before your conspiring
advance a freewill offering; that is
better for you and purer. Yet if you
find not means, God is All-forgiving,
    All-compassionate.
Are you afraid, before your conspiring,
to advance freewill offerings? If you
do not so, and God turns again unto
you, then perform the prayer, and
pay the alms, and obey God and
His Messenger. God is aware of
    the things you do.

15   Hast thou not regarded those who have taken
for friends a people against whom God is
wrathful? They belong neither to you nor
to them; and they swear upon falsehood,
    and that wittingly.
God has made ready for them a chastisement
terrible; surely they—evil are the things
    they have been doing.
They have taken their oaths as a covering,
and barred from God's way; so there awaits them
    a humbling chastisement.
Neither their riches nor their children
shall avail them anything against God;
those—they are the inhabitants of the Fire,
    therein dwelling forever.
Upon the day when God shall raise them up all
together, and they will swear to Him, as they
swear to you, and think they are on something.
    Surely, they are the liars!
20   Satan has gained the mastery over them, and
caused them to forget God's Remembrance.

Those are Satan's party; why, Satan's party,
    surely, they are the losers!

Surely those who oppose God and His Messenger,
those are among the most abject. God has
written, 'I shall assuredly be the victor,
I and My Messengers.' Surely God is
    All-strong, All-mighty.

Thou shalt not find any people who believe
in God and the Last Day who are loving to
anyone who opposes God and His Messenger, not
though they were their fathers, or their sons,
or their brothers, or their clan. Those—
He has written faith upon their hearts, and
He has confirmed them with a Spirit from
Himself; and He shall admit them into
gardens underneath which rivers flow, therein
to dwell forever, God being well-pleased with
them, and they well-pleased with Him. Those are
God's party; why, surely God's party—they are
    the prosperers.

LIX

THE MUSTERING

In the Name of God, the Merciful, the Compassionate

All that is in the heavens and the earth magnifies God;
    He is the All-mighty, the All-wise.

It is He who expelled from their habitations
the unbelievers among the People of the Book
at the first mustering. You did not think
that they would go forth, and they thought
that their fortresses would defend them
against God; then God came upon them from
whence they had not reckoned, and He cast
terror into their hearts as they destroyed
their houses with their own hands, and the
hands of the believers; therefore take heed,
    you who have eyes!
Had God not prescribed dispersal for them,
He would have chastised them in this world;
and there awaits them in the world to come
    the chastisement of the Fire.
That is because they made a breach with
God and His Messenger; and whosoever
makes a breach with God, God is terrible
    in retribution.

5   Whatever palm-trees you cut down, or
left standing upon their roots, that was
by God's leave, and that He might degrade
    the ungodly.
And whatever spoils of war God has given
unto His Messenger from them, against
that you pricked neither horse nor camel;
but God gives authority to His Messengers

over whomsoever He will. God is powerful
over everything.
Whatsoever spoils of war God has given to
His Messenger from the people of the cities
belongs to God, and His Messenger, and
the near kinsman, orphans, the needy
and the traveller, so that it be not a
thing taken in turns among the rich of you.
Whatever the Messenger gives you, take;
whatever he forbids you, give over.
And fear God; surely God is terrible
in retribution.
It is for the poor emigrants, who were
expelled from their habitations and their
possessions, seeking bounty from God
and good pleasure, and helping God
and His Messenger; those—they are
the truthful ones.
And those who made their dwelling in
the abode, and in belief, before them,
love whosoever has emigrated to them,
not finding in their breasts any need
for what they have been given, and
preferring others above themselves, even
though poverty be their portion. And
whoso is guarded against the avarice
of his own soul, those—they are
the prosperers.

10   And as for those who came after them,
they say, 'Our Lord, forgive us and our
brothers, who preceded us in belief,
and put Thou not into our hearts any
rancour towards those who believe. Our
Lord, surely Thou art the All-gentle,
the All-compassionate.'

Hast thou not regarded the hypocrites, saying
to their brothers of the People of the Book who
disbelieve, 'If you are expelled, we will go

forth with you, and we will never obey anyone
in regard to you. If you are fought against,
we will help you.' And God bears witness that
       they are truly liars.
If those are expelled, they will not go forth
with them, and if they are fought against, they
will not help them. Even if they helped them,
they would surely turn their backs, then they
       would not be helped.
Why, you arouse greater fear in their hearts
than God; that is because they are a people
       who understand not.
They will not fight against you all together
except in fortified cities, or from behind walls.
Their valour is great, among themselves; you
think of them as a host; but their hearts are
scattered; that is because they are a people
       who have no sense.

15   Like those who a short time before them tasted
the mischief of their action; there awaits them
       a painful chastisement.
Like Satan, when he said to man, 'Disbelieve';
then, when he disbelieved, he said, 'Surely
I am quit of you. Surely I fear God, the
       Lord of all Being.'
Their end is, both are in the Fire, there
dwelling forever; that is the recompense
       of the evildoers.

O believers, fear God. Let every soul
consider what it has forwarded for the
morrow. And fear God; God is aware of
       the things you do.
Be not as those who forgot God, and so He
caused them to forget their souls; those—
       they are the ungodly.

20   Not equal are the inhabitants of the
Fire and the inhabitants of Paradise.
The inhabitants of Paradise—they

are the triumphant.

If We had sent down this Koran upon a mountain,
thou wouldst have seen it humbled, split asunder
     out of the fear of God.
And those similitudes—We strike them for men;
     haply they will reflect.

He is God;
     there is no god but He.
He is the knower of the Unseen and the Visible;
He is the All-merciful, the All-compassionate.

He is God;
     there is no god but He.
He is the King, the All-holy, the All-peaceable,
     the All-faithful, the All-preserver,
     the All-mighty, the All-compeller,
          the All-sublime.
Glory be to God, above that they associate!

He is God,
     the Creator, the Maker, the Shaper.
To Him belong the Names Most Beautiful.
All that is in the heavens and the earth magnifies Him;
     He is the All-mighty, the All-wise.

LX

THE WOMAN TESTED

In the Name of God, the Merciful, the Compassionate

O believers, take not My enemy and your enemy
for friends, offering them love, though they
have disbelieved in the truth that has come to
you, expelling the Messenger and you because
you believe in God your Lord. If you go forth to
struggle in My way and seek My good pleasure,
secretly loving them, yet I know very well
what you conceal and what you publish; and
whosoever of you does that, has gone astray
      from the right way.
If they come on you, they will be enemies to
you, and stretch against you their hands and
their tongues, to do you evil, and they wish that
      you may disbelieve.
Neither your blood-kindred nor your children
shall profit you upon the Day of Resurrection;
He shall distinguish between you. And God sees
      the things you do.

You have had a good example in Abraham, and
those with him, when they said to their people,
'We are quit of you and that you serve, apart
from God. We disbelieve in you, and between
us and you enmity has shown itself, and
hatred for ever, until you believe in God alone.'
(Except that Abraham said unto his father,
'Certainly I shall ask pardon for thee; but I
have no power to do aught for thee against God.')
'Our Lord, in Thee we trust; to Thee we turn; to
      Thee is the homecoming.
5   Our Lord, make us not a temptation to those who

disbelieve; and forgive us. Our Lord, Thou art
    the All-mighty, the All-wise.'
You have had a good example in them for whoever
hopes for God and the Last Day. And whosoever
turns away, surely God is the All-sufficient,
    the All-laudable.
It may be God will yet establish between you
and those of them with whom you are at enmity
love. God is All-powerful; God is All-forgiving,
    All-compassionate.

God forbids you not, as regards those who have not
fought you in religion's cause, nor expelled you
from your habitations, that you should be kindly
to them, and act justly towards them; surely
    God loves the just.
God only forbids you as to those who have fought
you in religion's cause, and expelled you from
your habitations, and have supported in your
expulsion, that you should take them for friends.
And whosoever takes them for friends, those—
    they are the evildoers.

10   O believers, when believing women come to you
as emigrants, test them. God knows very well
their belief. Then, if you know them to be
believers, return them not to the unbelievers.
They are not permitted to the unbelievers,
nor are the unbelievers permitted to them.
Give the unbelievers what they have expended;
and there is no fault in you to marry them
when you have given them their wages. Do not
hold fast to the ties of unbelieving women,
and ask what you have expended, and let them
ask what they have expended. That is God's
judgment; He judges between you; and God is
    All-knowing, All-wise.
And if any of your wives slips away from you
to the unbelievers, and then you retaliate,

give those whose wives have gone away the like
of what they have expended. And fear God, in
    whom you believe.

O Prophet, when believing women come to thee,
swearing fealty to thee upon the terms that
they will not associate with God anything,
and will not steal, neither commit adultery,
nor slay their children, nor bring a calumny
they forge between their hands and their feet,
nor disobey thee in aught honourable, ask God's
forgiveness for them; God is All-forgiving,
    All-compassionate.

O believers, take not for friends a people
against whom God is wrathful, and who have
despaired of the world to come, even as the
unbelievers have despaired of the inhabitants
    of the tombs.

LXI

THE RANKS

In the Name of God, the Merciful, the Compassionate

All that is in the heavens and the earth magnifies God;
    He is the All-mighty, the All-wise.

    O you who believe, wherefore do you say
        what you do not?
Very hateful is it to God, that you say
        what you do not.
God loves those who fight in His way in
ranks, as though they were a building
        well-compacted.

5   And when Moses said to his people,
    'O my people, why do you hurt me,
    though you know I am the Messenger
    of God to you?' When they swerved,
    God caused their hearts to swerve;
    and God guides never the people
        of the ungodly.

        And when Jesus son of
        Mary said, 'Children of
        Israel, I am indeed the
        Messenger of God to you,
        confirming the Torah
        that is before me, and
        giving good tidings of
        a Messenger who shall
        come after me, whose
        name shall be Ahmad.'
Then, when he brought them the clear signs,
they said, 'This is a manifest sorcery.'

And who does greater evil than he who
forges against God falsehood, when he
is being called unto surrender?
And God guides never the people
      of the evildoers.

They desire to extinguish with their mouths the light
of God; but God will perfect His light, though
      the unbelievers be averse.
It is He who has sent His Messenger with
the guidance and the religion of truth, that
he may uplift it above every religion, though
      the unbelievers be averse.

10   O believers, shall I direct you to a
commerce that shall deliver you from
      a painful chastisement?
You shall believe in God and His
Messenger, and struggle in the way of
God with your possessions and your
selves. That is better for you,
      did you but know.
He will forgive you your sins and admit
you into gardens underneath which
rivers flow, and to dwelling-places
goodly in Gardens of Eden; that is
      the mighty triumph;
and other things you love, help from God
and a nigh victory. Give thou good tidings
      to the believers!

O believers, be you God's helpers, as
Jesus, Mary's son, said to the Apostles.
      'Who will be my helpers
      unto God?' The Apostles
      said, 'We will be helpers
      of God.'
And a party of the Children of Israel
believed, and a party disbelieved.

So We confirmed those who believed
against their enemy, and they became
masters.

LXII

CONGREGATION

In the Name of God, the Merciful, the Compassionate

All that is in the heavens and the earth magnifies God,
the King, the All-holy,
the All-mighty, the All-wise.
It is He who has raised up from among the common people
a Messenger from among them, to recite His signs to them
[and
to purify them, and to teach them the Book and the Wisdom,
though before that they were in manifest error,
and others of them who have not yet joined them. And He is
the All-mighty, the All-wise.

That is the bounty of God;
He gives it to whom He will,
and God is of bounty
abounding.

5 The likeness of those who have been loaded with the Torah,
then they have not carried it, is as the likeness of an ass
carrying books. Evil is the likeness of the people
who have cried lies to God's signs. God guides never
the people of the evildoers.

Say: 'You of Jewry, if you assert that
you are the friends of God, apart from
other men, then do you long for death,
if you speak truly.'
But they will never long for it, because of
that their hands have forwarded; God knows
the evildoers.
Say: 'Surely death, from which you flee,
shall encounter you; then you shall be

277

returned to the Knower of the Unseen and
the Visible, and He will tell you that
        you have been doing.'

O believers, when proclamation is made for prayer on
the Day of Congregation, hasten to God's remembrance
and leave trafficking aside; that is better for you,
        did you but know.

10 Then, when the prayer is finished, scatter in the land
and seek God's bounty, and remember God frequently;
        haply you will prosper.

But when they see merchandise or diversion
they scatter off to it, and they leave thee
        standing.
        Say: 'What is with God is better
        than diversion and merchandise.
        God is the best of providers.'

LXIII

THE HYPOCRITES

In the Name of God, the Merciful, the Compassionate

When the hypocrites come to thee they say,
'We bear witness that thou art indeed
the Messenger of God.' And God knows
that thou art indeed His Messenger, and
God bears witness that the hypocrites
        are truly liars.
They have taken their oaths as a covering,
then they have barred from the way of God.
Surely they—evil are the things they
        have been doing.
That is because they have believed, then
they have disbelieved; therefore a seal
has been set on their hearts, and they
        do not understand.
When thou seest them, their bodies please
thee; but when they speak, thou listenest
to their speech, and it is as they were
propped-up timbers. They think every cry
is against them. They are the enemy;
so beware of them. God assail them! How
        they are perverted!
5   And when it is said to them, 'Come now,
and God's Messenger will ask forgiveness
for you,' they twist their heads, and thou
seest them turning their faces away,
        waxing proud.
Equal it is for them, whether thou askest
forgiveness for them or thou askest not
forgiveness for them; God will never
forgive them. God guides not the people
        of the ungodly.

Those are they that say, 'Do not expend
on them that are with God's Messenger
until they scatter off'; yet unto God
belong the treasuries of the heavens
and of the earth, but the hypocrites
   do not understand.
They say, 'If we return to the City,
the mightier ones of it will expel
the more abased'; yet glory belongs
unto God, and unto His Messenger
and the believers, but the hypocrites
   do not know it.

O believers, let not your possessions
neither your children divert you from
God's remembrance; whoso does that,
   they are the losers.
10 Expend of what We have provided you
before that death comes upon one of you
and he says, 'O my Lord, if only
Thou wouldst defer me unto a near
term, so that I may make freewill
offering, and so I may become
   one of the righteous.'
But God will never defer any soul when
its term comes. And God is aware of
   the things you do.

LXIV

MUTUAL FRAUD

In the Name of God, the Merciful, the Compassionate

All that is in the heavens and the earth magnifies God.
    His is the Kingdom, and His is the praise,
        and He is powerful over everything.

It is He who created you. One of you is an unbeliever,
    and one of you a believer; and God sees
        the things you do.
He created the heavens and the earth with the truth,
and He shaped you, and shaped you well; and unto Him
        is the homecoming.
He knows whatever is in the heavens and the earth, and
    He knows what you conceal and what you publish.
    God knows the thoughts within the breasts.

5   Has there not come to you the tidings of those
    that disbelieved before, then tasted the mischief
    of their action, and there yet awaits them a
        painful chastisement?
That is because their Messengers came to them
with the clear signs, and then they said, 'What,
shall mortals be our guides?' Therefore they
disbelieved, and turned away; and God was in
no need of them. And God is All-sufficient,
        All-laudable.

    The unbelievers assert that they will
    never be raised up. Say: 'Yes indeed,
    by my Lord! You shall be raised up,
    then you shall be told the things you did.
        That is easy for God.'

Therefore believe in God and
His Messenger, and in the
Light which We have sent down.
And God is aware of the things you do.

Upon the day when He shall gather you
for the Day of Gathering; that shall
be the Day of Mutual Fraud. And
whosoever believes in God, and does
righteousness, God will acquit him
of his evil deeds, and admit him
into gardens underneath which
rivers flow, therein to dwell for
ever and ever; that is the mighty
triumph.

10 And those who disbelieved and cried
lies to Our signs, those shall be
the inhabitants of the Fire.
therein to dwell forever—an evil
homecoming!

No affliction befalls, except it be
by the leave of God. Whosoever
believes in God, He will guide his
heart. And God has knowledge of
everything.

And obey God, and obey the Messenger;
but if you turn your backs, it is
only for the Messenger to deliver
the Manifest Message.

God—
there is no god but He.
And in God let the believers
put their trust.

O believers, among your wives and children

there is an enemy to you; so beware of them.
But if you pardon, and overlook, and if you
forgive, surely God is All-forgiving,
     All-compassionate.
15   Your wealth and your children are
only a trial; and with God is
     a mighty wage.
So fear God as far as you are able,
and give ear, and obey, and expend
well for yourselves. And whosoever
is guarded against the avarice
of his own soul, those—they are
     the prosperers.
If you lend to God a good loan, He
will multiply it for you, and will
 forgive you. God is All-thankful,
     All-clement,
Knower He of the Unseen and the Visible,
    the All-mighty, the All-wise.

LXV

DIVORCE

In the Name of God, the Merciful, the Compassionate

O Prophet, when you divorce women, divorce them
when they have reached their period. Count the
period, and fear God your Lord. Do not expel
them from their houses, nor let them go forth,
except when they commit a flagrant indecency.
Those are God's bounds; whosoever trespasses
the bounds of God has done wrong to himself.
Thou knowest not, perchance after that God will
      bring something new to pass.
Then, when they have reached their term, retain
them honourably, or part from them honourably.
And call in to witness two men of equity from
among yourselves; and perform the witnessing
to God Himself. By this then is admonished
whosoever believes in God and the Last Day.
And whosoever fears God, He will appoint for him
a way out, and He will provide for him from
      whence he never reckoned.

    And whosoever puts his trust in God,
    He shall suffice him. God attains his
    purpose. God has appointed a measure
      for everything.

As for your women who have despaired of further
menstruating, if you are in doubt, their period
shall be three months, and those who have not
menstruated as yet. And those who are with child,
their term is when they bring forth their burden.
Whoso fears God, God will appoint for him, of His
      command, easiness.

5 That is God's command, that He has sent down
unto you. And whosoever fears God, He will
acquit him of his evil deeds, and He will give him
                a mighty wage.
Lodge them where you are lodging, according to
your means, and do not press them, so as to
straiten their circumstances. If they are with
child, expend upon them until they bring forth
their burden. If they suckle for you, give them
their wages, and consult together honourably.
If you both make difficulties, another woman shall
                suckle for him.
Let the man of plenty expend out of his plenty.
As for him whose provision is stinted to him,
let him expend of what God has given him. God
charges no soul save with what He has given him.
God will assuredly appoint, after difficulty,
                easiness.

        How many a city turned in disdain
        from the commandment of its Lord
        and His Messengers; and then We
        made with it a terrible reckoning
        and chastised it with a horrible
                chastisement.
        So it tasted the mischief of its
        action, and the end of its affair
                was loss.
10   God prepared for them a terrible
        chastisement. So fear God, O men
                possessed of minds!

    Believers, God has sent down to you, for a
    remembrance, a Messenger reciting to
    you the signs of God, clear signs, that
    He may bring forth those who believe
    and do righteous deeds from the shadows
    into the light. Whosoever believes in
    God, and does righteousness, He will

admit him to gardens underneath which
rivers flow; therein they shall dwell
for ever and ever. God has made for him
a goodly provision.

It is God who created seven heavens, and of earth their like,
between them the Command descending,
that you may know that God is powerful over everything
and that God encompasses everything in knowledge.

LXVI

THE FORBIDDING

In the Name of God, the Merciful, the Compassionate

O Prophet, why forbiddest thou what God has
made lawful to thee, seeking the good pleasure
of thy wives? And God is All-forgiving,
      All-compassionate.

God has ordained for you the absolution of
your oaths. God is your Protector, and He is
    the All-knowing, the All-wise.

And when the Prophet confided to one of his
wives a certain matter; and then, when she
told of it, and God disclosed that to him,
he made known part of it, and turned aside
from part; then, when he told her of it,
she said, 'Who told thee this?' He said,
'I was told of it by the All-knowing,
      the All-aware.'
If you two repent to God, yet your hearts
certainly inclined; but if you support one
another against him, God is his Protector,
and Gabriel, and the righteous among the
believers; and, after that, the angels are
      his supporters.

5   It is possible that, if he divorces you,
his Lord will give him in exchange wives
better than you, women who have surrendered,
believing, obedient, penitent, devout,
given to fasting, who have been married
      and virgins too.

Believers, guard yourselves and your families
against a Fire whose fuel is men and stones,
and over which are harsh, terrible angels who
disobey not God in what He commands them and
    do what they are commanded.
'O you unbelievers, do not excuse yourselves
today; you are only being recompensed for
    what you were doing.'
Believers, turn to God in sincere repentance;
it may be that your Lord will acquit you
of your evil deeds, and will admit you
into gardens underneath which rivers flow.

Upon the day when God will not degrade the Prophet
and those who believe with him, their light running
before them, and on their right hands; and they say,
'Our Lord, perfect for us our light, and forgive us;
    surely Thou art powerful over everything.'

O Prophet, struggle with the unbelievers and the hypocrites,
and be thou harsh with them; their refuge shall be Gehenna—
    an evil homecoming!

10   God has struck a similitude
for the unbelievers—the wife of
Noah, and the wife of Lot; for
they were under two of Our
righteous servants, but they
betrayed them, so they availed
them nothing whatsoever
against God; so it was said,
'Enter, you two, the Fire with
    those who enter.'
God has struck a similitude
for the believers—the wife of
Pharaoh, when she said, 'My
Lord, build for me a house in
Paradise, in Thy presence, and
deliver me from Pharaoh

and his work, and do Thou
deliver me from the people
    of the evildoers.'
And Mary, Imran's daughter,
who guarded her virginity,
so We breathed into her of
Our Spirit, and she confirmed
the Words of her Lord and His
Books, and became one of
    the obedient.

K

LXVII

THE KINGDOM

In the Name of God, the Merciful, the Compassionate

Blessed be He in whose hand is the Kingdom—
He is powerful over everything—
who created death and life, that He might try you
which of you is fairest in works; and He is
the All-mighty, the All-forgiving—
who created seven heavens one upon another.
Thou seest not in the creation
of the All-merciful any imperfection.
Return thy gaze; seest thou any fissure?
Then return thy gaze again, and again, and thy gaze comes
back to thee dazzled, aweary.

5 And We adorned the lower heaven with lamps, and made
⸢them
things to stone Satans; and We have prepared for them
the chastisement of the Blaze.

And for those who disbelieve in their Lord
there awaits the chastisement of Gehenna—
an evil homecoming!
When they are cast into it they will hear it sighing, the
while it boils and wellnigh bursts asunder with rage. As
often as a troop is cast into it, its keepers ask them,
'Came there no warner to you?' They say, 'Yes indeed, a
warner came to us; but we cried lies, saying, "God has
not sent down anything; you are only in great error."'

10 They also say, 'If we had only heard, or had understood,
we would not have been of the inhabitants of the Blaze.'
So they confess their sins. Curse the inhabitants of the Blaze!

Surely those who fear their Lord
in the Unseen—

there awaits them forgiveness
and a great wage.

Be secret in your speech, or proclaim it,
He knows the thoughts within the breasts.
Shall He not know, who created? And
He is the All-subtle, the All-aware.

15 It is He who made the earth submissive to you; therefore
walk in its tracts, and eat of His provision; to
Him is the Uprising.

Do you feel secure that He who is in heaven
will not cause the earth to swallow you,
the while it rocks?
Do you feel secure that He who is in heaven
will not loose against you a squall of pebbles,
then you shall know how My warning is?

Those that were before them also cried lies;
then how was My horror!

Have they not regarded the birds above them
spreading their wings, and closing them?
Naught holds them but the All-merciful. Surely
He sees everything.

20 Or who is this that shall be a host for you
to help you, apart from the All-merciful?
The unbelievers are only in delusion.
Or who is this that shall provide for you
if He withholds His provision? No, but
they persist in disdain and aversion.

What, is he who walks prone upon his face
better guided than he who walks upright
on a straight path?

Say: 'It is He who produced you, and

appointed for you hearing and sight and hearts;
   little thanks you show!'
Say: 'It is He who scattered you in the earth,
   and unto Him you shall be mustered.'

25 They say, 'When shall this promise come to pass,
       if you speak truly?'
   Say: 'The knowledge is with God; I am
       only a clear warner.'
Then, when they see it nigh at hand, the faces of
the unbelievers will be vexed, and it will be said,
   'This is what you were promised.'

   Say: 'What think you? If God destroys me
   and those with me, or has mercy on us,
   then who will protect the unbelievers from
       a painful chastisement?'
   Say: 'He is the All-merciful. We believe
   in Him, and in Him we put all our trust.
   Assuredly, you will soon know who is
       in manifest error.'
30 Say: 'What think you? If in the morning
   your water should have vanished into
   the earth, then who would bring you
       running water?'

LXVIII

THE PEN

In the Name of God, the Merciful, the Compassionate

Nun

By the Pen, and what they inscribe,
thou art not, by the blessing of thy Lord,
    a man possessed.
Surely thou shalt have a wage unfailing;
surely thou art upon a mighty morality.
So thou shalt see, and they will see,
    which of you is the demented.

Surely thy Lord knows very well
those who have gone astray from
His way, and He knows very well
    those who are guided.

So obey thou not those who cry lies. They
wish that thou shouldst compromise, then
    they would compromise.
10 And obey thou not every mean swearer,
backbiter, going about with slander,
hinderer of good, guilty aggressor,
coarse-grained, moreover ignoble,
because he has wealth and sons.
15 When Our signs are recited to him, he
says, 'Fairy-tales of the ancients!'
We shall brand him upon the muzzle!

Now We have tried them, even as We tried
the owners of the garden when they swore
    they would pluck in the morning
and they added not the saving words.

Then a visitation from thy Lord visited
 it, while they were sleeping,
20 and in the morning it was as if it were
  a garden plucked.
In the morning they called to one another,
'Come forth betimes upon your tillage,
 if you would pluck!'
So they departed, whispering together,
'No needy man shall enter it today
 against your will.'
25 And they went forth early, determined
 upon their purpose.
But when they saw it, they said, 'Surely
 we are gone astray;
nay, rather we have been robbed!'
Said the most moderate of them,
'Did I not say to you, "Why do you
 not give glory?" '
They said, 'Glory be to God, our Lord;
 truly, we were evildoers.'
30 And they advanced one upon another,
 blaming each other.
They said, 'Woe, alas for us! Truly,
 we were insolent.
It may be that our Lord will give us
in exchange a better than it; to our
 Lord we humbly turn.'

Such is the chastisement; and the chastisement
of the world to come is assuredly greater,
 did they but know.
Surely for the godfearing shall be Gardens of
 Bliss with their Lord.
35 What, shall we make those who have surrendered
 like to the sinners?

What ails you then, how you judge?
Or have you a Book wherein you study? Surely
therein you shall have whatever you choose!

Or have you oaths from Us, reaching to the
Day of Resurrection? Surely you shall have
   whatever you judge!
40   Ask them, which of them will guarantee that!
  Or do they have associates? Then
  let them bring their associates,
   if they speak truly.

Upon the day when the leg shall be bared, and they shall **be**
  to bow themselves, but they cannot; [summon**ed**
humbled shall be their eyes, and abasement shall overspread
          [them,
for they had been summoned to bow themselves while they
         [were whole.

  So leave Me with him who
  cries lies to this discourse!
  We will draw them on little by little
   whence they know not;
45   and I shall respite them—assuredly
   My guile is sure.

  Or askest thou them for a wage, and so they
   are weighed down with debt?
  Or is the Unseen in their keeping, and so
   they are writing it down?

So be thou patient under the judgment of thy Lord,
and be not as the Man of the Fish, when he called,
   choking inwardly.
Had there not overtaken him a blessing from his Lord
he would have been cast upon the wilderness,
   being condemned.
50 But his Lord had chosen him, and He placed him
   among the righteous.

  The unbelievers wellnigh strike thee down
  with their glances, when they hear the
  Reminder, and they say, 'Surely he is

a man possessed!'
And it is nothing but a Reminder
unto all beings.

LXIX

THE INDUBITABLE

In the Name of God, the Merciful, the Compassionate

The Indubitable!
What is the Indubitable?
And what will teach thee what is the Indubitable?

Thamood and Ad cried lies to the Clatterer.
5 As for Thamood, they were destroyed by the
Screamer;
and as for Ad, they were destroyed by a
wind clamorous, violent
that He compelled against them seven nights
and eight days, uninterruptedly, and thou
mightest see the people laid prostrate in it
as if they were the stumps of fallen down
palm-trees.
Now dost thou see any remnant of them?

Pharaoh likewise, and those before him,
and the Subverted Cities—they committed
error,
10 and they rebelled against the Messenger
of their Lord, and He seized them with a
surpassing grip.

Lo, when the waters rose, We bore you in
the running ship
that We might make it a reminder for you
and for heeding ears to hold.

So, when the Trumpet is blown with a single blast
and the earth and the mountains are lifted up and
crushed with a single blow,

15 then, on that day, the Terror shall come to pass,
and heaven shall be split, for upon that day it
   shall be very frail,
and the angels shall stand upon its borders, and
upon that day eight shall carry above them the
   Throne of thy Lord.
On that day you shall be exposed, not one secret
   of yours concealed.
Then as for him who is given his book in his right hand,
20 he shall say, 'Here, take and read my book! Certainly
I thought that I should encounter my reckoning.' So he
   shall be in a pleasing life
    in a lofty Garden,
     its clusters nigh to gather.
'Eat and drink with wholesome appetite for that you did
   long ago, in the days gone by.'
25 But as for him who is given his book in his left hand,
he shall say, 'Would that I had not been given my book
and not known my reckoning! Would it had been the end!
   My wealth has not availed me,
    my authority is gone from me.'
30 'Take him, and fetter him, and then roast him in Hell,
then in a chain of seventy cubits' length insert him!
Behold, he never believed in God the All-mighty, and
35 he never urged the feeding of the needy; therefore he
today has not here one loyal friend, neither any food
saving foul pus, that none excepting the sinners eat.'

   No! I swear by that you see
   and by that you do not see,
40 it is the speech of a noble Messenger.
   It is not the speech of a poet
    (little do you believe)
   nor the speech of a soothsayer
    (little do you remember).
A sending down from the Lord of all Being.

   Had he invented against Us any sayings,
45 We would have seized him by the right hand,

then We would surely have cut his life-vein
and not one of you could have defended him.

Surely it is a Reminder to the godfearing;
but We know that some of you will cry lies.
50   Surely it is a sorrow to the unbelievers;
yet indeed it is the truth of certainty.

Then magnify the Name of thy Lord, the All-mighty.

LXX

THE STAIRWAYS

In the Name of God, the Merciful, the Compassionate

A questioner asked of a chastisement about to fall
    for the unbelievers, which none may avert,
        from God, the Lord of the Stairways.
To Him the angels and the Spirit mount up in a day
    whereof the measure is fifty thousand years.

5   So be thou patient with a sweet patience;
            behold, they see it as if far off, but We
                see it is nigh.

    Upon the day when heaven shall be as molten copper
        and the mountains shall be as plucked wool-tufts,
10   no loyal friend shall question loyal friend, as
    they are given sight of them. The sinner will wish that he
    might ransom himself from the chastisement of that day even
    by his sons, his companion wife, his brother, his kin who
    sheltered him, and whosoever is in the earth, all together,
            so that then it might deliver him.

15   Nay, verily it is a furnace
                snatching away the scalp,
                calling him who drew back
                    and turned away,
                who amassed and hoarded.

            Surely man was created fretful,
20   when evil visits him, impatient,
            when good visits him, grudging,
                save those that pray
            and continue at their prayers,
        those in whose wealth is a right known

25   for the beggar and the outcast,
who confirm the Day of Doom
and go in fear of the chastisement of their Lord
(from their Lord's chastisement none feels secure)
and guard their private parts
30   save from their wives and what their right hands own,
then not being blameworthy
(but whoso seeks after more than that,
they are the transgressors),
and who preserve their trusts
and their covenant,
and perform their witnessings,
and who observe their prayers.
35   Those shall be in Gardens, high-honoured.

What ails the unbelievers, running with outstretched necks
[towards thee
on the right hand and on the left hand in knots?
What, is every man of them eager to be admitted to a Garden
[of Bliss?
Not so; for We have created them
of what they know.

40   No! I swear by the Lord of the Easts and Wests,
surely We are able
to substitute a better than they; We shall
not be outstripped.

Then leave them alone to plunge and play
until they encounter that day of theirs
which they are promised,
the day they shall come forth from the
tombs hastily, as if they were hurrying
unto a waymark,
humbled their eyes, overspreading
them abasement. That is the day
which they were promised.

LXXI

NOAH

In the Name of God, the Merciful, the Compassionate

We sent Noah to his people, saying,
'Warn thy people, ere there come on **them**
    a painful chastisement.'
He said, 'O my people, I am unto you
    a clear warner,
saying, "Serve God, and fear Him, and
    obey you me,
and He will forgive you your sins, and
defer you to a stated term; God's term,
when it comes, cannot be deferred,
    did you but know." '

5   He said, 'My Lord, I have called my
people by night and by day, but my
calling has only increased them
    in flight.
And whenever I called them, that Thou
mightest forgive them, they put their
fingers in their ears, and wrapped them
in their garments, and persisted, and
    waxed very proud.
Then indeed I called them openly;
then indeed I spoke publicly
unto them, and I spoke unto them
    secretly,
and I said, "Ask you forgiveness
of your Lord; surely He is ever
    All-forgiving,

10   and He will loose heaven upon you
    in torrents
and will succour you with wealth
and sons, and will appoint for you

302

gardens, and will appoint for you
    rivers.
What ails you, that you look not for
    majesty in God,
seeing He created you by stages?
Have you not regarded how God
created seven heavens one upon
    another,
15   and set the moon therein for a light
    and the sun for a lamp?
And God caused you to grow out of
    the earth,
then He shall return you into it,
    and bring you forth.
And God has laid the earth for you
    as a carpet,
that thereof you may thread ways,
    ravines." '
20   Noah said, 'My Lord, they have
rebelled against me, and followed him
whose wealth and children increase him
    only in loss,
and have devised a mighty device
and have said, "Do not leave your
gods, and do not leave Wadd,
    nor Suwa',
Yaghuth, Ya'uq, neither Nasr."
And they have led many astray.
Increase Thou not the evildoers
    save in error!'
25   And because of their transgressions
they were drowned, and admitted
    into a Fire,
for they found not, apart from God,
    any to help them.
And Noah said, 'My Lord, leave not
upon the earth of the unbelievers
    even one.
Surely, if Thou leavest them, they

will lead Thy servants astray, and
will beget none but unbelieving
      libertines.
My Lord, forgive me and my parents
and whosoever enters my house
as a believer, and the believers,
men and women alike; and do
Thou not increase the evildoers
      save in ruin!'

LXXII

THE JINN

In the Name of God, the Merciful, the Compassionate

Say: 'It has been revealed to me that a
company of the jinn gave ear, then they
said, "We have indeed heard a Koran
    wonderful,
guiding to rectitude. We believe in it,
and we will not associate with our Lord
    anyone.
He—exalted be our Lord's majesty!—
has not taken to Himself either consort
    or a son.
The fool among us spoke against God
    outrage,
5 and we had thought that men and jinn
would never speak against God
    a lie.
But there were certain men of mankind
who would take refuge with certain men
of the jinn, and they increased them in
    vileness,
and they thought, even as you also
thought, that God would never raise up
    anyone.
And we stretched towards heaven, but we
found it filled with terrible guards and
    meteors.
We would sit there on seats to hear; but
any listening now finds a meteor in wait
    for him.
10 And so we know not whether evil is
intended for those in the earth, or
whether their Lord intends for them

rectitude.
And some of us are the righteous, and
some of us are otherwise; we are sects
            differing.
Indeed, we thought that we should never
be able to frustrate God in the earth,
neither be able to frustrate Him
            by flight.
When we heard the guidance, we believed
in it; and whosoever believes in his
Lord, he shall fear neither paltriness nor
            vileness.
And some of us have surrendered,
and some of us have deviated.
Those who have surrendered sought
            rectitude;

15   but as for those who have deviated,
they have become firewood for
            Gehenna!" '

Would they but go straight on the way,
We would give them to drink of water
            copious,
that We might try them therein.
And whosoever turns away from the
Remembrance of his Lord, He will
thrust him into chastisement
            rigorous.
The places of worship belong to God;
so call not, along with God, upon
            anyone.
When the servant of God stood calling
on Him, they were wellnigh upon him
            in swarms.

20   Say: 'I call only upon my Lord,
and I do not associate with Him
            anyone.'
Say: 'Surely I possess no power

over you, either for hurt or for
 rectitude.'
Say: 'From God shall protect me not
 anyone,
and I shall find, apart from Him, no
 refuge,
excepting a Deliverance from God
and His Messages. And whoso rebels
against God and His Messenger,
for him there awaits the Fire of
Gehenna; therein they shall dwell
 forever.'

25 Until, when they see that which
they are promised, then they will know
who is weaker in helpers and fewer in
 numbers.
Say: 'I do not know whether that
which you are promised is nigh, or
whether my Lord will appoint for it
 a space;
Knower He of the Unseen, and
He discloses not His Unseen to
 anyone,
save only to such a Messenger as
He is well-pleased with; then He
despatches before him and behind him
 watchers,
that He may know they have delivered
the Messages of their Lord; and He
encompasses all that is with them,
and He has numbered everything in
 numbers.'

LXXIII

ENWRAPPED

In the Name of God, the Merciful, the Compassionate

O thou enwrapped in thy robes,
keep vigil the night, except a little
(a half of it, or diminish a little,
or add a little), and chant the Koran
very distinctly.

5 Behold, We shall cast upon thee a weighty word;
surely the first part of the night is heavier in
tread, more upright in speech,
surely in the day thou hast long business.
And remember the Name of thy Lord, and devote thyself
very devoutly.   [unto Him
Lord of the East and the West;
there is no god but He;
so take Him for a Guardian.

10 And bear thou patiently what they say,
and forsake them graciously.
Leave Me to those who cry lies,
those prosperous ones, and respite them a little,
for with Us there are fetters, and a furnace, and
food that chokes, and a painful chastisement,
upon the day when the earth and the mountains shall quake
and the mountains become a slipping heap of sand.

15 Surely We have sent unto you a Messenger
as a witness over you, even as We sent to
Pharaoh a Messenger,
but Pharaoh rebelled against the Messenger,
so We seized him remorselessly.
If therefore you disbelieve, how will you
guard yourselves against a day that shall make
the children grey-headed?

Whereby heaven shall be split, and its promise
      shall be performed.

    Surely this is a Reminder; so let
    him who will take unto his Lord
        a way.

Thy Lord knows that thou keepest vigil
nearly two-thirds of the night, or a half
of it, or a third of it, and a party of
those with thee; and God determines
the night and the day. He knows that you
will not number it, and He has turned
towards you. Therefore recite of the Koran
so much as is feasible. He knows that some
of you are sick, and others journeying
in the land, seeking the bounty of God,
and others fighting in the way of God. So
recite of it so much as is feasible.
And perform the prayer, and pay the alms,
and lend to God a good loan. Whatever
good you shall forward to your souls'
account, you shall find it with God as
better, and mightier a wage. And ask
God's forgiveness; God is All-forgiving,
      All-compassionate.

LXXIV

SHROUDED

In the Name of God, the Merciful, the Compassionate

O thou shrouded in thy mantle,
              arise, and warn!
              Thy Lord magnify
              thy robes purify
5   and defilement flee!
Give not, thinking to gain greater
and be patient unto thy Lord.

For when the Trump is sounded
              that day will be a harsh day,
10   for the unbelievers not easy.
Leave Me with him whom I created alone,
and appointed for him ample wealth
              and sons standing before him,
              and made all things smooth for him;
15   then he is eager that I should do more.
Nay! He is forward unto Our signs;
and I shall constrain him to a hard ascent.
Lo! He reflected, and determined—
              death seize him, how he determined!
20   Again, death seize him, how he determined!
              Then he beheld,
              then he frowned, and scowled,
              then he retreated, and waxed proud.
He said, 'This is naught but a trumped-up sorcery;
25   this is nothing but mortal speech.'
I shall surely roast him in Sakar;
and what will teach thee what is Sakar?
It spares not, neither leaves alone
              scorching the flesh;
30   over it are nineteen.

We have appointed only angels to be
masters of the Fire, and their number
We have appointed only as a trial for
the unbelievers, that those who were
given the Book may have certainty,
and that those who believe may increase
        in belief,
and that those who were given the Book
and those who believe may not be
        in doubt,
and that those in whose hearts there is
sickness, and the unbelievers, may say,
'What did God intend by this as a
        similitude?'
So God leads astray whomsoever He will,
and He guides whomsoever He will; and
none knows the hosts of thy Lord but He.
And it is naught but a Reminder to
        mortals.

35   Nay! By the moon
      and the night when it retreats
      and the dawn when it is white,
   surely it is one of the greatest things
      as a warner to mortals,
40   to whoever of you desires to go forward or lag behind.
Every soul shall be pledged for what it has earned,
      save the Companions of the Right;
in Gardens they will question concerning the sinners,
     'What thrusted you into Sakar?'
They shall say, 'We were not of those who prayed, and
45   we fed not the needy,
   and we plunged along with the plungers,
   and we cried lies to the Day of Doom,
     till the Certain came to us.'
Then the intercession of the intercessors shall not profit them.

50   What ails them, that they turn away
      from the Reminder,

as if they were startled asses fleeing
   before a lion?
Nay, every man of them desires to be
   given scrolls unrolled.
No indeed; but they do not fear the
      Hereafter.
No indeed; surely it is a Reminder; so
   whoever wills shall remember it.
55   And they will not remember, except that
God wills; He is worthy to be feared,
      worthy to forgive.

LXXV

THE RESURRECTION

In the Name of God, the Merciful, the Compassionate

No! I swear by the Day of Resurrection.
No! I swear by the reproachful soul.
What, does man reckon We shall not gather his bones?
Yes indeed; We are able to shape again his fingers.
5   Nay, but man desires to continue on as a libertine,
asking, 'When shall be the Day of Resurrection?'

But when the sight is dazed
and the moon is eclipsed,
and the sun and moon are brought together,
10   upon that day man shall say, 'Whither to flee?'
No indeed; not a refuge!
Upon that day the recourse shall be to thy Lord.
Upon that day man shall be told his former deeds and his
nay, man shall be a clear proof against himself,   [latter;
15   even though he offer his excuses.

Move not thy tongue with it
to hasten it;
Ours it is to gather it, and to recite it.
So, when We recite it, follow thou its recitation.
Then Ours it is to explain it.

20   No indeed; but you love the hasty world,
and leave be the Hereafter.
Upon that day faces shall be radiant,
gazing upon their Lord;
and upon that day faces shall be scowling,
25   thou mightest think the Calamity has been wreaked on them.

No indeed; when it reaches the clavicles

and it it said, 'Who is an enchanter?'
and he thinks that it is the parting
and leg is intertwined with leg,
upon that day unto thy Lord shall be the driving.

30   For he confirmed it not, and did not pray,
but he cried it lies, and he turned away,
then he went to his household arrogantly.

        Nearer to thee and nearer
35   then nearer to thee and nearer!
What, does man reckon he shall be left to
roam at will?
Was he not a sperm-drop spilled?
Then he was a blood-clot, and He created and formed,
and He made of him two kinds, male and female.
40   What, is He not able to quicken the dead?

LXXVI

MAN

In the Name of God, the Merciful, the Compassionate

Has there come on man a while of time
when he was a thing unremembered?

We created man of a sperm-drop, a mingling, trying him;
and We made him hearing, seeing.
Surely We guided him upon the way
whether he be thankful or unthankful.
Surely We have prepared for the unbelievers
chains, fetters, and a Blaze.
5   Surely the pious shall drink of a cup
whose mixture is camphor,
a fountain whereat drink the servants of God,
making it to gush forth plenteously.
They fulfil their vows, and fear a day whose evil is
upon the wing;
they give food, for the love of Him, to the needy,
the orphan, the captive:
'We feed you only for the Face of God;
we desire no recompense from you, no
thankfulness;
10   for we fear from our Lord a frowning day,
inauspicious.'
So God has guarded them from the evil of
that day, and has procured them radiancy
and gladness,
and recompensed them for their patience
with a Garden, and silk;
therein they shall recline upon couches,
therein they shall see neither sun nor
bitter cold;
near them shall be its shades, and its clusters hung

meekly down,

15   and there shall be passed around them vessels of
silver, and goblets of crystal,
crystal of silver that they have measured
very exactly.
And therein they shall be **giv**en to drink a cup whose
mixture is ginger,
therein a fountain whose name is called Salsabil.
Immortal youths shall go about them;
when thou seest them, thou supposest them
scattered pearls,

20   when thou seest them then thou seest bliss
and a great kingdom.
Upon them shall be green garments of silk
and brocade; they are adorned with
bracelets of silver, and their Lord shall
give them to drink a pure draught.
'Behold, this is a recompense for you, and
your striving is thanked.'

Surely We have sent down the Koran on thee,
a sending down;
so be thou patient under the judgment of thy Lord,
and obey not one of them, sinner or unbeliever.

25   And remember the Name of thy Lord
at dawn and in the evening
and part of the night; bow down before Him
and magnify Him through the long night.

Surely these men love the hasty world, and
leave be behind them a heavy day.
We created them, and We strengthened their
joints; and, when We will, We shall exchange
their likes.

Surely this is a Reminder; so he
who will, takes unto his Lord
a way.

30   But you will not unless God wills;

surely God is ever All-knowing,
  All-wise.
For He admits into His mercy
whomsoever He will; as for the
evildoers, He has prepared for them
  a painful chastisement.

LXXVII

THE LOOSED ONES

In the Name of God, the Merciful, the Compassionate

By the loosed ones successively
storming tempestuously
by the scatterers scattering
and the severally severing
and those hurling a reminder
5   excusing or warning,
surely that which you are promised is about to fall!

When the stars shall be extinguished,
when heaven shall be split
10   when the mountains shall be scattered
and when the Messengers' time is set,
to what day shall they be delayed?
To the Day of Decision.
And what shall teach thee what is the Day of Decision?
15   Woe that day unto those who cry it lies!

Did We not destroy the ancients,
and then follow them with the later folk?
So We serve the sinners.
Woe that day unto those who cry it lies!

20   Did We not create you of a mean water,
that We laid within a sure lodging
till a known term decreed?
We determined; excellent determiners are We.
Woe that day unto those who cry it lies!

25   Made We not the earth to be a housing
for the living and for the dead?
Set We not therein soaring mountains?

Sated you with sweetest water?
Woe that day unto those who cry it lies!

Depart to that you cried was lies!
30   Depart to a triple-massing shadow
unshading against the blazing flame
that shoots sparks like dry faggots,
sparks like to golden herds.
Woe that day unto those who cry it lies!

35   This is the day they shall not speak
neither be given leave, and excuse themselves.
Woe that day unto those who cry it lies!

'This is the Day of Decision; We have joined you with the
                                    [ancients;
if you have a trick, try you now to trick Me!'
40   Woe that day unto those who cry it lies!

Truly the godfearing shall dwell amid shades and fountains,
and such fruits as their hearts desire:
'Eat and drink, with wholesome appetite, for
that you were working.'
Even so do We recompense the good-doers.
45   Woe that day unto those who cry it lies!

'Eat and take your joy a little; you are sinners!'
Woe that day unto those who cry it lies!

When it is said to them, 'Prostrate yourselves!' they pros-
                                    [trate not.
Woe that day unto those who cry it lies!

50   In what discourse after this will they believe?

LXXVIII

THE TIDING

In the Name of God, the Merciful, the Compassionate

Of what do they question one another?
Of the mighty tiding
whereon they are at variance.
No indeed; they shall soon know!
5   Again, no indeed; they shall soon know!

Have We not made the earth as a cradle
and the mountains as pegs?
And We created you in pairs,
and We appointed your sleep for a rest;
10   and We appointed night for a garment,
and We appointed day for a livelihood.
And We have built above you seven strong ones,
and We appointed a blazing lamp
and have sent down out of the rain-clouds water cascading
15   that We may bring forth thereby grain and plants,
and gardens luxuriant.

Surely the Day of Decision is an appointed time,
the day the Trumpet is blown, and you shall come in troops,
and heaven is opened, and become gates,
20   and the mountains are set in motion, and become a vapour.
Behold, Gehenna has become an ambush,
for the insolent a resort,
therein to tarry for ages,
tasting therein neither coolness nor any drink
25   save boiling water and pus
for a suitable recompense.
They indeed hoped not for a reckoning,
and they cried loud lies to Our signs;
and everything We have numbered in a Book.

30   'Taste! We shall increase you not save in chastisement.'

Surely for the godfearing awaits a place of security,
gardens and vineyards
and maidens with swelling breasts, like of age,
and a cup overflowing.
35   Therein they shall hear no idle talk, no cry of lies,
for a recompense from thy Lord, a gift, a reckoning,
Lord of the heavens and earth, and all that between them is,
the All-merciful
of whom they have no power to speak.
Upon the day when the Spirit and the angels stand in ranks
they shall speak not, save him to whom the All-merciful has
given leave, and who speaks aright.

That is the true day; so whosoever wills
takes unto his Lord a resort.
40   Lo, We have warned you of a nigh chastisement,
upon the day when a man shall behold what his hands have
[forwarded,
and the unbeliever shall say, 'O would that I were dust!'

LXXIX

THE PLUCKERS

In the Name of God, the Merciful, the Compassionate

By those that pluck out vehemently
and those that draw out violently,
by those that swim serenely
and those that outstrip suddenly
5   by those that direct an affair!

Upon the day when the first blast shivers
and the second blast follows it,
hearts upon that day shall be athrob
and their eyes shall be humbled.
10   They shall say, 'What, are we being restored
as we were before?
What, when we are bones old and wasted?'
They shall say, 'That then were a losing return!'
But it shall be only a single scare,
and behold, they are awakened.

15   Hast thou received the story of Moses?
When his Lord called to him in the holy
valley, Towa: 'Go to Pharaoh; he has
waxed insolent. And say, "Hast thou the
will to purify thyself, and that I
should guide thee to thy Lord, then thou
20   shalt fear?" ' So he showed him the great
sign, but he cried lies, and rebelled,
then he turned away hastily, then he
mustered and proclaimed, and he said,
'I am your Lord, the Most High!' So
25   God seized him with the chastisement
of the Last World and the First.
Surely in that is a lesson for him who fears!

322

What, are you stronger in constitution
or the heaven He built?
He lifted up its vault, and levelled it,
and darkened its night, and brought forth its forenoon;
30   and the earth—after that He spread it out,
therefrom brought forth its waters and its pastures,
and the mountains He set firm,
an enjoyment for you and your flocks.

Then, when the Great Catastrophe comes
35   upon the day when man shall remember what he has striven,
and Hell is advanced for whoever sees,
then as for him who was insolent
and preferred the present life,
surely Hell shall be the refuge.
40   But as for him who feared the Station of his Lord
and forbade the soul its caprice,
surely Paradise shall be the refuge.

They will question thee concerning
the Hour, when it shall berth.
What art thou about, to mention it?
Unto thy Lord is the final end of it.
45   Thou art only the warner of him who fears it.
It shall be as if, on the day they see it,
they have but tarried for an evening, or its forenoon.

LXXX

HE FROWNED

In the Name of God, the Merciful, the Compassionate

He frowned and turned away
that the blind man came to him.
And what should teach thee? Perchance he would cleanse him,
or yet remember, and the Reminder profit him.
5   But the self-sufficient,
to him thou attendest
though it is not thy concern, if he does not cleanse himself.
And he who comes to thee eagerly
and fearfully,
10   to him thou payest no heed.

No indeed; it is a Reminder
(and whoso wills, shall remember it)
upon pages high-honoured,
uplifted, purified,
15   by the hands of scribes noble, pious.

Perish Man! How unthankful he is!
Of what did He create him?
Of a sperm-drop
He created him, and determined him,
20   then the way eased for him,
then makes him to die, and buries him,
then, when He wills, He raises him.
No indeed! Man has not accomplished His bidding.

Let Man consider his nourishment.
25   We poured out the rains abundantly,
then We split the earth in fissures
and therein made the grains to grow
and vines, and reeds,

and olives, and palms,
30   and dense-tree'd gardens,
and fruits, and pastures,
an enjoyment for you and your flocks.

And when the Blast shall sound,
upon the day when a man shall flee from his brother,
35   his mother, his father,
his consort, his sons,
every man that day shall have business to suffice him.
Some faces on that day shall shine
laughing, joyous;
40   some faces on that day shall be dusty
o'erspread with darkness—
those—they are the unbelievers, the libertines.

LXXXI

THE DARKENING

In the Name of God, the Merciful, the Compassionate

When the sun shall be darkened,
when the stars shall be thrown down,
when the mountains shall be set moving,
when the pregnant camels shall be neglected,
5   when the savage beasts shall be mustered,
when the seas shall be set boiling,
when the souls shall be coupled,
when the buried infant shall be asked for what sin she was
10   when the scrolls shall be unrolled,   [slain,
when heaven shall be stripped off,
when Hell shall be set blazing,
when Paradise shall be brought nigh,
then shall a soul know what it has produced.

15   No! I swear by the slinkers,
the runners, the sinkers,
by the night swarming,
by the dawn sighing,
truly this is the word of a noble Messenger
20   having power, with the Lord of the Throne secure,
obeyed, moreover trusty.

Your companion is not possessed;
he truly saw him on the clear horizon;
he is not niggardly of the Unseen.

25   And it is not the word of an accursed Satan;
where then are you going?

It is naught but a Reminder

unto all beings,
for whosoever of you who would go straight;
but will you shall not, unless God wills,
the Lord of all Being.

LXXXII

THE SPLITTING

In the Name of God, the Merciful, the Compassionate

When heaven is split open,
when the stars are scattered,
when the seas swarm over,
when the tombs are overthrown,
5   then a soul shall know its works, the former and the latter.

O Man! What deceived thee as to thy generous Lord
who created thee and shaped thee and wrought thee in
[symmetry
and composed thee after what form He would?

No indeed; but you cry lies to the Doom;
10   yet there are over you watchers
noble, writers
who know whatever you do.

Surely the pious shall be in bliss,
and the libertines shall be in a fiery furnace
15   roasting therein on the Day of Doom,
nor shall they ever be absent from it.

And what shall teach thee what is the Day of Doom?
Again, what shall teach thee what is the Day of Doom?
A day when no soul shall possess aught to succour another
[soul;
that day the Command shall belong unto God.

LXXXIII

THE STINTERS

In the Name of God, the Merciful, the Compassionate

Woe to the stinters
who, when they measure against the people, take full measure
but, when they measure for them or weigh for them, do skimp.
Do those not think that they shall be raised up
5   unto a mighty day
a day when mankind shall stand before the Lord of all Being?

No indeed; the Book of the libertines is in Sijjin;
and what shall teach thee what is Sijjin?
A book inscribed.
Woe that day unto those who cry it lies,
10   who cry lies to the Day of Doom;
and none cries lies to it but every guilty aggressor.
When our signs are recited to him, he says,
'Fairy-tales of the ancients!'
No indeed; but that they were earning has rusted
upon their hearts.
15   No indeed; but upon that day they shall be veiled
from their Lord,
then they shall roast in Hell.
Then it shall be said to them, 'This is that you cried lies to.'

No indeed; the book of the pious is in Illiyun;
and what shall teach thee what is Illiyun?
20   A book inscribed,
witnessed by those brought nigh.
Surely the pious shall be in bliss,
upon couches gazing;
thou knowest in their faces the radiancy of bliss
25   as they are given to drink of a wine sealed
whose seal is musk—so after that let the strivers strive—

329

and whose mixture is Tasnim,
a fountain at which do drink those brought nigh.

Behold, the sinners were laughing at the believers,
30   when they passed them by winking at one another,
and when they returned to their people they returned blithely,
and when they saw them they said, 'Lo, these men are astray!'
Yet they were not sent as watchers over them.
So today the believers are laughing at the unbelievers,
35   upon couches gazing.
Have the unbelievers been rewarded what they were doing?

LXXXIV

THE RENDING

In the Name of God, the Merciful, the Compassionate

When heaven is rent asunder
and gives ear to its Lord, and is fitly disposed;
when earth is stretched out
and casts forth what is in it, and voids itself,
5   and gives ear to its Lord, and is fitly disposed!

O Man! Thou art labouring unto thy Lord laboriously,
and thou shalt encounter Him.
Then as for him who is given his book in his right hand,
he shall surely receive an easy reckoning
and he will return to his family joyfully.
10   But as for him who is given his book behind his back,
he shall call for destruction
and he shall roast at a Blaze.
He once lived among his family joyfully;
he surely thought he would never revert.
15   Yes indeed; his Lord had sight of him.

No! I swear by the twilight
and the night and what it envelops
and the moon when it is at the full,
you shall surely ride stage after stage.

20   Then what ails them, that they believe not,
and when the Koran is recited to them they do not bow?
Nay, but the unbelievers are crying lies,
and God knows very well what they are secreting.

So give them good tidings of a painful chastisement,
25   except those that believe, and do righteous deeds—
theirs shall be a wage unfailing.

LXXXV

THE CONSTELLATIONS

In the Name of God, the Merciful, the Compassionate

By heaven of the constellations,
by the promised day,
by the witness and the witnessed,
slain were the Men of the Pit,
5   the fire abounding in fuel,
when they were seated over it
and were themselves witnesses of what they did with the
⌈believers.
They took revenge on them only because they believed in
the All-mighty, the All-laudable,   ⌈God
to whom belongs the Kingdom of the heavens and the earth,
and God is Witness over everything.

10   Those who persecute the believers, men and women,
and then have not repented, there awaits them the
chastisement of Gehenna, and there awaits them
the chastisement of the burning.
Those who believe, and do righteous deeds, for them
await gardens underneath which rivers flow; that is
the great triumph.

Surely thy Lord's assault is terrible.
Surely it is He who originates, and brings again,
and He is the All-forgiving, the All-loving,
15   Lord of the Throne, the All-glorious,
Performer of what He desires.

Hast thou received the story of the hosts,
Pharaoh and Thamood?
Nay, but the unbelievers still cry lies,
20   and God is behind them, encompassing.

Nay, but it is a glorious Koran,
in a guarded tablet.

LXXXVI

THE NIGHT-STAR

In the Name of God, the Merciful, the Compassionate

By heaven and the night-star!
And what shall teach thee what is the night-star?
The piercing star!
Over every soul there is a watcher.

5   So let man consider of what he was created;
he was created of gushing water
issuing between the loins and the breast-bones.
Surely He is able to bring him back
upon the day when the secrets are tried,
10   and he shall have no strength, no helper.

By heaven of the returning rain,
by earth splitting with verdure,
surely it is a decisive word;
it is no merriment.

15   They are devising guile,
and I am devising guile.
So respite the unbelievers; delay with them awhile.

LXXXVII

THE MOST HIGH

In the Name of God, the Merciful, the Compassionate

Magnify the Name of thy Lord the Most High
who created and shaped,
who determined and guided,
who brought forth the pasturage
5 then made it a blackening wrack.

We shall make thee recite, to forget not
save what God wills;
surely He knows what is spoken aloud
and what is hidden.
We shall ease thee unto the Easing.

Therefore remind, if the Reminder profits,
10 and he who fears shall remember,
but the most wretched shall flout it,
even he who shall roast in the Great Fire,
then he shall neither die therein, nor live.

Prosperous is he who has cleansed himself,
15 and mentions the Name of his Lord, and prays.

Nay, but you prefer the present life;
and the world to come is better, and more enduring.

Surely this is in the ancient scrolls,
the scrolls of Abraham and Moses.

LXXXVIII

THE ENVELOPER

In the Name of God, the Merciful, the Compassionate

Hast thou received the story of the Enveloper?

Faces on that day humbled,
labouring, toilworn,
roasting at a scorching fire,
5   watered at a boiling fountain,
no food for them but cactus thorn
unfattening, unappeasing hunger.

Faces on that day jocund,
with their striving well-pleased,
10   in a sublime Garden,
hearing there no babble;
therein a running fountain,
therein uplifted couches
and goblets set forth
15   and cushions arrayed
and carpets outspread.

What, do they not consider how the camel was created,
how heaven was lifted up,
how the mountains were hoisted,
20   how the earth was outstretched?
Then remind them! Thou art only a reminder;
thou art not charged to oversee them.

But he who turns his back, and disbelieves,
God shall chastise him with the greatest chastisement.
25   Truly, to Us is their return;
then upon Us shall rest their reckoning.

LXXXIX

THE DAWN

In the Name of God, the Merciful, the Compassionate

By the dawn and ten nights,
by the even and the odd,
by the night when it journeys on!
Is there in that an oath for a mindful man?

5   Hast thou not seen how thy Lord did with Ad,
Iram of the pillars,
the like of which was never created in the land,
and Thamood, who hollowed the rocks in the valley,
and Pharaoh, he of the tent-pegs,
10   who all were insolent in the land
and worked much corruption therein?
Thy Lord unloosed on them a scourge of chastisement;
surely thy Lord is ever on the watch.

As for man, whenever his Lord tries him,
and honours him, and blesses him,
15   then he says, 'My Lord has honoured me.'
But when he tries him and stints for him
his provision,
then he says, 'My Lord has despised me.'

No indeed; but you honour not the orphan,
and you urge not the feeding of the needy,
20   and you devour the inheritance greedily,
and you love wealth with an ardent love.

No indeed! When the earth is ground to powder,
and thy Lord comes, and the angels rank on rank,
and Gehenna is brought out, upon that day
man will remember; and how shall the Reminder be for him?

M

25   He shall say, 'O would that I had forwarded for
my life!' Upon that day none shall chastise as
He chastises,
none shall bind as He binds.

'O soul at peace, return unto thy Lord,
well-pleased, well-pleasing!
Enter thou among My servants!
30   Enter thou My Paradise!'

XC

THE LAND

In the Name of God, the Merciful, the Compassionate

No! I swear by this land,
and thou art a lodger in this land;
by the begetter, and that he begot,
indeed, We created man in trouble.
5 What, does he think none has power over him,
saying, 'I have consumed wealth abundant'?
What, does he think none has seen him?

Have We not appointed to him two eyes,
and a tongue, and two lips,
10 and guided him on the two highways?
Yet he has not assaulted the steep;
and what shall teach thee what is the steep?
The freeing of a slave,
or giving food upon a day of hunger
15 to an orphan near of kin
or a needy man in misery;
then that he become of those who believe
and counsel each other to be steadfast,
and counsel each other to be merciful.

Those are the Companions of the Right Hand.
And those who disbelieve in Our signs,
they are the Companions of the Left Hand;
20 over them is a Fire covered down.

XCI

THE SUN

In the Name of God, the Merciful, the Compassionate

By the sun and his morning brightness
and by the moon when she follows him,
and by the day when it displays him
and by the night when it enshrouds him!
5   By the heaven and That which built it
and by the earth and That which extended it!
By the soul, and That which shaped it
and inspired it to lewdness and godfearing!
Prosperous is he who purifies it,
10   and failed has he who seduces it.

Thamood cried lies in their insolence
when the most wretched of them uprose,
then the Messenger of God said to them,
'The She-camel of God; let her drink!'
But they cried him lies, and hamstrung her,
15   so their Lord crushed them for their sin, and levelled them:
and He fears not the issue thereof.

XCII

THE NIGHT

In the Name of God, the Merciful, the Compassionate

By the night enshrouding
and the day in splendour
and That which created the male and the female,
surely your striving is to diverse ends.

5   As for him who gives and is godfearing
and confirms the reward most fair,
We shall surely ease him to the Easing.
But as for him who is a miser, and self-sufficient,
and cries lies to the reward most fair,
10   We shall surely ease him to the Hardship;
his wealth shall not avail him when he perishes.

Surely upon Us rests the guidance,
and to Us belong the Last and the First.

Now I have warned you of a Fire that flames,
15   whereat none but the most wretched shall be roasted,
even he who cried lies, and turned away;
and from which the most godfearing shall be removed,
even he who gives his wealth to purify himself
and confers no favour on any man for recompense,
20   only seeking the Face of his Lord the Most High;
and he shall surely be satisfied.

XCIII

THE FORENOON

In the Name of God, the Merciful, the Compassionate

By the white forenoon
and the brooding night!
Thy Lord has neither forsaken thee nor hates thee
and the Last shall be better for thee than the First.
5   Thy Lord shall give thee, and thou shalt be satisfied.

Did He not find thee an orphan, and shelter thee?
Did He not find thee erring, and guide thee?
Did He not find thee needy, and suffice thee?

10   As for the orphan, do not oppress him,
and as for the beggar, scold him not;
and as for thy Lord's blessing, declare it.

XCIV

THE EXPANDING

In the Name of God, the Merciful, the Compassionate

Did We not expand thy breast for thee
and lift from thee thy burden,
the burden that weighed down thy back?
Did We not exalt thy fame?

5   So truly with hardship comes ease,
truly with hardship comes ease.
So when thou art empty, labour,
and let thy Lord be thy Quest.

XCV

THE FIG

In the Name of God, the Merciful, the Compassionate

By the fig and the olive
and the Mount Sinai
and this land secure!
We indeed created Man in the fairest stature
5   then We restored him the lowest of the low—
save those who believe, and do righteous deeds;
they shall have a wage unfailing.

What then shall cry thee lies as to the Doom?
Is not God the justest of judges?

XCVI

THE BLOOD-CLOT

In the Name of God, the Merciful, the Compassionate

Recite: In the Name of thy Lord who created,
    created Man of a blood-clot.
Recite: And thy Lord is the Most Generous,
    who taught by the Pen,
5   taught Man that he knew not.

No indeed; surely Man waxes insolent,
    for he thinks himself self-sufficient.
Surely unto thy Lord is the Returning.

What thinkest thou? He who forbids
10   a servant when he prays—
What thinkest thou? If he were upon guidance
    or bade to godfearing—
What thinkest thou? If he cries lies, and turns away—
    Did he not know that God sees?

15   No indeed; surely, if he gives not over,
    We shall seize him by the forelock,
        a lying, sinful forelock.
So let him call on his concourse!
We shall call on the guards of Hell.

No indeed; do thou not obey him,
    and bow thyself, and draw nigh.

XCVII

POWER

In the Name of God, the Merciful, the Compassionate

Behold, We sent it down on the Night of Power;
And what shall teach thee what is the Night of Power?
The Night of Power is better than a thousand months;
    in it the angels and the Spirit descend,
  by the leave of their Lord, upon every command.
5   Peace it is, till the rising of dawn.

XCVIII

THE CLEAR SIGN

In the Name of God, the Merciful, the Compassionate

The unbelievers of the People of the Book
and the idolaters would never leave off,
till the Clear Sign came to them,
a Messenger from God, reciting pages purified,
therein true Books.
And they scattered not, those that were given the Book,
excepting after the Clear Sign came to them.
They were commanded only to serve God,
making the religion His sincerely,
men of pure faith, and to perform
the prayer, and pay the alms—that is
the religion of the True.

5   The unbelievers of the People of the Book
and the idolaters shall be in the Fire of Gehenna,
therein dwelling forever;
those are the worst of creatures.
But those who believe, and do righteous deeds,
those are the best of creatures;
their recompense is with their Lord—
Gardens of Eden, underneath which rivers flow,
therein dwelling for ever and ever.
God is well-pleased with them, and they are well-pleased
[with Him;
that is for him who fears his Lord.

XCIX

THE EARTHQUAKE

In the Name of God, the Merciful, the Compassionate

When earth is shaken with a mighty shaking
and earth brings forth her burdens,
and Man says, 'What ails her?'
upon that day she shall tell her tidings
5   for that her Lord has inspired her.

Upon that day men shall issue in scatterings to see their
                [works,
and whoso has done an atom's weight of good shall see it,
and whoso has done an atom's weight of evil shall see it.

C

THE CHARGERS

In the Name of God, the Merciful, the Compassionate

By the snorting chargers,
by the strikers of fire,
by the dawn-raiders
blazing a trail of dust,
5   cleaving there with a host!
Surely Man is ungrateful to his Lord,
and surely he is a witness against that!
Surely he is passionate in his love for good things.
Knows he not that when that which is in the tombs is over-
[thrown,
10   and that which is in the breasts is brought out—
surely on that day their Lord shall be aware of them!

CI

THE CLATTERER

In the Name of God, the Merciful, the Compassionate

The Clatterer! What is the Clatterer?
And what shall teach thee what is the Clatterer?
The day that men shall be like scattered moths,
and the mountains shall be like plucked wool-tufts.

5   Then he whose deeds weigh heavy in the Balance
shall inherit a pleasing life,
but he whose deeds weigh light in the Balance
shall plunge in the womb of the Pit.
And what shall teach thee what is the Pit?
A blazing Fire!

CII

RIVALRY

In the Name of God, the Merciful, the Compassionate

Gross rivalry diverts you,
even till you visit the tombs.
No indeed; but soon you shall know.
Again, no indeed; but soon you shall know.
5 No indeed; did you know with the knowledge of certainty,
you shall surely see Hell.
Again, you shall surely see it with the eye of certainty
then you shall be questioned that day concerning true bliss.

CIII

AFTERNOON

In the Name of God, the Merciful, the Compassionate

By the afternoon!
Surely Man is in the way of loss,
save those who believe, and do righteous deeds,
and counsel each other unto the truth,
and counsel each other to be steadfast.

CIV

THE BACKBITER

In the Name of God, the Merciful, the Compassionate

Woe unto every backbiter, slanderer,
who has gathered riches and counted them over
thinking his riches have made him immortal!

No indeed; he shall be thrust into the Crusher;
and what shall teach thee what is the Crusher?
The Fire of God kindled
roaring over the hearts
covered down upon them,
in columns outstretched.

CV

THE ELEPHANT

In the Name of God, the Merciful, the Compassionate

Hast thou not seen how thy Lord did with the Men of the
[Elephant?
Did He not make their guile to go astray?
And He loosed upon them birds in flights,
hurling against them stones of baked clay
5 and He made them like green blades devoured.

CVI

KORAISH

In the Name of God, the Merciful, the Compassionate

For the composing of Koraish,
their composing for the winter and summer caravan!

So let them serve the Lord of this House
who has fed them against hunger.
and secured them from fear.

CVII

CHARITY

In the Name of God, the Merciful, the Compassionate

Hast thou seen him who cries lies to the Doom?
That is he who repulses the orphan
and urges not the feeding of the needy.

So woe to those that pray
5   and are heedless of their prayers,
to those who make display
and refuse charity.

CVIII

ABUNDANCE

In the Name of God, the Merciful, the Compassionate

Surely We have given thee abundance;
so pray unto thy Lord and sacrifice.
Surely he that hates thee, he is the one cut off.

CIX

THE UNBELIEVERS

In the Name of God, the Merciful, the Compassionate

Say: 'O unbelievers,
I serve not what you serve
and you are not serving what I serve,
nor am I serving what you have served,
neither are you serving what I serve.

5   To you your religion, and to me my religion!'

CX

HELP

In the Name of God, the Merciful, the Compassionate

When comes the help of God, and victory,
and thou seest men entering God's religion in throngs,
then proclaim the praise of thy Lord, and seek His forgive-
for He turns again unto men.　　　　.[ness;

CXI

PERISH

In the Name of God, the Merciful, the Compassionate

Perish the hands of Abu Lahab, and perish he!
His wealth avails him not, neither what he has earned;
        he shall roast at a flaming fire
    and his wife, the carrier of the firewood,
5   upon her neck a rope of palm-fibre.

CXII

SINCERE RELIGION

In the Name of God, the Merciful, the Compassionate

Say: 'He is God, One,
God, the Everlasting Refuge,
who has not begotten, and has not been begotten,
and equal to Him is not any one.'

CXIII

DAYBREAK

In the Name of God, the Merciful, the Compassionate

Say: 'I take refuge with the Lord of the Daybreak
  from the evil of what He has created,
  from the evil of darkness when it gathers,
  from the evil of the women who blow on knots,
5 from the evil of an envier when he envies.'

CXIV

MEN

In the Name of God, the Merciful, the Compassionate

Say: 'I take refuge with the Lord of men,
the King of men,
the God of men,
from the evil of the slinking whisperer
5   who whispers in the breasts of men
of jinn and men.'

INDEX

GEORGE ALLEN & UNWIN LTD

Head Office:
40 Museum Street, London, W.C.1
Telephone: 01–405 8577

Sales, Distribution and Accounts Departments
Park Lane, Hemel Hempstead, Herts.
Telephone: 0442 3244

Athens: 7 Stadiou Street, Athens 125
Barbados: P.O. Box 222, Bridgetown
Bombay 103/5 Fort Street, Bombay 1
Calcutta: 285J Bepin Behari Ganguli Street, Calcutta 12
Dacca: Alico Building, 18 Montijheel, Dacca 2
Hong Kong: 105 Wing On Mansion, 26 Hankow Road, Kowloon
Ibadan: P.O. Box 62
Johannesburg: P.O. Box 23134, Joubert Park
Karachi: Karachi Chambers, McLeod Road Karachi 2
Lahore: 22 Falettis' Hotel, Egerton Road
Madras: 2/18 Mount Road, Madras 2
Manilla: P.O. Box 157, Quezon City, D-502
Mexico: Serapio Rendon 125, Mexico 4, D.F.
Nairobi: P.O. Box 30583
New Delhi: 1/18 B Asaf Ali Road, New Delhi 1
Ontario: 2330 Midland Avenue, Agincourt
Singapore: 36c Prinsep Street, Singapore 7
Sydney N.S.W.: Bradbury House, 55 York Street
Tokyo: C.P.O. Box 1728, Tokyo 100–91
Wellington: P.O. Box 1467, Wellington, New Zealand